More Lifeways

Finding support and inspiration in family life

Edited by
Patti Smith and Signe Eklund Schaefer

Introduction by
Gudrun Davy and Bons Voors

Hawthorn Press

Published by Hawthorn Press,
Hawthorn House, 1 Lansdown Lane, Lansdown, Stroud,
Gloucestershire, GL5 1BJ
Tel (01453 757040)   Fax (01453) 751138

The ideas expressed within this book are not necessarily those of the publisher.

Designed and typeset by Lynda Smith
Cover artwork by Karin Schaefer
Cover typography by Patrick Roe, Glevum Graphics
Printed by Redwood Books, Wiltshire

British Library Cataloguing in Publication Data
A catalogue record for this book is available from the British Library.

ISBN 1 869 890 86 8

Contents

Foreword

Patti Smith and Signe Eklund Schaefer

We were warned when we first thought of compiling a new volume of *Lifeways* that it would be far more time consuming and demanding than we could imagine. We shrugged: 'Oh, it couldn't be so bad, asking colleagues and friends to write articles about subjects that matter to them.' In fact, most people we asked did agree to write; and most came through in the end. (We trust they will forgive our increasingly insistent prodding!) What we have learned over the last four years, as the job, indeed, demanded much more than our initial enthusiasm, was that even with intriguing and passionate stories to tell, few of us could easily translate our insights into written text. Most often the subject matter led us into quite unexpected growth.

This book is an experiment. Our thesis is that everyone has thoughts and experiences of value to share with others. What most of us lack is the confidence or the opportunity to rise above the insecurity that prevents us from voicing them. We can feel so isolated, and also perplexed by life's challenges. The voices in *More Lifeways* articulate this confusion and our individual struggles for balance and understanding.

For the authors of this book, the writing process itself has been a journey of self-discovery. 'Catharsis' was a word we heard again and again. Each writer has dared to share her or his quest with strangers. In editing the book we have seen the humility, integrity, self-doubt, self-knowledge and growth that are involved in the writing process. That you, as reader, become engaged with what is written and follow your own process of discovery, will be testament to our belief that as adults we can influence our troubled world in positive ways, when we try to articulate our genuine questions, when we listen to the questions and responses of others.

We ask you to read these offerings as if you were having a conversation with a trusted friend. Too often we read as we listen—our own thoughts like fisted hands, ready for a punch. Our intention with this book is to provide a space for companionship and encouragement. You are invited to enter this space with good will and let our voices inspire your own. We imagine you will find things to agree with, and things you seriously question; we hope you will find moments to laugh and moments of being deeply moved.

Each contribution is preceded by a short biography. Writers were asked to speak about themselves in relation to the questions addressed. We have come to these topics from personal experience, and our authority rests on our efforts to extract meaning and direction for further development. It will be obvious that the views and insights expressed belong to each author. Even amongst ourselves we do not always agree; in fact, some of our areas of disagreement have been great spurs to deepening individual understanding.

Organizing the book was difficult. We had assumed that we would follow a similar format to the one in the original *Lifeways*, but the topics did not easily fit into uniform categories. Many topics are interconnected. The chapter about sports doubles easily as an article on fathering, as could the chapters on media. Stories about death share pictures of birth. Remembering Ariadne's golden thread—that life-sustaining clue which freed Theseus from the devouring Minotaur in Greek mythology—we chose to weave our way through the labyrinth of questions, letting one chapter move into the next, knowing there were other turns we might have made.

We begin with a chapter on inner development, a subject which resonates in every article and is at the core of the *Lifeways* work. We then hear reflections on adult life and parental concerns. A single parent's story is echoed in the tale of a single-parented child; adoptive parents share their experiences and are followed by the questions of one who is adopted. Educators address child development, and families bravely tell of meeting death. We enter the intense world of adolescence, hearing the painful and demanding self-discoveries of youth. Listening requires attention to suffering we were never trained to endure, a sacrifice many adults are not able to make. There are rewards to be celebrated by those who do take the risk, and these stories are also here. The book turns out to have a surprising number of chapters about adolescents, a reflection, we feel, of their vulnerability and need in our chaotic times.

The last three contributions are reworkings of lectures given at the First Annual Conference of the Center for Life Studies of Sunbridge College in Spring Valley, New York. The Conference was entitled "Who is Raising our Daughters? Women Coming of Age for the 21st Century" and took place in April, 1995. The Center for Life Studies is very much connected to this book; in fact, it developed, in part, out of workshops and classes inspired by the original *Lifeways*. Since the fall of 1994, the Center has been part of Sunbridge College, an adult education center based on the work of Rudolf Steiner. The Center offers outreach activities in support of families and individuals at different stages of life.

There are many people we want to thank for bringing *More Lifeways* to completion. Firstly, our writers have earned our deepest respect and gratitude for their perseverance and honest sharing. Dale Bennett, our tireless manuscript editor, brought to each contribution imagination, tact, and a magical capacity to suggest helpful transformations. This book could not exist without her painstaking work. Joanna Williams skillfully deciphered our many different scribbles, and Jeff Olson was always ready to offer computer advice in the preparation of the final manuscript.

When we began this project we were simultaneously developing the Center for Life Studies, and our colleague in those early days, Jennifer Brooks-Quinn, offered many helpful suggestions in the book's evolving. Gudrun Davy and Bons Voors, the editors of the original *Lifeways*, were firm supporters from the very beginning. They also contributed much-appreciated funding toward expenses, from the royalty money from the first book. Our plan is that money from the royalties for *More Lifeways* will similarly be available for a variety of projects in support of parents and children, through the Center for Life Studies. Additional funding for this book came from *The Cultural Freedom Foundation* and *The Foundation for Rudolf Steiner Books*.

We also thank our colleagues in the Center for Life Studies Development Group and at Sunbridge College for their encouragement and belief that the book really would come together. Linda Norris, with her warm get-away cottage for quiet writing, also gave unswerving support. It is a special joy that Karin Schaefer and David Hale brought their artistry to the cover design. Martin Large has been a most patient and encouraging publisher, who showed understanding for the inevitable delays.

To Andy and Chris, and to our children, a special thanks for all the ways we share our lives.

Patti Smith and Signe Eklund Schaefer   *June 1996*

Introduction
Gudrun Davy and Bons Voors

In England in 1980 a small group of women assembled in order to discuss a request for a book on 'parenting.' The request came to our group because we had been working on family questions, mainly in connection with Emerson College, a center for adult education based on the work of Rudolf Steiner. Students from all over the world attend Emerson to find inspiration and direction for their personal search or professional training in education or other fields. In the seventies, many students arrived there with children, especially from the United States. The quest for a personal path and professional training became one of also finding new ways of looking at family life.

We know from our experience of compiling *Lifeways*, that such an impulse can bring about a warm response and an enormous sense of gratitude. We have received many responses to the book, for example: 'I know now that I am no longer alone in my struggles, it is helpful to hear that others share the path of loneliness, disappointment and small triumphs.' Some comments came back about the book being too idealistic and too 'goody goody', leaving readers with feelings of inadequacy or guilt. For the most part, readers felt met, strengthened, inspired, sometimes 'saved' by the book lying half-read on the bedside table!

That a group of 'experiencers in the field' rather than 'experts', wrote a book was certainly new and accounts for *Lifeways'* success. It was surprising that these stories were translated into Dutch, German and Italian, and that the book was reprinted five times within ten years. Our little boat from the original cover, in fact, sailed international waters. It carried Bons and Gudrun into numerous countries to start groups and to give workshops. It harbored at its home port every summer for a week to call together adults and children at Emerson College for a Lifeways week.

Each year children and adults (sometimes grand-parents instead of parents) meet to enrich their family life. The adults attend workshops while activities are provided for the children. The older children build camps and the younger ones share rooms or tents with the adults who bring them. In the afternoons everyone participates in crafts, art, music and dance. Evening activities are also shared with the older children. The week culminates in a Harvest of the Week, a big bonfire and dance. The week has become a successful tradition at the College, serving hundreds of families.

Such a week costs money and is supported by the royalties from the *Lifeways* book. The original group decided that the royalties would be placed in a fund at Emerson College to develop and support activities for families. Families, otherwise unable to contemplate a 'Lifeways Week,' have benefited from this fund. We bought a children's Caravan and a large sand-pit. We financed the translation of an important book on drug addiction and sent one person to Russia on the 'Cultural Caravan.' We provided seed money for two 'Life Centers' to be developed, to give this work a permanent home-base. Lastly, since life and death cannot be separated, we paid for a beautifully sculpted stone to mark the place where the ashes of our colleagues and friends, such as John Davy, (who coined the word Lifeways), and Francis Edmunds, are laid.

We are asked by the editors of this new book to say something of a more personal nature of what has happened to us since 1983. So, in conclusion, we will take up our 'personal pens.'

Gudrun

Less than a year after the publication of *Lifeways*, my husband, John Davy, whom the readers of the first book have met through his important contributions, was dead. We lived for six months with the knowledge of a fatal brain tumor. To speak about this intense, terrible and wonderful journey could fill another book. The year before his own death, we shared in the long drawn out process of the dying of his mother. In retrospect, that experience prepared us for what was to come.

We were privileged to find a group, centered around one nurse, to take this arduous 24 hour nursing on as a common task. The group consisted of one closely connected household helper, some young students, our wonderful nurse and the two of us. Everybody had his or her shift, and John's frail father, well into his eighties, often took on the most difficult times with exceptional devotion. Six months after John's death, I had to find another group to do the same for this remarkable man. This time we relied on morning and evening help from the official National Health nurses to teach us about turning the patient hourly and other skills, about which we knew nothing. The students who helped me, mainly men, felt very deeply moved and enriched through this experience.

During these three nursing and death experiences, I often felt blessed in the sense that it seemed that we, the caring groups, were pioneering something which went far beyond our personal tasks. I know that we were not the only pioneers of such a 'destiny-group' forming around a dying person. Others have found a similar way to help friends or relatives die, as did people in earlier times. This process feels like confirmation of what life is all about. In the future we may not be able to rely on state and hospital support. In many situations of any social difficulty, 'destiny-groups', groups who come together in support of an individual, will have to take on the work together. We can no longer do it alone. I was reminded of the somewhat humorous remark my husband made, when he knew he had cancer: 'It is as if I have joined a club.'

'Destiny groups' have in recent years become necessary and relevant for almost any problem, from supporting relatives of those with Alzheimer's Disease, to those who suffer addiction or abuse. The AA is a forerunner to this much needed development. In this vein, the two *Lifeways* books represent the gathering of two 'destiny groups', which came together to struggle with the challenges that arise for families and individuals in these ever changing times.

In my own life, birth—in the form of eleven grandchildren—followed death. Inwardly, I could relive all the agonies and joys of the first few months with a newborn without actually being the main care-giver. One could fill pages of observations about these new, very awake souls arriving on this Earth. Also startling was the arrival of four new partners to my four children, coming from totally other backgrounds and world views than our own. This was a very great challenge and learning experience, and I had not expected it in quite this way.

I should like to end by mentioning two new themes which come into my life: Color and Community. I finished my art therapy training in 1984 and have been developing a 'color path', relating to John Davy's article called 'Discovering Hope', in *Hope, Evolution and Change*, Hawthorn Press 1985. It is an ongoing research project, but lends itself directly to working therapeutically with people in crisis. The second theme is a proper *Lifeways* theme: Learning to live in a Community. I have moved to a Homelife Support Community, consisting of about 70 people of all ages. We have our own work and housing but own the grounds and gardens communally. We share the work of looking after it, and we also share celebrations. It feels right to be here. It feels right that this new book is going out into the world. May it find those who are looking for it and those for whom it will be an exciting surprise!

Bons

More Lifeways is on the rails. The road through family life is as challenging, punishing and rewarding as ever and certainly not less hazardous. There are fewer forms of support, yet more choices and exciting diversions available for the traveller.

My own journey has just started a new phase, when—after 23 years— my husband and I find ourselves at the kitchen table without any children. A rather big contrast to the last ten years, when we were joined by a total of twelve extra teenagers: children who lived with us during school time and rejoined their own parents during the holidays. In our experience, it was definitely easier to have more teenagers than less teenagers! There was more noise, but more laughter, more exams and more drama, more homework and infinitely more laundry! There were hundreds of parent evenings at school, and so many wonderful plays and thrilling performances: a lot more exposure to all the different temperaments, more painful insights but also more fun. No space for lethargy and much more life and fire in the family-pot!

All the boarders are now gone, and our own three children are studying and traveling. Our parental task is (we'd like to think) still ongoing and vital. Life is getting more serious for young people in their twenties. Major life choices have to be taken with regard to studies, jobs, relationships and choice of country. Contact is maintained with high telephone bills, through the odd, but important letter and by infrequent, short bursts of invasions: children with their changed plans and their changing partners!

I have continued my counseling work in a medical setting, where I am privileged to hear the biographies of clients, and where family life unfolds in endless color and variation in my counselling room. I have been involved in creating 'destiny groups', as Gudrun has rightly coined them: groups of patients with a variety of difficulties—such as phobias, anxieties, those that are wheelchair-bound or have cancer—within which people find support and where they say: 'This is my new family, really.' These groups help people take up the thread of destiny again, through building confidence and friendships: not by focusing on problems only, but through singing, poetry, writing stories, outings and plant study, forging a new link to nature and life.

Working in a doctor's surgery I meet very depressed young people, who are confused and lost, in search of meaning in the face of hopelessness. Finding the spark, the spirit in each human being—masked by whatever phobia, addiction, or garb—is the task at hand, the challenge I face.

Our hope for *More Lifeways* is that, through the contributions of these individuals, others may be inspired to face the challenges that come toward them and find support to journey on as parents, partners and human beings.

Signe Eklund Schaefer

In a familiar moment of distraction, as I try to write something about myself, I notice that I am surrounded by papers. Is this who I am? ... scraps with ideas for a talk, reminders of today's requirements, household tasks needing attention, manuscripts piled up waiting for final editing, folders of correspondence, half-finished letters. Is it possible that in this state of semi-organized chaos (an apparent contradiction, I know, but such is life!) I could possibly have written a chapter on inner development?

Actually, when I began this chapter, I was on holiday by the ocean. For two hours each morning my husband and I would write—sharing the same gentle breezes and warm sunshine in a backyard patio, but otherwise engrossed in our own projects. The words flowed out, and I imagined I could write whole books in this peaceful rhythm. But then our vacation was over, and I returned to my more usual life with an unfinished chapter. Committed as I am to my work at Sunbridge College, directing the Orientation Year and developing the Center for Life Studies, I found no regular time to keep writing; and so a year passed by. In the summer of 1995, I began a six-month sabbatical and set myself the task of completing this chapter before heading out on a round-the-world adventure made possible by seven weeks of work in Australia and New Zealand. Such a battle between intention and anticipation! The deadline worked, but when I returned from my trip, I had some serious revisions still to do.

Inner development—it's been a theme of longing, guilt, and dedication for all my adult life. At twenty, I discovered Rudolf Steiner's work and knew I had found a central thread of my life. Within a few years, as a young wife and mother of a daughter and a son, I began to interweave this thread with my interest in feminism. During the 1970's, while living in England, I was part of developing Ariadne, an international women's group. Those were years rich in friendship and discovery; and this work to understand feminine and masculine as qualities interacting in the individual and in the evolution of consciousness, was essential to all I have become. It was also during those years in England that I was involved in working on the first *Lifeways* book.

As I head into my fifties, my passion for human development finds expression in my teaching, in work with biography and karma, in the never-ending gifts and challenges of a long marriage partnership, in the joy of continuing to grow with my adult children, and in the nourishment of deep friendships. Ten years ago I stumbled into acting in Rudolf Steiner's *Mystery Dramas* and have been immeasurably enriched by this work, now coming to a close with the performance of the fourth play. I look forward to more time in the future to write.

1

Life development and inner learning: a path of becoming

What is it about inner work that seems so daunting? The very idea elicits feelings of inadequacy, of discouragement, of longing. Caught up as we so often are—especially as parents of young children—in the requirements and the rush of everyday life, we can imagine inner development as something that could happen only on a secluded mountain top. Or maybe it is only the privilege of others: single friends, students on a spiritual path, our spouse.

What image do we hold of inner development? Is it practicing meditative exercises, working with mantra, stilling our buzzing mind? Or is it growing inner wakefulness, attentiveness that lives in ever more moments, consciousness that begins to permeate our life experiences and penetrate to ever deeper levels of understanding? Do we define it as something outside our sphere of possibility, requiring a retreat from everyday life, something reserved for others, or do we see it as a process of growing and learning that can be entered wherever we are, in whatever phase of life we find ourselves?

Many years ago a friend shared an experience with me that vividly captures the tensions that I and so many women friends have felt around the question of focused inner work. She had asked her husband to watch their infant daughter while she hurried through a variety of household chores. The baby was gurgling and kicking happily on their bed, and so the man thought this would be a good time to do some meditative exercises. While he was concentrating on his meditation, the baby fell off the bed. Fortunately, she was not hurt, but my friend, who was daily feeling spiritually inadequate in comparison to her husband because she could not seem to find time or energy for inner work, was aghast that her husband was oblivious to the immediate situation around him while ostensibly seeking 'higher' knowledge. She knew, from a place deep within her, that her encompassing attention would never have let the baby fall. And yet it was just this encompassing attention, this sense for dimension in all that was going on around her, that made focused inner work so difficult.

I share this example not to bind the experiences within gender differences—I know many men who identify with the woman in this story, and many women who could have acted as this man did. Yet, there is something objective about the nurturing role that asks for a certain wholeness of consciousness—and I call this a feminine awareness whether it manifests in a woman or a man. This is qualitatively different from a determined sense of self, a directed feeling of individual identity that can close off the impressions of the surrounding world and concentrate on its chosen focus. This latter capacity is connected, I believe, to a masculine consciousness whether it is being exercised by a man or a woman. [1]

Often when one is busy with young children, with the multi-sided responsibilities of caring for family life, it is easy to lose sight of oneself as a distinct individual. I speak out of my experiences as a mother who was for several years the 'at home' carrier of our developing family. I do not want to exclude either men, or women who are not mothers, from my comments, but I am aware how much the daily realities of my life have colored my thoughts. Each of us will know our own particular struggle to find balance between that in us which inclines toward the needs of others, which seeks to nurture and care and carry the totality, and that other part of us which yearns for self-expression and individual achievement. In the years since the Women's Movement brought so many of women's, and men's, previously accepted roles into question, this challenge for balance has become an ever more pressing question of consciousness. I imagine that readers of this book know this challenge and are seeking ways to bridge the growth that can come through attending to the needs of others—particularly through the responsibilities of parenting—with the equally real growth that is the fruit of consciously pursued self-development.

Our culture has long undervalued the role of nurturer. The assertive self-starter has tended to be the one to receive attention and praise. We have depended on nurturing, of course, and are in fact now suffering its lack in myriad ways, both individually and as a society. But it is only fairly recently that we have begun to see the tremendous developmental possibilities available to those who take nurturing seriously, who enter it with all the energy, enthusiasm and attentiveness usually reserved for one's career outside the family. Quite the reverse of being a detour on one's path of individual becoming, parenting offers us so many opportunities for real, tangible self-development. I know that it has been one of the most profound gifts to my inner and outer becoming.

A modern path of inner schooling, such as the one articulated by Rudolf Steiner, includes many exercises to awaken reverence, foster inner quiet, promote self-knowledge, and activate observation and focused attention. These exercises are to be practiced again and again in order to enhance one's soul capacities, in order to develop heightened perception and an ever greater possibility to know the dimensions of reality. As responsible parents, we are daily doing the work that these exercises suggest. We may feel we have no time for spiritual exercises, but if we look carefully at what is asked of us everyday, we will find how often we are practicing just what a student on a spiritual path seeks to exercise. However, we do not necessarily pause to notice and appreciate what we are doing. We often overlook the opportunities for conscious self-learning that stand before us. How can we come to know and work more attentively with these opportunities so that our daily tasks become substance for our evolving inner life?

Opportunities awaiting consciousness

In describing the basic conditions for a path of spiritual schooling, Rudolf Steiner speaks of a fundamental mood of soul upon which all genuine inner development depends; he calls this an attitude of reverence, a devotion to truth and knowledge.[2] He acknowledges, as we all must, how genuine feelings of reverence, of awe and wonder, have been severely undermined in the modern age. Since childhood we have been taught to look critically at the world, to find the flaw, the missing piece. Indeed, it is hard not to feel cynical in the face of much that confronts us in society and even in our personal relationships. Right judgment certainly has its place and must be cultivated; but if feelings of admiration and veneration can find no room to grow within us, we close ourselves off to so much that would otherwise be ours to see.

When my children were young, I would go into their rooms at night before I went to bed. Sometimes I would stand there in the quiet, listening to their gentle breathing, remembering the fullness and activity of the day, and I would be filled with the mystery of these mighty beings who were now in my care. In those moments, I knew they were so much more than 'my little children.' I do not mean to imply that I could see into their previous lives, but I knew beyond a doubt that they had had them, and that somehow we had agreed that in this life, I would care for them as mother. The truth of this agreement, with its enormous responsibility and its unparalleled gift, was tangibly present for me. Whenever I read in Rudolf Steiner, '...one knows that every feeling of true devotion unfolded in the soul produces an inner strength or force that sooner or later leads to knowledge,'[3] I know that he is right.

In conversations over the years on the subject of reverence, I have again and again heard people bring examples of experiences with their children. For many, childbirth was a moment of profound awakening; the wonder they felt in the face of this mystery opened quite unexpected dimensions of knowing. Here was truth; here was being. Life would never be quite the same again, for in that moment, a veil had parted, and although it closed again, the living experience could never be denied.

So many moments as parents invite our reverence. For example, we watch our children take so many first steps—from walking, to discovering what their hands or their minds can do, to falling in love. We stand daily in front of the truth and the mystery of development. Material to inspire our reverence is never lacking; it is we who are too tired, too burdened or pre-occupied to notice. Can we try to recognize each day the feelings of devotion which hover in our sub-conscious? Can we make more space for them, allow them to become conscious, to resound within us?

Often the reverence so naturally present in our child can open our eyes to what we would have missed otherwise. How many wonders lie beyond a whispered 'Look Mommy!': rainbows of light in an oily puddle, a beetle rich with pre-historic lore, flower petals of a color we cannot name. I am so grateful to my children for opening my eyes—and my heart—in such varied directions. I remember their eager young faces as we would light the candles on the Advent wreath. The light in their eyes invited me into an experience of growing anticipation and inner preparation that I had never before known at the approach of Christmas. Through the children, many festivals took on new dimensions of inner experience for me. I must say that as the years went by, I also realized the temptation to depend on the children to inspire my own reverence in such situations. Luckily, children do not stay the same and so we, too, are challenged to keep growing.

Even when they were teenagers—not generally a very visibly reverent age—I often found myself feeling genuine awe for the ways they chose to assert their individualities. The courage of self-expression behind my daughter's green hair, the self-protecting shut-down my son imposed on my maternal questions...whenever I could find respect for the phenomena before me, could feel how absolutely right and appropriate this behavior was for this particular child (and I do not mean to suggest that this was easy!), then doorways of understanding for human development opened within me. Ever and again, I experience that the key to such opening is in my attitude. When I can allow feelings of reverence to accompany my encounter with others, or with ideas or natural phenomena, I inevitably meet more than what is only on the surface.

Observing reality

Another condition that belongs to a path of inner schooling is the exercising of one's capacity of observation. Plant studies, working with simple man-made objects, observing natural processes or human social behavior: these are but a few of the many suggestions to foster more acute and objective observation skills.[4] We are told to choose an object and then to stay attentive to it, taking in its details, opening ourselves to what makes it what it is, to the particular thought that underlies its being. We try to allow ourselves to experience more than a generic or automatic identification, more than a scientific analysis, to really meet this particular object and how it reveals whatever archetype may lie within it.

Students on a spiritual path must seek out objects for careful observation; conscientious parents are, in fact, doing this work naturally all the time. I think it is a rare parent who cannot be interested in his or her child, who is not drawn to notice a myriad of details—the tiny miraculous infant toenails, the concentrated scowl as chubby fingers tie a shoe lace, the 'I can do it!' joy of jumping off a wall. What mother is unable to discern the different cries of hunger, wet diaper, crankiness or a wish for company? We are observing all the time, and growing in confidence and skill as we do so. But do we recognize this developing faculty, and could we work with it more consciously?

To experience parenting as a path of conscious inner growing requires us to move beyond instinctive behavior, however effective it may be. Interest that is simply there—because of our innate fascination with everything about our child—needs to become more aware, more self-directed and objective. Learning about child development is enormously helpful—just as study belongs to any path of schooling; but the information can only be helpful if we also school our observing. Then we will be able to experience the truth of what we have learned, and we will find confirmation through our study of what we have seen for ourselves.

As we observe our child, we can notice what characteristics seem to belong to the phase of development he or she is in, what gestures are present through imitation of family members or friends, what habits indicate temperament [5], and what qualities seem to belong uniquely to this child. Distinguishing the sources of a particular behavior can be so helpful in determining how we respond. It often takes a long time to understand what lies behind certain ways of being, and we sometimes interpret things quite inadequately; but the learning from looking back at our mistakes, and looking again and again at the phenomena before us, becomes the substance for real growth in both our parenting and in our inner development.

My eldest child, for example, was quite a late walker. I was puzzled that she would support herself round and round a low table, or seem quite tireless toddling along holding my hand, but would never venture forward on her own, not even to my husband's or my open arms. She seemed quite resolute in what looked like a refusal to take that solitary step. And then one day in a large room full of people, she freely stood up in the middle of the floor, looked around, took sixteen steps, looked around, and sat down with obvious satisfaction. Luckily, I was there to see this, and it filled me with both joy and questions. What need in her refused to take a less than perfect step? How had she mastered this without the build-up of two-steps, four-steps? Had she been secretly practicing? Or were these very questions more a reflection of how I might have approached the task?

Some years later when we were living in Holland, she would actively refuse our suggestions that she greet the milkman or a neighbor with the simple Dutch phrases we were learning. I would find out from her kindergarten teacher what story was being told each week so that I could tell the same one at home in English. Nevertheless, her teacher said she never spoke any Dutch although she seemed happy enough chattering to herself in English. And then one day—perhaps five or six weeks after we had arrived—when I went to pick her up at school, the teacher greeted me with great excitement and announced: 'She speaks fluent Dutch! She started first thing in the morning and has hardly shut her mouth since.' Suddenly, I remembered how she had begun walking, and I knew there was a connection and that I was observing something essential about her individuality. Many other puzzling—and at times frustrating—moments with her came to my mind, and I saw with new clarity that she simply had to do new things her own way. She needed our help to be led gently toward what she did not know, but her fierce independence had to be respected. I had been observing isolated phenomena for years, but only gradually could they reveal to me this central gesture of her being. This insight was incredibly helpful over the years —when I was awake enough to remember it—and through it I learned a bit more about trusting my observations, sooner or later, to yield me greater understanding.

In a very helpful lecture entitled *Practical Training in Thought*, Rudolf Steiner describes several exercises to strengthen our power of image-making, to build confidence in our ability to foresee possible consequences, and to trust that we will have the right thoughts when we need them.[6] All these exercises are based on accurate and careful observation of phenomena—whether in nature, in human interaction or in memory. They encourage activity that as parents we are engaged in all the time.

For example, two of the exercises deal with observing some aspect of human behavior and either building a concrete mental picture of what will follow on from the observed phenomena or reflecting on what has caused it to manifest. In the one case, we are imagining into the future, in the other, into the past. As parents, we very often engage in similar thought processes: we see the children disappearing out the door with pillows and a bedspread, the broom and the mop. We imagine they intend to make a camp. Will it be a peaked tent by the woods or a furling canopy above the picnic table with cushioned thrones at either end for king and queen? Our ten-year-old comes home from school under a cloud. He will not speak beyond monosyllables and looks on the verge of tears: did his best friend go off with someone else, or was the teacher cross with him? Did something happen on the bus ride home? Parental interest or concern quite naturally causes us to speculate from the present into the future or the past. But are we thorough in imagining the pictures? And do we then follow through by checking out what does or did, in fact, occur? These are the critical steps in the exercises Steiner describes, and even further he advises us to correct the inner pictures if the ones we first made were proved wrong. This step, I think, we do not so readily take naturally, yet it is fundamental for our inner growth. The act of self-correction in the face of reality heightens our attention to what is approaching us, encourages us to confront inappropriate pride in our insights, and strengthens our capacity to admit consequence as part of any process.

Moments of inner quiet

Another challenge of parenting that belongs to any path of inner development is learning to discern the essential from the non-essential. We can so easily get lost in the details of a day, in the needs for scheduling, in the endless tasks of cleaning, washing, shopping, cooking; we can sometimes forget that these activities are there to serve life not to consume it. Or, we can see our young teenager with what seem to us like too many holes in her jeans, or in her ears, or perhaps he is shrouded all in black, his hair cropped off or pony-tailed. How are we to know if what we see is a warning of some deep problem or simply the going style, or the need to hide a bit, or a message that if we want to know them, we must go beneath the surface?

Rudolf Steiner suggests that in order to practice distinguishing the essential from the non-essential, we should create moments of inner quiet, times when we pull away from the ongoing requirements of our day.[7] How shall we find these times when some person or task seems to need us every waking moment? And not only parenting but much else in modern life works against the possibilities of inner tranquillity: we are bombarded by ever-changing sense impressions through the media, Muzak, traffic, and what can feel like a kind of universal rush. Even if we catch a moment for ourselves, we often feel an inner buzz continuing; or we fall asleep from pure exhaustion. Yet, because it is so hard, I think we know how important it is to find those moments apart, those times when we can consciously let our experiences reverberate and reveal their deeper meaning, when we can collect ourselves and allow a healthy transition between activities.

Steiner encourages us to take the time—five minutes he says will do—to review each day before we go to sleep.[8] Instead of getting caught up again in feeling through our experiences, he suggests we try to stand outside the flow of the day and view it as a stranger. Or we can think of ourselves looking down on the day from a higher place, where what was important stands out and the non-essential falls away. The fruits of such a review will be enhanced if we go backwards from evening to morning—for this we must be more active, more awake, and so we will be less likely to slip into automatic replay. Most people I know who have made this review a part of their lives, find it invaluable; it helps to bring the day to a close, to prepare us for a deeper sleep. To be honest, many have fallen asleep in the process of doing it, which, of course, is not the aim! As with all inner work, perseverence does help, and so does sitting up while doing the review. The temptation to do it when already lying in bed is very great and is an invitation to instant sleep.

A complementary exercise to this daily review, and one again that is very helpful in parenting, is to take a few minutes in the morning to listen to the mood with which we enter the day, and to preview what the day will bring. Acknowledging the basic challenges in front of us can give us strength. Of course, we know that the unexpected will also meet us, but a momentary look at what we do know lies ahead can give us pivotal points to work with, can create anticipated breathing spaces, and allow us to return in memory during the rush of the day to this moment when we felt centered and attentive. Perhaps it seems impossible to imagine even two minutes in the morning for such a daily preview—the baby's cry or a bouncing child is our wake-up call and it's full steam ahead from then on. But we do take time to brush our teeth; is two more minutes for soul hygiene any less important?

Centering oneself

I would now like to describe a group of six exercises which Rudolf Steiner emphasized as particularly important in fostering and balancing inner growth. I think of them as practices in centering ourselves; they help us to be more attentive in our thinking, feeling and willing and encourage us to look beyond our all too frequent automatic reactions of criticism and dismissal. Steiner describes them as essential accompanying activities in the development of a conscious spiritual life, but they are also incredibly strengthening for a more wakeful and fruitful participation in everyday life. As exercises, they can seem surprisingly simple on first hearing; perhaps it is this simplicity that makes them so difficult to sustain. Yet, it is the dedicated effort of working with them that builds confidence and inner equilibrium.[9]

In our roles as parents, we are challenged to develop qualities like positivity, openness and balance. To take up these centering exercises would be to engage more consciously in a structured working on such qualities. We are working on them everyday anyway, but often in a quite haphazard way; we confront a situation and respond most often out of instinct— sometimes wisely but also many times in ways we later regret. We see this happening; we want to become more centered, and yet it is so difficult to take five minutes to work on inner exercising.

I think back on my years as a mother of young children and remember how each year as summer approached, I would somehow find time for leg-lifts and sit-ups—at least a few minutes everyday. Was I only motivated by the imagined shame of my winter-white self exposed on a beach? This seems so shallow; surely I also wanted to feel more fit. But where did time for this come from? And what about my more energetic friends who found regular time to jog or do aerobics? Why is it so much harder to find five or ten minutes for inner fitness?

Sometimes I think we resist this inner work because we know how life-changing it will be. Perhaps we already feel so inundated with responsibilities that we shy away from what will lead us to be more responsible. We know somewhere that if we are more centered, we will perceive more around us; we will experience more joy but also more of the world's pain. As our capacities of perception grow, so too may increase what is asked of us. And we are already so tired. I think this field of conflicting desires and fears, competing demands for our time and energy, is known to most conscientious parents. Yet I continually find that whenever I overcome my resistances and give myself those few minutes to attend to my inner life, quite the opposite of what I had dimly worried about actually occurs. Yes, my increasing perception brings with it new responsibilities, but rather than draining my forces, I find that even a few minutes of regular inner work gives renewed strength and an unimagined source of energy with which to meet life.

Thinking

For many modern people it is difficult to stay concentrated on a particular thought. We start out thinking about something but become easily distracted by an association, a memory, a worry, or a physical sensation. We feel scattered, unfocused and confused. Modern life seems to present us with such complex issues, and we easily doubt our capacity to penetrate the layers of phenomena. Thought clichés, often borrowed unconsciously from the media, permeate our inner meanderings and our conversations with others. We observe ourselves wandering around with our thoughts, and yet feel quite mystified by how we can be thinking or saying such a thing. All of these experiences can leave us wondering: Is anyone at home here? Am I really present?

The first of Steiner's 'six exercises' helps us to become centered in thinking activity. The aims of the exercise are to develop more objectivity and inner firmness and to help us enter the thought processes which inform our world. We choose a simple everyday object (cup, button, paperclip, needle...) and inwardly try to concentrate our attention on the thoughts which belong to it. We may begin, for example, thinking the shape and color of the object, its straightness or concavity or texture. We resist the temptation to dart from impression to impression but try to enter carefully the living thoughts which the object makes manifest. Through our own power of determination, we think through, as factually as we can, the different aspects of the object (form, method of manufacture, function, etc.)

In this exercise, we do not observe an actual physical object in front of us, but rather reflect on the object in our thinking. It generally helps to do this with closed eyes. We are trying to strengthen our inner activity and to gradually release our dependence on the sense world. We use man-made objects because it is easy to see that they are embodiments of ideas—that thought underlies their creation. And we use simple objects in order to resist relying on attraction or outside interest as a motivating force. Steiner suggests that we might stay with the same object for several days. The challenge is to think freshly and actively each time, not to rely on thoughts from yesterday's exercise. We might, in fact, think the same thoughts, but each time this must be an activity of the present, not an act of memory.

There are obvious difficulties which arise with this exercise. To keep your thinking focused for five minutes on one object asks for real wakefulness. It is incredibly easy to drift off and find your attention on last summer's holiday or making a grocery list. If you find yourself far from the 'button' (and I can assure you that you will!), just go back. Don't waste time berating yourself or wondering how you ended up in eighth grade math class or braiding your daughter's hair; this would only be a further indulgence in distraction. But after finishing the exercise, it is useful to look back and see where and how you wandered off. You may notice re-occurring weak spots where you tend to free associate, for example, whenever you make a transition from thinking through the form of the object to considering its origin. After this kind of review, you may be able to focus more attentively in future exercises. You may also notice things about how you think—in dialogue, in images, in concepts—and so be able to intentionally practice what is less natural to you.

For parents, this exercise is particularly helpful in our efforts to discern the essential from the non-essential and to trust our abilities to meet the challenges we face each day with a heightened sense of self-control. We are so inundated with advice about parenting that we can begin to doubt our own capacity to know what our child needs. Doing this exercise over time fosters living thinking activity and builds confidence in our capacity to penetrate reality. It helps us to see through the thought clichés that deaden us and our culture. This living thinking is vital to an awakened inner life. It gives us access to the world of spirit activity, as a freely participating individual.[10]

Willing

After we begin to feel more active and centered in our thinking, we can add
an exercise for the will. I think it is easy to see why we might benefit from
attending to our will activity. How often have you set out to do a task and
found yourself in the midst of something altogether different without any
consciousness of having changed your plans? Do you ever part from a
chance encounter with an acquaintance saying, 'Let's get together...I'll call
you'? How many of your 'to do' lists begin with perennial intentions (clean
the toy chest, write to Aunt Sue, sort through the laundry room...) that
never quite get done?

So much of our daily activity is motivated by outside requirements. We
respond to what we must but are often unable to follow through on aims
that arise within us. Perhaps we are unsure of what we want to do, or we
feel cramped in our efforts to be self-determining. It can be very useful at
the end of a day to reflect on the following questions: How centered was I
in the working of my will today? What moved me...outer obligations, inner
intentions, the needs of others, my own desires...? Did I have a plan? Was it
realistic? Did it become a prison? Did I follow through with my real
intentions? Was I flexible in meeting the unexpected? Was I aimless or
scattered?

After reflecting on questions like the above, we may feel more motivated
to attempt the exercise for becoming centered in the will. Steiner suggests
that we undertake to do some small unnecessary act (re-tie a shoelace,
scratch your ear, look out the window) at a certain time in the day. This is
to be repeated day after day. An apparently insignificant action is chosen
because it is the self-determining nature of the act that is important.
Feeding the dog does not count because the dog needs to be fed; and
something particularly interesting would pull us toward it. The central
requirement in this exercise is that we consciously follow through with our
own intention.

After a few days of remembering to do the chosen deed, people will
often forget they ever meant to do it at all. Perhaps days will go by before
they remember it again with shock and frustration. What is essential is to
keep trying. If what is to be practiced were easy, we would have no need to
do the exercise. As it becomes more possible to fulfill the chosen task, it is
good to add further ones. In accomplishing these small acts of initiative, we
gradually strengthen our will for more significant activity, not only in those
intentions which are required by our outer life, but also those which arise
within us.

For parents, this exercise can be particularly beneficial. Too often we feel pulled through our days by a force that seems to have little to do with us. We may feel as if we are on 'automatic pilot'; we function through our many tasks but feel barely present. We may set ourselves clear goals: I *will* get the children to school on time, I *will* sort through the summer clothes, I *will* say no to that extra project at work. But often our many goals come into conflict, and at the end of the day we are tired and discouraged by our lack of follow-through. We may, at first, disdain this 'small' exercise to become centered in our will, out of the sense that we have much bigger tasks to accomplish. But it is precisely the regular practicing of these small deeds that strengthens the inner capacity of will for when we really need it.

Feeling

The exercise for becoming more centered in one's feeling life often arouses controversy and resistance. In our psychological age, we worry that somehow this may be an invitation to repression; do we even *want* to control our feelings? Don't we want to be able to truly express what is on our minds or in our hearts? It is, in fact, just this that Steiner encourages us to work on—but to do it knowingly and in a way that fits the situation. From a foundation of inner calm, can we become our own 'ruler over expressions of joy and sorrow, of pleasure and pain?'[11]

I have often experienced that in the midst of an intense feeling, I too easily lose myself. Later, I find myself wondering: 'What happened then? Where was I?' I know that I lost my sense of being centered, that I was, in fact, 'beside myself.' It fascinates me how much our language has to tell us about the domain and the importance of this exercise. Why would we ever want to be in a state of 'blind rage', or 'panic stricken', or 'racked with grief'? Do we really want to be overcome, drained, swept away, or consumed by feelings? When we can be centered in a moment of genuine feeling and let its expression be appropriate to the moment, how much richer is our experience. We are awakened and our feeling can reveal unexpected truths beyond the merely personal.

But how to practice such an exercise? How to catch the habits of snapping back at a whining child, or sinking into depression at another's (perhaps unintended) slight? As with the exercise for the will, it helps to bring attention to one's feeling experience by reviewing at the end of the day. Where was I in my feeling life? What threw me off center? When did I feel an inner enlivening? Were there moments when I felt hollow, stone-like, volcanic or dull? When did I feel authentic, when false in my feeling expressions? Were there times that my feeling expressions brought forth consequences that were very different from what I intended? In reflecting on a particular situation that occurred, can I also imagine—in living inner pictures—a more centered feeling participation than actually occurred? Do I see patterns of how I become beside myself, or particular situations that produce this state?

Of course, the aim of this exercise is not merely to review when one was or was not centered; the real purpose is *to bring feeling consciousness into the present moment.* Through reflection, we can often realize where we stepped away from appropriate and genuine expression. Gradually, our attending can wake us up in the moment of slipping off, and then we have a choice to become more centered. We might, for example, catch ourselves about to lash out in anger when our child ignores our request to pick up toys. We know from previous experience that our expression of anger will lead to tears, to guilt, to toys still scattered on the floor. If we can center ourselves, we may recognize our irritation, or tiredness, and know that to inflict this on our child is useless. Then we may find the inner strength to seek another method of encouragement for the task.

We have so many habitual feeling responses, echoes of our own parent's edicts or religious commandments, memories of social pressures that may play into even the simplest situation. How are we to know what is 'appropriate' behavior? This question can suggest to us why Rudolf Steiner introduces this exercise after the ones for thinking and willing. We need to have some control over our thoughts and intentions to be able to discern our own feeling responses with equanimity and let them find authentic expression in ways that suit the moment.

It is significant that Rudolf Steiner cautions us as much about too little feeling engagement as he does about too much. The person who cannot laugh or cry is as in need of centering activity as the one who giggles or weeps uncontrollably.[12] We each must discover our own challenges: we may become too quickly angry, or fearful, impatient or detached. When our feeling moves almost automatically into outward expression, its genuine message to our soul can be dissipated. Where we must struggle to develop equanimity, we build inner strength which will serve us well for our spiritual development. In *How to Know Higher Worlds*, Rudolf Steiner speaks of letting a feeling become 'a messenger, instructing us about the world.'[13] Far from distancing us from the world around us, a consciously attended, calm and centered feeling life opens us to ever richer and deeper realms of experience and inner knowledge.

Positivity

The fourth exercise is to seek out, even in the most difficult situation, something that is good or true or beautiful. As previously stated, we live in an age when a critical faculty is highly valued: we are schooled from early childhood to see 'what is wrong with this picture.' All too easily we take the good for granted and focus on the flaws—in another person, in a relationship, in nature or in social phenomena.

How many times do we catch ourselves inadvertently running through the inadequacies of our spouse, our child's teacher, our town, or the weather? Even with people with whom we clearly have a deep and loving connection we can fall into times where all we take note of are their less than desired traits. This exercise challenges us to expand our thinking and guide our feelings in order to seek out qualities we can admire. This does not mean ignoring the bad, or the ugly, or what needs improvement; it simply asks that we also notice something good.

In describing this exercise, Rudolf Steiner referred to a legend about Christ and some of his followers encountering a dead dog lying by the road. The others were all repulsed and turned away from the decaying corpse, but Christ admired the dog's beautiful teeth.[14] This story captures very graphically the challenge of this exercise: can we discover the 'beautiful teeth' in what otherwise presents itself to us as flawed?

As with the previous exercises, we can become aware of how positivity lives in us by reviewing our day to see where we exercised it, and where it was lacking. Should we begin to feel depressed about how readily we fall into negativity, it is important to remember that we could not freely develop positivity—as a conscious accomplishment of our 'I'—if we never felt critical. Automatic positivity lacks individual consciousness. It is in the effort to see clearly through what is difficult to what is also good that we refine our capacity for right and responsible judgment.

To practice positivity, we can consciously look for what we may have initially missed. For example, we can stop to notice what our otherwise lazy and self-centered teenager did today that was right, helpful, or kind. Perhaps we may even be able to appreciate something developmentally appropriate in his or her self-absorption. If we have become aware of slipping into negativity in a careless conversation with others, we can resolve next time to bring a more balanced picture, even praise if it is due, and so lift a future conversation from the grip of gossip.

Another way to practice this exercise is to try to think even one positive thought about something that is distressing us, such as pollution, a difficulty at work, or a friend's illness. Many years ago, I found myself becoming increasingly obsessed with all that was wrong with a colleague. I could see nothing worthy about him and so asked my husband if he could help me. I could agree to the positive qualities my husband would mention, but each time I would reply, 'Yes, but...' Finally, my husband said, 'Just stop at the 'yes', leave the 'but' for some other time.' Gradually, I came to see much more deeply into my colleague's virtues and to appreciate how the difficulties I still perceived were, in fact, important clues into the riddle of this particular human being.

This practice in looking for the positive can also be very helpful in trying to accept some of our children's interests or friends. Often we can be aghast at their choices; we wonder where we have gone wrong that our daughter seeks out such a friend, that our son has such taste in music or in reading matter. These situations can make us despair for the future, or we can face the challenge to look deeper: to appreciate her initiative or compassion, to value that he is reading at all. We grow in our capacity to understand, and when necessary, to bring helpful balancing forces, when we can expand our attention beyond negative impressions to encompass the good as well.

Openness

The fifth exercise is to practice being open and receptive to new experiences, to things one does not yet know. Often, we go through our days with an attitude of dismissal toward anything that might contradict our previous experiences. Again, our use of language can alert us to how we close ourselves off from what might challenge our sense of security. Have you ever found yourself thinking, or saying: 'That's ridiculous', 'I never heard of such a thing', 'I can't stand that person, she is always so...', or 'That's not how I do it'?

John Davy spoke of this exercise as practicing a 'readiness to learn'[15], and I find this a very helpful term. The world offers us endless possibilities to grow in consciousness, but are we ready to learn? Are we open to new impressions? Of course, the new must be weighed against our previous experience; this is not an invitation to ignore what we know, but rather to allow it to expand. We need to use our clear thinking and also our will to stay open to the unexpected.

We can become familiar with the challenge of this exercise by asking ourselves as part of a daily review: were there times when I closed down today? Can I get in touch with why?—habit, fear, lack of awareness of being closed... When was I open to something new? What prompted this—a surprise, another's insistence, my own effort...?

We may be closed to new ideas because they create new responsibility in us. For example, if we hear that television has detrimental effects on children, we may react with: 'It didn't hurt me' or 'My child doesn't watch much' or 'The children love to play Power Rangers—TV stimulates their imaginations.' We do not necessarily want to hear something that might push us to look deeper into other experiences we *also* have, such as that the children often end up fighting after a stint of TV watching, or that they sit around a lot with glazed eyes, acting bored when the TV is turned off. Can we find the courage to open ourselves to new ideas knowing that we may be changed in the process? Can we welcome these opportunities for self-development?

At times we shut down because our sense of identity is challenged by something new. How often do we think: I can't draw...or sing...; I don't like guitar music...or big cities...or spinach? Often our actual experience contradicts these narrow self-definitions, but we cling to them out of a need for security. Can we be open to our own possibilities to grow, to become more than we are at present? And can we grant the same possibilities to others? Do we meet the people in our lives with ever-renewing interest, ready to experience something unexpected in them, open to their small or large steps of development?

This exercise asks us to seek daily opportunities to learn something new: new ideas, capacities, impressions of others or of the world. In our experiences of nature, we have endless possibilities to meet newness, to release ourselves from the fixed boxes of learned concepts: the sky is blue (except when it is white, or pink, yellow or grey...); tree bark is brown (and red, green, white, and black...). So many miracles of expanding awareness greet us in every flower, in water babbling over rocks, in falling leaves. As parents, we have the gift of our children's open-heartedness to the world to invite us along on a journey of discovery. By nature they bring wonder and fresh perspectives to what they meet; if we are receptive and will consciously attend to where they lead us, we will find never-ending opportunities to grow.

Harmonizing

The final practice of these 'six exercises' is to bring the previous five together as a part of daily life. If each exercise has been practiced daily for at least a month, and earlier ones are not completely dropped as new ones are added, then eventually we are challenged to balance these different evolving capacities: centeredness in thinking, will and feeling, as well as positivity and openness. For me, a helpful image for this balance has been the five-pointed star. Each point is important in its own right, and when the five are brought together, something quite new comes into focus, begins to shine and radiate new force. This coming together as a star is what the sixth exercise allows—a harmonizing and enlivening consciousness. Over time, this kind of attention can foster self-confidence, inner tranquillity, objectivity, interest and strength with which to meet life's challenges, with which to grow in spiritual perception.

All our life experiences are substance for our inner development. The question is: will we let ourselves be overwhelmed or dulled, made hopeless or violent or apathetic by the troubles of modern life and, more specifically, by the challenges of modern parenting? Or will we take up the opportunities for inner work and school our attention to meet the world, and ourselves, and our children in ever deeper and more responsible ways? I think that many of us have come to feel that taking our inner lives seriously is actually a matter of survival, both for ourselves and through us for our children. If we are not to be mercilessly buffeted by the pace and the complexity of modern life, we need to strengthen our inner core, our ability to perceive the real needs around us, and our capacity to be self-directing. Furthermore, earnest attention to our own self-development is not only about ourselves; it will serve our children and it is also essential for the earth and for a healthy social future. Rudolf Steiner often expressed the idea that to truly find ourselves, we must look into the world, and to know the world around us, we must look within ourselves.[16]

Steiner presented spiritual science as a path of knowledge that can awaken in us an appreciation of our full human nature and responsibility. One way of translating the name he gave his work—Anthroposophia—is *awareness of our humanity*. It captures something of the path we follow as human beings, a path toward the conscious recovery of divine wisdom, known to the ancients as Sophia. As parents, we are allowed to witness and to guide the process of our children's human becoming. We are truly on a path of mutual development: their needs for care ask us to grow, and our love and attention nourish their unfolding. As adults, we can also go this journey with ever more inner attention, and so come to know ourselves in our own evolving.

Notes

1. See *Ariadne's Awakening* (Margli Matthews, Signe Schaefer and Betty Staley; Stroud: Hawthorn Press, 1986) for a discussion of how feminine and masculine qualities interweave within individual women and men, and also as cultural forces within the evolution of human society.

2. Rudolf Steiner, *How to Know Higher Worlds* (New York: Anthroposophic Press, 1994), 16.

3. Ibid., 18.

4. Ibid., exercises to enhance observation can be found particularly in Chapter 2, as well as in Rudolf Steiner, 'Practical Training in Thought' in *Anthroposophy in Everyday Life* (New York: Anthroposophic Press, 1995).

5. For an introduction to the idea of temperament see the chapter by Ann Druitt in Gudrun Davy and Bons Voors, *Lifeways: Working with Family Questions* (Stroud: Hawthorn Press, 1983), 200-213; and Rudolf Steiner 'The Four Temperaments' in *Anthroposophy in Everyday Life*.

6. R. Steiner, *Practical Training in Thought*, Rudolf Steiner Press, London and in *Anthroposophy in Everyday Life*.

7. R. Steiner, *How to Know Higher Worlds*, 26.

8. Rudolf Steiner, *An Outline of Occult Science* (New York: Anthroposophic Press, 1984), 291-292.

9. Ibid., 283-290.

10. Rudolf Steiner's *Intuitive Thinking as a Spiritual Path* (New York: Anthroposophic Press, 1995) addresses the question of living thinking as a path toward freedom. (Earlier translations of this book are titled *The Philosophy of Spiritual Activity* or *The Philosophy of Freedom*.)

11. R. Steiner, *An Outline of Occult Science*, 286.

12. Ibid., 287-288.

13. R. Steiner, *How to Know Higher Worlds*, 24.

14. R. Steiner, *An Outline of Occult Science*, 288.

15. John Davy, *Hope, Evolution and Change* (Stroud: Hawthorn Press, 1985).

16. This idea permeates Rudolf Steiner's work. It is also captured in many meditative verses; see for example: *Verses and Meditations* (London: Rudolf Steiner Press, 1972), 49 and 59.

Joseph Rubano and Patricia Rubano

Joseph Rubano

Life has been good to me—when I find something that I love I am allowed to follow it. As a kid I played sports. In my early 20s I found yoga and meditation which opened me to singing and dancing, which opened me to writing. I kept a journal and have been writing for myself for close to 25 years. In that time life has given me many teachers who have guided me into the worlds of marriage and fatherhood, herbs and healing, dreams, inner work and counselling, Native American wisdom and ceremonies, tai chi, anthroposophy, meditation and particularly into the world of relationships.

For many years, the world of work managed to grab only small pieces of me—I worked with teenagers in a home for runaways, painted houses, did carpentry, owned an herb company, taught in an Environmental Education Center, and coordinated maintenance in a spiritual community. Now, as I turn toward the world and offer myself to be eaten, the world is taking bigger bites. I am counselling, teaching tai chi, studying Spatial Dynamics, reading and writing poetry, leading workshops, and trying to be a good husband and father. As the world asks more, I shake, pull in a little out of fear, say yes anyway and cry out for help. I am blessed with many spirited friends, artists and healers, who open new worlds to me. Everyday I realize what a gift every 'you' is to me. We are borne by each other and born out of each other.

Meeting people in an alive, creative way is central to my life: I keep at it even though I fail over and over again! This article is the fruit of the work that Patricia and I have done through countless failings during twenty years of marriage. So it should be no surprise that writing the article was a struggle, one of the hardest things I've been asked to do. I wrote and rewrote it many times. Friends read it and with a loving pointed sword pierced me deep with their comments. I wrote some more—it kept getting stuck. Sometimes I'd think: this is going into a book, many people are going to read it. I'd get scared. My private world of writing was going public, was I ready? Was I good enough? I wanted to quit several times. I did for months at a time. But every time I thought I simply couldn't get it done by the deadline, the deadline was extended—I couldn't get out of it! I persevered with the continued help and encouragement from Patricia and friends—I turned a corner in my writing. I am grateful. I hope that the words I wrote can help others to open to, and honor the tremendous gift that every other human being is in their life.

Patricia Rubano

I consider myself a human being in training. And at 42 I feel that life up to this point has only been a preparation for what's to come. I have learned that I know nothing and that feels like the first hint of wisdom.

I was born in Kentucky of very mixed breeding (a real American mutt). My life has been blessed with loving parents, brothers I like, good friends, a few exceptional teachers (especially Mr. Shipley), two beautiful children and a willing partner. Who could ask for more?

More was provided however. There was Christianity that watered the seeds of love, truth, and freedom that were sleeping in my soul, Eastern philosophies that filled in some gaps, and finally anthroposophy bridged the two. Buddhist teachings of mindfulness and compassion along with Native American ceremonies of prayer and sacrifice have done a lot to open my heart.

I have spent the past 20 years working with young children, mostly in Waldorf schools. My dearest hope is that I can take what I have learned from the little ones and transform it to be a worthy offering for the big ones.

I think that the real world is the invisible one that weaves between— between people, between all beings, between the worlds. And I want to be a weaver when I grow up. But the chrysalis isn't finished yet and the butterfly is only a dream.

It took Joseph to write the words of this article in the end, but I think it took us both to create the substance of it. Thank you Joseph.

2
Listening and the art of relationship

Poles apart, I'm the color of dying, you're the color of being born.
Unless we breathe in each other, there can be no garden.

Rumi (1984, p.14)

Everyone must journey now, to the other end. Extreme to extreme.
Understanding each other is not meeting in the middle. Balance
does not come from offsetting the extremes. You must come to where
I am and I must come to where you are.
The middle is nowhere.

Juan Mobili (unpublished)

Here we are, two separate individuals, poles apart, living our lives together.
If we wish to grow something beautiful, we must breathe each other in. If
we wish to understand each other, we must leave the place where we stand
and walk to the other. In both pictures there is movement. This movement
is the relationship. It is what happens between individuals. For a
relationship to be life-giving something needs to be passing back and forth
between the two that carries nourishment and creates a spark.

One way that we take each other in and travel over the land in which the
other lives is by listening. The poet Antonio Machado said: 'To talk to
someone, ask a question first, then—listen.' Listening is the key to
understanding because when we listen we make it easier for another to
show us who they are. When we speak, if we attempt to put into words our
present experience openly, honestly, and from the heart we help another to
understand us. This moving back and forth via speaking and listening is
conversation. Through conversation we reveal who we are, we reach across

to each other, we breathe each other in. And where a true conversation lives between two people there you will find life. However, when the word is not spoken from the heart and received into the heart, or does not move freely between the two, the relationship begins to dry up and die just like a plant that is cut off from water and sunlight.

In this article, we hope to convey something about the art of entering into conversation and the activity of trying to understand another person. We will offer some pictures of what to strive for in a relationship, touch on the times we live in and introduce some thoughts on why intimate relationships are so difficult. We will talk about learning to make and maintain contact with someone you care about and the importance of listening and speaking the truth in the process. The process is one of creating a new kind of space into which another person may enter and feel at home. This conscious space-making activity allows us to get closer to someone while at the same time staying in touch with ourselves.

Striving for a new image

How are we with each other? How do we perceive and hold each other in our minds and hearts? What happens in us when we meet? Here is a picture of what we can strive toward:

Faithfulness
Create for yourself a new, indomitable perception of faithfulness. What is usually called faithfulness passes so quickly. Let this be your faithfulness:

You will experience moments—fleeting moments—with the other person. The human being will appear to you then as if filled, irradiated with the archetype of his spirit.

And then there may be, indeed will be, other moments, long periods of time, when human beings are darkened. But you will learn to say to yourself at such times: 'The spirit makes me strong. I remember the archetype. I saw it once. No illusion, no deception shall rob me of it.'

Always struggle for the image that you saw. This struggle is faithfulness. Striving thus for faithfulness, we shall be close, one to another, as if endowed with the protective powers of angels.

Rudolf Steiner

Steiner is talking about how we perceive, hold and carry the other person within ourselves. Many of us have had the gift of another person who sees the strength, light and beauty in us. With that person we become more than we think we are—we are freed and elevated by that person's perception of us. And we carry ourselves into our daily life with a clarity and inner joy that is calming, exhilarating, and refreshing. This happens when we fall in love. What Steiner is talking about is not falling in love, but a conscious striving to see the best in the other.

This is an important practice for it supplies the light and warmth, the invisible substance, which is essential for a relationship to flourish. It is a difficult practice because it requires us to go to that place in our heart where true seeing dwells. It is an activity that comes out of ourselves, it is not given from the outside. It can be helpful to remind yourself that you are a divine being and the person next to you or across from you is also divine. You can stand in awe inwardly asking the question: 'Who is this one that stands before me?'

The times we live in and the difficulty of intimate relationships

In thinking about relationships, the obvious question comes—why are relationships so difficult? Why is it so difficult to bridge the gap that separates any two people? What creates this gap to begin with?

Talk with almost anybody and you will hear a desire to be connected with others and to live and work together in harmony. We are social beings and we want to be social beings. So what is the problem? In his lecture, 'Social and Anti-social Forces in the Human Being,' Rudolf Steiner says: 'Precisely because one finds social impulses or desires in human nature, one also finds the opposite.' These he calls anti-social impulses or forces which separate one person from another. Today we have to reckon with both of these forces. (1982, p.3)

Those who are familiar with the work of Rudolf Steiner know that he talks over and over again of the evolution of human consciousness. In each age, humanity is faced with new challenges and must develop new capacities. The task for us today is to become free and independent human beings capable of making choices and taking a conscious part in the shaping of the world. Life does not simply happen to us—we are co-creators of our life and the life of the world. Each of us can make a difference. But to do so we are challenged to free ourselves from the influences of others and to become self-reliant in the sense of being able to see, understand and make judgments on our own. The activity of doing this requires that people move away from one another. In this way, we are anti-social. Each individual must evolve these anti-social forces for his or her own development. 'The anti-social forces are the pillars on which personal independence rests.' (1982, p. 2) Steiner goes on to say that for human beings to accomplish their task, these forces will continue to develop and become more powerful for another 1,000 years.

In the past, humanity had a 'natural' ability to be social. Today it is more 'natural' to be anti-social and egotistical, for distance to be created between people. We can see by this that relationships are necessarily difficult—we are not terrible people, guilty of some grave misdeed because this is the case—but there is work to be done. This means that if we want to be social, if we want to come to know and understand one another, it has to be made conscious and will require an inner effort. How do we come to understand and acknowledge each other? How do we free ourselves from our egotistical strivings enough to see another person clearly?

Influences from the past

Anything which keeps us trapped in our own world and unable to make genuine contact with others, we can call egotistical and anti-social. It is commonly acknowledged that we all carry pieces of our past around with us. We have been shaped and molded by our past relationships and life experiences, by our parents, teachers, culture and ancestry, and by the fact that we are male or female. We are inclined to identify with who we have become based on our past. The effects of this identification with the past is that we become less able to relate in the present moment.

Imagine that you are some kind of light being in the center of an energetic, mobile sphere of substance created out of accumulated past experiences, attitudes, beliefs, hopes, fears, likes and dislikes. By virtue of its makeup, the sphere, unlike the center, is somewhat darkened. In places it is energetic and moving, in places it is unmoveable, frozen and stiff. What and how you go through your life is influenced by your life experiences. But, remember, who you are is not your life experience. You are the light being in the center. The light being, when it is strong and bright enough, can illumine and penetrate into life experiences with love and understanding, thus enabling the experiences to serve the light being. When the light is not strong enough, the accumulated experiences take on a life of their own, become self-serving and confuse the light into believing it is also that experience. Mostly this is what happens: they take on a life of their own and we identify with them.

Because of this identification, when we meet another person or life situation, we do not meet it simply and directly center to center, but we meet it at some distance from our center in the mobile sphere that surrounds us. Some meetings are naturally and effortlessly illumined by the light from the centers when each person recognizes and is sparked by the other. Other meetings are not so illumined. Whenever and wherever we react to another person or life situation we are being controlled by the forces within the sphere which have a life of their own. In this sense we are not free of the burdens of the past. Our unfreedom is a result of a life experience that has not been fully understood or processed, that has not been illumined from the center. In the moment of reacting, these forces are stronger than our current ability to be alive, present and attentive to the moment. If our vision were not clouded by the past, if we were awake and aware of our present thoughts and feelings and able to express them appropriately, we would not react with antipathy or judgment. We would respond honestly and directly to what or who was in front of us.

In an intimate relationship, we are constantly living in the midst of the interplay of a variety of forces, some light-filled, some unfree. And since we open so much to each other, our love, our trust, all of our old wounds, we become extremely sensitive and vulnerable. The more time we spend together, the more opportunity there is for some conflict or interlocking of forces to occur. We can imagine that these forces, being unfree, act on each other in a mechanical, conditioned fashion. Something like this happens when two people fall into a fixed way of relating to each other, where they meet the same uncomfortable, stuck place over and over again. Sometimes we find ourselves responding to situations out of habit—we hear our father's voice in what we say or do or we find ourselves feeling and reacting just like we did as a child. We do not choose to be like this but we are not in control. We notice our response comes, not from the freedom of our own conscious choice but from an unconscious energy pattern from the past. In a relationship these forces are at work any place where life energy does not flow: in topics that people will not talk about, in how people avoid, push away or shut down around each other.

You can experience how these unfree energy patterns take on a life of their own and interact with each other in a dramatic way if you observe two people who are intimately related discussing something important. I have often witnessed couples begin talking about a specific incident or subject.

A word or emotion or particular way of perceiving something by one person triggers a reaction in the other which triggers another reaction. Often memories or connected topics or grievances are brought into play. Very soon a real battle is going on or a thick fog of confusion settles in while the original topic of conversation is lost or forgotten. The people end up miles apart and the bad feelings which are generated can hang around for days (or years). Most people don't understand what happened. Some force took over and carried them away. The two individuals at the center never met.

These forces will continue to work in our relationships. If they are not to take over, active participation and attention from each of us are needed. In a relationship, if even one person begins to observe him or herself closely enough to recognize how he or she is limited by all the past conditioning, the play of reactive forces is diminished. We can imagine that these locked-in experiences or attitudes want to be freed. We have the opportunity in an intimate relationship to set them free when we learn to acknowledge these forces and see through them to honor and understand the individual who is the light being in the center. In fact some things we cannot see by ourselves. The only way to free ourselves is with the help of an intimate partner.

Something new is being asked of us

We need to be independent, and the forces of the past are strong factors in our moving away from each other. Equally strong is our desire to be in relationship. I have asked many couples what they want in relationship. Most people answer in one form or another that they want to be wanted, to be seen and heard, and to be understood. Each wants to be loved and to love. And each wants space to be him or herself and to live his or her own life. It sounds so very basic and simple and ordinary. Of course we want these things. But if we look closely we can see that what people are asking for in relationship is really quite new. Can you imagine your grandparents or parents saying they want to be seen, heard, understood and acknowledged as unique individuals? I can't. I think that the turmoil and struggle in many relationships is because something new is trying to be born through them. When something new tries to be born, there is great resistance and often pain. Something has to die or be ripped open. What is the new that is seeking birth?

In *The Work of the Angels in Man's Astral Body*, Steiner says: 'The basis of all free religious feeling that will unfold in humanity in the future will be the acknowledgment, not merely in theory but in actual practice, that every human being is made in the likeness of the Godhead. When that time comes there will be no need for any religious coercion; for then every meeting between one person and another will be itself in the nature of a religious rite, a sacrament.'

We are being asked to nurture the sacramental in our relationships by learning to cultivate a deep honoring of ourselves and our partner. We are being asked to create the love-being of our relationship through our thoughts, words and deeds. In the old days more marriages held together. A different kind of glue was used then. It was applied from the outside— the glue of duty, custom, economic necessity, church, clan, close-knit family unit. This glue is cracking and you can only buy it in remote corners of the world. Today for a relationship to hold together and really serve the life of the two individuals and the community, the two individuals must really want it and be willing to work for it. This is the new kind of glue—it comes from the inside, it is created by our own intentions. We are left on our own. In fact we often get more encouragement from friends and professional counselling to get out of a relationship when we find ourselves stuck and unhappy, than to work through the difficult times. Serve yourself, do what is good for you, free yourself—these are the cries we all hear. Most of us do not know how to be free while in relationship. We do not know what the work is or how to go about doing it.

Fortunately, we are not completely stranded. There are a growing number of teachers, many husband and wife teams, who are discovering that it is possible to have fulfilling, long-term intimate relationships. Many books are available and workshops offered where people are taught how to work from the inside out to create a relationship that works. Patricia and I are walking the road in this direction. We would certainly not say that we have a completely fulfilling relationship and some days we really wonder if we have the right to say anything at all about relationship, but we can say that each year it's getting better. Each year we open a little more to each other. We were married in 1976, so that's 20 years. We want to encourage people to go through the struggles of relationship and to look for sources of help and support.

Dialogue—making contact, creating space

The ground work is set. We see the problems and some possible explanations. We see the high goals before us. We are back to the beginning.

How do we come to know and understand each other? Through listening and speaking; through entering into conversation with our partner. Let's face it, the only way we can know what is going on with another person and to find out what he or she really wants is by asking. I am convinced that the reason Patricia and I continue to want to be together is because we have been willing to take the time to talk in an effort to build a bridge of understanding between us.

Language has power, the word, passing between two people, has power. Georg Kuhlewind, in *From Normal to Healthy*, makes a tremendous statement when he says: 'Language really exists so that man can exercise and realize his humanity through it. Without speaking, a human is not really a human, and this means that without an interlocutor a human is not really human. In earlier times this partner in conversation was the godhead—his first 'thou'—and today it is the nearest godhead: his neighbor, another human being.'

We have each other as partners, so we might as well take advantage of this opportunity to help ourselves become more human. I know of no better way to reveal myself to another, actively and consciously, nor a better way to strive to understand another person than through dialogue. Through dialogue we reveal ourselves, through revealing we come to understand, through understanding we come to love each other.

We have found in our many hours of talking that we were not only building a bridge. Each time we are able to listen openly and to speak honestly we are creating a space for each other to enter into and be just as we are—in fact more than we know ourselves to be.

> Only the I within itself, has the power of stepping back and giving shelter to another (being). If the Ego were destroyed this shelter would also be lost. Love lives precisely in this: That two "I"s (Egos) give each other interior room or shelter.
>
> R. Frieling (*Christianity and Islam*)

How do we sit down and be with another person? In a poem titled 'Lost', David Wagoner (1976) has these lines:

> Wherever you are is called here
> And you must treat it as a powerful stranger
> Must ask permission to know it and be known.

In a lecture on 'Psychosophy', Steiner talks about the difference between perceiving a tree, hearing the sound of a bell, and listening to a person speak. In listening to a person we are concerned not with the sounds but with the inner life of the person; your inner being confronts the other's soul directly. And in so doing, you take good care not to intrude. He gives the picture of 'halting as in timid awe before the inner substance, before the matter that really concerns us.' In this halting we do homage to the inner soul activity of the other. So this is the necessary attitude—to stand before the other with awe and reverence, taking care not to intrude, asking permission to know and be known.

Even when you meet someone that you have lived with for 18 years don't think you know that person or that she knows you. If you think you know someone, you will not see or understand that person. You will not be attentive to the newness that is arising in the moment. Sit before that person as you would before a stranger. And when you sit with her, learn to be quiet yourself and open yourself to receive who this other is. Be interested and wonder—Who is this person?—Really wonder, listen, look with full attention: Who is this person, how can I understand this person? If we hold this attitude and attention, everything will take care of itself and both people will feel seen, understood, and alive. They will experience a living force between them and within them.

Basic guidelines and exercises

Early in our relationship, Patricia and I struggled a lot. We did not know how to open to each other, to meet specific problem areas directly or how to speak or listen to each other. We were fortunate though in meeting a man who was a student of Charles Berner, who was pioneering communication work in Northern California. From this man we learned a simple technique of sitting across from each other, speaking and listening openly to one another.

There were only a few basic guidelines to follow. Sit across from each other in a comfortable position. Make eye contact. Realize that the person across from you is a divine spiritual being and keep your attention on that divine being. (For some people the truth of this idea is instantly recognized and experienced, for others it is an idea that needs to be worked with.) We worked with specific questions or instructions that we asked or stated to our partners. The first ones that we worked with were: tell me something you like about me; tell me something that you think we agree on; tell me something about yourself that you think I should know; how can I help you;

how can you help me; what is going on with you right now; what is love; tell me who you are.

One person gives the instruction or asks the question from the place inside that is genuinely interested. He then places his full attention on his partner and listens as deeply as he can. The other person receives the instruction, contemplates it, and then speaks as openly and honestly as he is able. Each person speaks or listens for five minutes, then switches roles. Berner talks about communication as being the activity of transferring a thought from one person to another. The activity begins when one person wishes to get something across to another person. He then speaks, gestures, or does whatever he needs to do to communicate his thoughts or feelings. The one listening must receive what is expressed and make it known that he has understood. This is referred to as a completed communication cycle—one in which there is a choice to relate, the activity of relating and the felt sense of understanding and being understood by both people. Any breakdown in this cycle results in a miscommunication and ends in some degree of separation between the two people.

When Patricia and I began working on our ability to communicate, I was challenged to develop the courage to stay in contact and not retreat into myself, while also developing my ability to speak. Patricia was challenged to develop the courage and ability to listen while learning to hold back. We did these exercises for 10-40 minutes at a time. Sometimes we would do them every night for weeks. We practiced. We practiced just the two of us and we practiced in weekend workshops with total strangers. Slowly I developed trust. I had a hard time trusting Patricia with my deepest thoughts and feelings because she was always so quick to respond or react—I never felt enough space to reveal myself. Because of the structure and the importance placed on listening, I could remain open and speak, knowing I had space for at least five minutes! It was a great relief. Patricia found in the imposed listening that much of what she thought needed to be said to foster communication was unnecessary and that silence and stillness often served as far more powerful tools.

I must say that sometimes I felt silly using such a structured format—certainly we should be able to talk to each other without having to do it just this way! However, it was working. When we practiced like this we felt better about ourselves and better about our relationship. There are so many forces distracting us from really meeting each other that unless we develop certain skills and have a deep interest and intention to understand each other, the forces of separation will take over. The structure protected us and helped us to develop the necessary skills to communicate more ably and freely. It is like learning any art or skill—you must practice very specific techniques and exercises to establish the foundation and tools to express yourself artistically and fluidly. And if you don't love the practice, you won't be able to perform the art.

These exercises, while simple, have incredible power for they exercise important faculties in us and give us a deep experience of communion that we are each seeking. We are exercising what Georg Kuhlewind in his book, *From Normal to Healthy*, calls *right speech* and *right listening*. In right speech, we speak from what is going on inside us right now, from what we are experiencing in the present moment. In this moment we are free from the past. In right listening, we strive to understand the other. We meet the other with an inner stillness and put our full attention on the divine human being who speaks. In *Knowledge of Higher Worlds*, Steiner writes...'When one practices listening without criticism,...one learns, little by little, to blend with the being of another and become identified with it. Then one hears through the words into the soul of the other.' Buddhism aims to develop the capacity to listen so deeply that understanding is fostered not only in the listener, but also in the person who speaks.

Right speech arises out of right listening. Silence gives birth to the word. When we speak in this way and are received in this way, we experience a great relief. A space inside is opened and we feel an inner cleansing and feel alive. We have been held by the listening presence of another person and been allowed to touch something real and true inside of us that is often difficult to touch on our own. We feel understood and close to the person across from us.

Working out problems

> I was angry with my friend
> I told my wrath, my wrath did end.
> I was angry with my foe
> I told it not, my wrath did grow.
>
> W. Blake (Poison Tree)

Problems often arise in relationships. The problem can be big or small, obvious or subtle. The question is the same—how to deal with this problem together. Charles Berner says that every problem in relationship is a result of incomplete communications. This thought has guided me for many years and is one that I have contemplated many times. I offer it as a thought which may help others. Another guiding thought is that the responsibility for getting a thought across and being understood is up to the person speaking, not the person listening. Of course there is a working together, but the one speaking is making the decision to relate and it is up to him or her to get the message across to his partner. If we really work with this thought we can no longer blame someone for not understanding us, but must take on the responsibility for finding another way to express ourselves so that we are understood.

When a problem arises in your relationship, you can begin asking yourself—how can I make contact, what am I not hearing, what needs to be communicated, what do I not understand about the other person or situation, what does the other not understand about me or the situation? I have learned in my own relationship and in working with couples that problems can only be solved (or allowed to move and shift), misperceptions can only be clarified when there is a dialogue between the two people which addresses the problem directly. There must be an ability to identify what is going on, and a willingness to be honest and not hide or withhold feelings or information.

I have seen people get stuck at a certain place in their relationship and yet the relationship goes on for years in a jagged state because important issues or problems have not been faced directly. When we work with the biography of their relationship, often we uncover an issue or pattern of relating that revealed itself early on but was never talked about or worked through. Too often we don't express what is going on, we hold it in, stuff it down. Or we simply don't ask the right question of ourselves or each other that would allow us to investigate or even acknowledge what is going on. Sometimes people don't want to bring an issue up because they know it will be uncomfortable. (Some common issues which are avoided are how we relate to and deal with money, sex, problems with in-laws, having or raising children, past or present affairs, etc.) Many people would rather live with the known discomfort than meet the issue head on. Sometimes people are reluctant to say or reveal something because they are afraid of hurting their partner, or are afraid to appear petty, or are ashamed to admit what they have done or thought. Sometimes it is just a matter of habit—perhaps we have never experienced anything except avoiding facing issues.

Experience has proved to me that facing problems directly and speaking the truth set us free even when they cause some immediate, but temporary pain. The acute pain of the truth is far better than the dull chronic ache of untruth and hiding. Truth pain never lingers—it is always healing—a pain that feels good. It is better to tell your partner what you want or expect from him, rather than expect him to read your mind or figure that you'll never get what you want anyway so why ask. It is better to tell your partner what you don't like about how he or she is, or how she does something, or how you react inwardly to him or her, than to allow your reactions, judgments and criticisms to fester. It may even be better to admit to having an affair than to let semi-conscious knowing eat away at the two of you. The important thing in this truth-speaking is that our intention be to heal, not to hurt. Even as much as we are cut off from each other, we also know on some level what is really going on. At a certain point in a relationship it becomes obvious that we do not lead separate lives. We live into each other—we are interdependent. We are always influencing and affecting one another. We are creating something together. The question is: do we want to create something that is a lie or something that is true? Do we want to create something beautiful?

Facing problems directly

I have learned important principles for relationships from my practice of Tai Chi. In Tai Chi there is an exercise called Push Hands where two people face each other and push against one another gently trying to feel for where the other is tight or off center. The idea is to help your partner release holding and to maintain his center. When you push against each other you always maintain contact, never break contact, and you always keep moving. In a relationship we want to make contact, maintain contact and keep the energy moving. Ideally we want to help our partner to release any holding and to meet us from a relaxed, centered place.

The first step in dealing with any problem is identifying the fact that there is a problem. There is a problem whenever there is a break in contact and the flow of life energy is either not moving between the two people or when it is destructive. In a relationship we all need contact and we all need space from each other—too much contact or too much space is a problem. That is, contact which is not also space-making and taking space which is not also a staying in contact is a sign, if it goes on for too long, that the relationship is not healthy. Sometimes the problem is obvious—the tension, conflict and unhappiness is very clear to both individuals. Sometimes the problem is subtle and may only be felt or acknowledged by one person. There may be a feeling sense that something is wrong, a feeling that there is no real contact, a feeling of being alone or not understood.

Making contact

When there is a problem, identify it and set up a time to talk with your partner. It doesn't work well to catch your partner unawares and launch into
him or her with a problem you are having—make time, prepare yourself to
meet your partner over this particular issue. When you meet, agree to talk
about a specific issue or issues. Be careful to stick to those issues—don't
drag in all kinds of unrelated grievances you might have. Meet in a space
where you both are comfortable. Make yourself comfortable. You might feel
anxious or excited. You ought to feel anxious when you are about to meet
your partner face to face like this. You ought to be scared and shaky when
you decide to open yourself to let another person in, when you decide to
let down your guard, to be honest, or when you agree to be vulnerable.
Learn to welcome the anxiety. It is telling you that what you are about to
face is important. Honor that.

Maintaining contact

Decide who is to speak first, and who is to listen first. Always, for a dialogue
to work, one person speaks, the other listens. Remember the listening is the
most important: listening silence creates the space for the word to be
spoken into. (With many couples, one will always bring an issue up and
speak first. If this is the case, let that one listen first.) You can start with a
simple question or statement like: What is going on with you? or Tell me
what is going on with you. Or, what do you have to say about this or that?
When you first begin to work like this, it is a good idea to put a time limit
on how long a person can talk at one time—three to five minutes is a good
amount. After you have become practiced in listening and speaking without
interrupting you can just let the conversation flow without time limitations.
When one person speaks, the other listens. At this point you can work in
one of two ways: (1) The person listening, listens for the full five minutes,
then repeats back what he understands his partner as saying. If the person
speaking feels that she is understood, you go on and switch roles. If not,
then she speaks again to make herself understood. The person listening
repeats back what he understands until the speaker is satisfied she is
understood. You should practice this kind of listening until you feel that you
are both good at it and that you can understand the content of what is
being said regularly and easily. (2) Once this is achieved, the listener can
interrupt to ask questions of clarification when he does not understand

what the speaker is saying. Once he feels he understands, he continues listening. Questions can also be used to help the speaker go deeper into what he is saying: Can you tell me more about that? or What do you mean when you say that? are open questions which serve this deepening. After the five minutes are up, you switch roles.

Again, one person speaks and the other listens. The person who speaks wants to say what is going on for him in the moment—he wants to communicate his thoughts and feelings to his partner. It is very important that you are aware of your feelings and that you can name them. It is essential for the life of the relationship that you communicate them without making the other person wrong or insisting that things are as you interpret them to be. For instance, it is better to say: 'I am feeling hurt and upset because you made plans to go out with your friends without checking it out with me. I feel that you don't care about me when you do that', rather than: 'You piss me off. You're so self-centered. You only think about yourself and your friends, just like your father does.' The first way leaves more room for a response, while the second is more likely to lead to defensiveness and a moving away. The point is to have the other person understand you, not to make the other feel guilty or for you to come out looking like the good guy and the other the bad guy. The person listening must allow what his partner is saying to enter him. He must hold back any reaction or sudden urge to interrupt. If judgments or criticisms rise up, hold them back. Resist formulating a response, drop it and return to listening. Your job is to understand the other person, not to defend yourself or retaliate. It can be helpful while listening to inwardly ask yourself: How has this person come to think like this or feel in this way? Use your thinking attention to try to understand.

For both the speaker and the listener, it is an opening. The speaker opens to himself, enters into the depths of his soul to find what is true and real, and attempts to put his thoughts and feelings into words. He also opens to the other person to sense if that person is really connected to him and following what he is saying. The listener opens to the other while quieting himself and holding himself back so that there is room for the other to enter. Both people's attention is on the speaker. In this way the speaker is able to speak the truth if that is his intention. It is a real working together.

Continue talking in this way for 40—60 minutes and then bring it to a close. Agree to meet again to continue talking about the issue. Take as many sessions as you need until the two of you feel there is some resolution or the problem shifts in some way. The goal in this kind of talking is not that you solve your problems or that you agree with each other. The goal is that you understand each other. You may think that you need to resolve a problem right away and that you need to talk it out until it is resolved. You many think that if you had the right tools you could go in there and fix the problem just like a mechanic would fix a broken machine. You do not need to talk it out until it is solved. You do need to fix something that is broken. You need to talk in such a way that creative life forces are engaged and things begin to shift and move. This happens when you address an issue directly and create a listening space in which you can speak true and come to see the other person's point of view. When you work in this way—striving toward understanding, rather than resolving a problem—you will find that problem-solving becomes an artistic process. You will discover how seeing another's point of view can be a revelation and totally shifts the energy in an exchange. We are looking for these shifts in the energy state. If a shift has happened, you can know that you have spoken true and that you have been heard. If no shift happens you are still holding on too tight. Maybe you don't feel understood, maybe you haven't spoken from the heart—usually the listening space was not properly created. By a shift in state I mean that you will feel something open and relax deep inside, you will experience a peaceful aliveness—maybe tears will come, maybe laughter, maybe a deep sigh and inner smile. In any true meeting there is always this shifting and moving, there is an inner peace and a free-flowing exchange of life energy. The old stuck places begin to soften and open and new ideas are allowed to enter. New insights come; the problem shifts.

Example from my life

I would like to give an example to make more concrete some of the ideas that I have presented. In it there is a minor problem and distancing, there is the recognition that something is wrong, a wanting to make contact and a willingness to investigate what is going on with the intention to understand. In this case simple questioning with the right mood and intention allowed the energy to shift. Sometimes all that is required is for one person to have the presence of mind to observe what is going on and point it out without criticizing or passing judgment. To acknowledge and accept what is, in itself brings movement and a sense of relief.

One day Patricia and I took a day off and went to the shore together. We rented a room on the beach and had a full day and a half to be on vacation. Patricia enters right in to her being-on-vacation space and becomes contented and child-like. I should be happy to be around her. But no, I get grumpy and feel that whatever we are doing is not good enough, that we are wasting our time and money. I close up and withdraw into myself. Patricia is used to this and doesn't take it personally any more. She has learned to ask me what is going on. So she asks. I tell her I am not happy. She asks again: 'Why are you not happy?' Well now, we are getting close to something scary. Part of the reason I am not happy is that I am judging Patricia to be a mindless, superficial, middle class, American housewife who wants to have fun and indulge her senses. I don't tell her this right off. I say something safe like: 'Oh I'm worried about this paper I have to write, and I'm worried about my business.' She listens and asks again: 'Why else are you not happy?' Now she is pushing it. OK, if she asks, I will tell her. And I do. When I tell her, I am immediately relieved. She is wise enough not to take it seriously. She knows that what is going on with me is my problem and not her fault. I begin to loosen up. Patricia inquires further: 'What about my being superficial, indulgent and mindless is a problem for you?' Now I have to think and investigate my judgments and feelings. As I move further into myself and see that Patricia is not reacting I become more and more relaxed and open. I am able to say that I have a hard time letting go and just allowing myself to enjoy myself and I am envious of how easily she is able to do so. Because Patricia took an interest in me and gave me the space to say whatever was going on with me, I began to loosen up and was able to understand myself and the state I was in better. And I was able to let go of it and to really be with her again. I then asked Patricia how it was for her to hear me say the things I did about her. She told me, I listened and asked a few more questions. Patricia was in a good place within herself and didn't need to say much. It was a good meeting; we were together again. Playfulness began to live and move between us. We ate dinner, walked in the rain by the ocean, enjoyed each other's company and self-rejuvenated.

Of course, our conversations don't always run so smoothly. In this case, Patricia was relatively free inside to begin with and remained that way throughout. Usually both people are caught somewhere and the process of understanding is more difficult. But the basic work is the same. Create a listening space, focus on a specific issue, and speak truthfully with the intention to understand.

It is easy to fall into an unfree place inside. There are many opportunities to close down, react or hide. We can say that that fallen place is not a truly human place. To be human is to be spontaneous, creative, loving—is to be actively participating in life. We need each other to reclaim our humanity. We need to enter into conversation with each other, or probably more accurately, to recognize and make space for conversation that lives between us.

The Persian poet, Rumi, often talks about what lives between people. Here he addresses a question that many people ask who find themselves in conversation with a partner who is not willing or able to speak freely.

What if a man cannot be made to say anything?
How do you learn his hidden nature?

I sit in front of him in silence, and set up a ladder made of patience,
and if in his presence a language from beyond joy and beyond grief
    begins to pour from my chest
I know that his soul is as deep and bright
    as the star Canopus rising over Yemen.

And so when I start speaking a powerful right arm of words sweeping
    down,
I know him from what I say, and how I say it,
because there's a window open between us,
mixing the night air of our beings.

(Rumi *We are Three*)

The essential elements are listening and coming to the realization that we are intimately connected and that we want that intimate connection to be recognized. If one person is quiet enough to recognize the other, it is likely that the barriers between the two will begin to dissolve and what wants to happen next will also begin to reveal itself.

Notes

Kuhlewind,G. (1988) *From Normal to Healthy* Great Barrington MA: Lindisfarne Press

Rumi (1984) *Open Secret* Pulmy Vt: Threshold Books and *We are Three* Athansiga, Maypole Books, p. 71

Steiner, R. *Anthroposophy, Psychology, Neumotosphy* Lecture 2 'Action and Interaction of the Human Soul Forces'

Steiner, R. (1982) *Social and Anti Social Forces in the Human Being* Spring Valley, NY: Mercury Press

Wagoner, D. (1976) *Collected Poems 1956—76* Bloomington ID: Indiana University Press p. 182

Robert McDermott

In response to an invitation from my friend Patti Smith, I have agreed to express some reflections and feelings which might be interesting to readers of a volume exploring the varied challenges and joys of shared experience. Most readers of this volume have had to grapple with several of the concepts treated in this essay. Surely all of us interested in *Lifeways* are deep in the tangles of the unholy trinity—money, sex and power—and most, if not all of us move regularly between spirit and shadow.

Of the six terms in my title, I feel most comfortable sharing about wonder. For more than thirty years, I have been reading, teaching and writing philosophy, which, as Aristotle tells us, begins in wonder. Although the fifth of eight children, of sanguine temperament and a New Yorker for fifty years, I do occasionally take time to wonder, and when I do it is often about one or more of the other five terms in my title—money, sex, and power, spirituality and shadow.

I have been paying attention to money since age eleven when I began delivering newspapers after school. Money took on greater significance when I had to select an economic level for a family of four, and recommend values for institutions whose boards I have chaired (e.g., Rudolf Steiner [summer] Institute, 1983-93; Sunbridge College, 1988-92; and Rudolf Steiner College, 1990-present). I have certainly wondered about sex for at least as long as I have wondered about money, and for the past thirty-one years, my wonderings have been inseparable from my marriage to Ellen Dineen McDermott. Before we moved to San Francisco in 1990, Ellen was a Waldorf nursery teacher at the Rudolf Steiner School in New York City, and now, in addition to advising Waldorf schools and teachers, works with me on behalf of the California Institute of Integral Studies, of which I have been president for the past six years.

I have been interested in power throughout my professional career. My current position has provided an unusually rich opportunity for dealing with power as a spiritual schooling. The complexity of my responsibilities can be gleaned from this institution's mission statement: 'The California Institute of Integral Studies is an accredited institution of higher learning and research which strives to embody spirit, intellect and wisdom in the service of individuals, communities and the Earth.' The Institute community of 1200 students and approximately 150 faculty and staff has introduced me to the realities of anxiety, projection and New Age psycho-spiritual complexities for which I was totally unprepared by my twenty-five years as a professor in New York.

Like power, money and sex are also opportunities for spiritual schooling. To write about these three concepts would require not just knowledge and insight but an ability to detect and resist the temptation to smooth over rough spots, and to put a happy face on the difficult areas of my private and public life. The extent to which I fail to inform these three activities by spiritual ideals may be referred to as shadow—always unconscious—in my thinking, feeling and willing.

I hope and expect that what I have written has been influenced by the thoughts of Rudolf Steiner, albeit indirectly. There are no references to sex or power, and only bibliographical references to money, in the 450 pages of my *Essential Steiner*. Similarly, in the more than one hundred public lectures

I have delivered on the teachings and significance of Rudolf Steiner, I have scarcely ever discussed money, sex or power. Thanks to the opportunity given me by the editors of this volume, I hope that I will now begin to apply some of Rudolf Steiner's ideas to money, sex and power, as well as to the subtle dance of shadow in all phases of spirituality.

3
Money, sex and power: spirituality, shadow and wonder

My friend Roxanne (Jean) Lanier has written a perfect opener for an essay on sex:

> 'A man sits up in bed next to a woman. 'Was it good for you?' he asks apprehensively. 'It was marvelous,' she replies. Satisfied with her response, he rolls over and tries to sleep. She too tries to sleep. Instead of sleeping, however, they each lie awake, wondering in silence.'[1]

My comments on this topic, perhaps juicy in apprehension, will prove in the end to be not much more than a series of wonderings. I will be pleased if they are wonderings and not merely commonsense assumptions dressed up for publication. I wonder about this difference: given the effects of professional training and mores, how can we detect when, and to what extent, we are thinking, speaking, writing, and wondering authentically, or when merely receiving conventional ideas?

I suspect that our 'wondering in silence,' as in the passage by Roxanne Lanier, above, is almost always more authentic than our wondering for public consumption. If posturing is scarcely avoidable in general, it would seem completely inescapable from any one of the six concepts in this essay. It is especially unproductive to write on the shadow of one's experience since shadow, by definition, refers to those elements and forces which work unconsciously. To be so conscious of one's motives in money, sex or power games as to be able to write about them would leave them as problems, but not as shadow.[2]

I want to approach the first three terms in the title of my essay—money, sex and power—from a spiritual perspective; but to claim spirituality concerning even one of them is to risk hubris and almost certainly run foul of shadow. Hence, I wonder whether I can say anything concerning my relation to them that isn't at least a mix of spirit and shadow, and perhaps all shadow dressed in spiritual garb? And is this caution which claims to issue from modesty not also shadow? I wonder.

This is the same kind of wonder I experienced in college philosophy courses when I first read existentialists such as Jean-Paul Sartre: Is it possible to escape, to be an exception to, self-deception? Now, after thirty-five years of reading philosophy—and after thirty-one years of marriage—I'm still wondering.

As Sartre rightly argued, not to know about self-deception is itself a form of self-deception; not to admit to the reality of the shadow in our own individual psycho-spiritual experience is itself shadow. By self-deception, Sartre doesn't just mean ignorance of self, of my true thoughts and feelings; he means an active, disabling protection of my self from my own inner, deeper, disturbing self, including self-protecting and self-enhancing motives and needs. Sartre's is only one version of many post- and neo-Freudian accounts of our increasingly well-documented ability to self-deceive. Scarcely any activities of our lives provide such rich opportunities for self-deception and shadow behavior as our relationship to money, sex and power.

Do we ever escape this shadowy realm, this cave of self-aggrandizement? I wonder. Perhaps Roxanne's essay might help.

'While there is nothing so disappointing as the emptiness we can feel after 'having sex,' there is nothing quite so fulfilling as the ecstasy we experience in truly meeting and joining with another person in the spirit of reverence for the total being of that person. It is in such encounters that we can know and love the God who is love. This love has nothing to do with possession or obsession. It has to do with freedom, with spirit.'(p. 20)

With Roxanne's sage words in my mind, I asked for guidance that I too might write something helpful and truthful concerning the relationship between my daily life and the high teachings, particularly those of Rudolf Steiner, on which I have been pondering, writing, and lecturing for the past several decades. How is it possible to get from 'having sex,'—or making money, using power—to an experience of God, spirit, or freedom?

Since my teen years, money, sex and power have been driving forces in, or of, my life but almost always packaged or colored by other values. The important topics are usually mediated, wrapped and veiled by a mix of positive and negative goals and pressures such as responsibility, service, sympathy and affection, as well as control, manipulation, opposition, and antipathy. When I set out to say something about these three concepts, I have to get at them through relationships, within the context of my original family, my wife and children, my career and position, my karmic situation, and, as Roxanne Lanier reminds us, within my relation to being, to spirit and to freedom.

Part of the schooling with respect to money-sex-power, as well as with spirituality and shadow, is to strive to know what I have brought to this life, to this incarnation, including the experiences and relationships appropriately lying in wait for me, and the capacities I should ideally develop this time around. From what source of guidance, and by what markers, can I know to what extent I am approximately in the right set of relationships and the right work?

Neither a map nor the terrain alone can give us full knowledge. Living contact with terra firma can be tremendously enhanced by a picture of that place in relation to others, and the layers of places, and relation of layers, etc. So, too, with the self: each lived experience is both unique and part of a context of meanings. Hence, the utility of maps for biographical as well as spatial experience. Contemporary social sciences, including most recent Western philosophies and psychologies, tend to ignore or deny both the unique and the inner in favor of the generic, or what we might call the trackable or mapable. According to the modern western paradigm, all else is marginal or fictional.

By contrast, Rudolf Steiner's spiritual scientific research emphasizes the unique experience of the 'I,' or spirit, the spiritual Self which stands behind the astral body or soul, etheric body and physical body. If we aspire to the inner experience of the true 'I,' of the unique yet infinite and universal reality, there might be a tendency to focus on this achievement at the expense of the other levels or layers of experience. We should note that Rudolf Steiner describes anthroposophy as 'a path of knowledge to lead the spiritual in the individual to the spiritual in the universe.' [3]

This description might give the mistaken impression that anthroposophy is concerned with the spiritual 'I,' but not particularly with the astral or soul life. Such an understanding would be distressing for all of us who seem to function only occasionally, and then with a mix of effort and grace, at the level of our spiritual 'I.' Most of the time, I seem to be functioning at, and caught in, a level removed from my essential-spiritual self, whether in the astral, etheric or physical mode of consciousness. To be at the 'I' or spirit level is to be, at least momentarily, in a state of grace, outside the Platonic Cave, free from the Buddhist wheel of samsara—in short, at a very high and rare state of consciousness.

C. G. Jung's account of the Self covers much of the same ground as Steiner's psychology, though Steiner offers many artistic, social and epistemological ways of developing the relationships between the spiritual self and the spiritual which dwells within all dimensions of reality. Unfortunately, Jung doesn't tell us any more than Steiner does about money, sex and power, but Jung tells us a great deal about shadow (it is essentially a Jungian concept), and Steiner tells us more than we can absorb, and, I believe, more than any other contemporary teacher, about the reality of spirit. Steiner also describes very effective ways to relate spiritually to oneself and to the rest of the universe.

Three significant parts of the universe through which we can realize our spiritual nature, and the spiritual nature of the universe, fall under the headings of money, sex and power. Realizations of the spiritual through these three channels are inevitably mixed with shadow—unconscious psychic energies working against our conscious, and confident, attempts to work spiritually. My efforts to reach a deeper, truer, more spiritual plane by sexual acts, by the exercise of power, by financial decisions, are all partly caught in a mix of unconscious not-so-spiritual motives. As a white male with professional credentials, I am invested in holding on to privilege even while working to empower individuals and groups with relatively less power. I am generally careful, and secretive even to myself, in my determination to help those individuals empower themselves who will not do so at my expense.

I want my wife Ellen to have more power but I do not want any less. Whether with respect to my wife or colleagues, I want more power for those whom I love or to whom I am committed in some way, but unconsciously, and habitually, I want them to take more, as it were, from another pile, as though money and power were quantities. Materialism is widespread. Even sex lends itself to this kind of thinking—not so much in terms of measurable units as in hopelessly unfruitful wondering about who gets what, and my just deserts. Money, sex and power are not negative but they do invite some negative modes of consciousness. When we relate to any one of these activities in an enlightened and spiritually free way, the material realm is also freed and illumined. We thereby create a thing of beauty, truth and love concerning which gods, angels and bodhisattvas can join in celebrating with the entire human community.

Two of Steiner's foundational books, *Intuitiive Thinking as a Spiritual Path* [4] and *How to Know Higher Worlds* [5], are intended to help us to relate spiritually to all realms of experience. These books, along with his approach to education, to sciences, and various artistic activities, can enable us to experience the spiritual dimension of processes such as sexual thoughts, feelings and actions; the handling of uneven power relationships; and the stirring of financial energies. Steiner doesn't tell his followers, or readers, what to do or what to think, but he does offer excellent advice on how to improve our thinking, feeling and willing so as to see into the secret life of complex and mysterious processes such as salaries, insurance and philanthropy; the relationship of eros and karma, eros and beauty, sexuality and love; power and service, power and domination, power and gender, power and temperament.

With respect to most of these situations and processes, I typically find myself to be working from a level removed from the 'I,' but I know that my reading countless volumes by Rudolf Steiner, and other efforts which are essential for progress in spiritual science, have had some effect if only because I am increasingly aware of the contrast between my ordinary relationship to money, sex and power and a truly spiritual, 'I'-based relationship. I hope it is not merely my 56 years, but the 21 years of struggling with the help of anthroposophy, that have enabled me to be slightly less satisfied by, or attached to, surfaces. Whitemaleness, professional status, career-successful family members, are superficial characteristics in competition with the reality of inner life and genuine individuality.

Although I am deep into idolatry with respect to money, sex and power, I now can name the idols and know them for what they are, even while continuing to love them. To love idols [6] is the essence of modern western consciousness; to work past idols to spiritual realities is the purpose of anthroposophy.

'Being caught in idolatry' is another way of describing thinking, feeling and willing on the etheric and physical levels of consciousness separate from the spiritual 'I', or thinking, feeling and willing bereft of imagination. When removed from the 'I' and from imagination, objects and relationships are more generic: money, sex and power, each in its myriad ways, become an 'it,' a 'having.' In these modes, I seem to be able to locate, characterize and evaluate my experience, but only as appearance or surface. Actions and desires not rooted in my spiritual self are not relational. They are neither for the other nor for the universe; they are 'all mine.'

In such relationships, and in such a mode of consciousness, money, sex, and power seem to me inseparable, and perhaps indistinguishable. They each have something of the 'I want,' 'it's mine' feel against which Buddha, the Dalai Lama and Gandhi, as well as Christians such as Simone Weil and Dorothy Day, are especially insightful and exemplary. It seems safe to claim that virtually all spiritual teachings and disciplines aim to some extent at the transformation of desire and attachment consciousness.

Anthroposophy, the spiritual science of Rudolf Steiner, provides a particularly effective way of getting to the root of deep and complex processes such as money, sex and power, but in the effort to penetrate to inner reality we are liable to meet shadow mixed with spirit. Many spiritual teachers have been heard to remind their students, as we get closer to the light, we cast a longer shadow. This is why Rudolf Steiner's spiritual path, as explained in *How to Know Higher Worlds*, begins with humility and reverence.

Since most of us have to deal with money, sex and power, and since shadow is a permanent accompaniment of spirit, humility and reverence are indispensable if we are to have any hope of relating to money, sex or power in, or from, a spiritual consciousness, from the spiritual being that I essentially am, however dimly I perceive my true being. It would be excellent for each of us and for those whom we love if we were to make the most positive possible relationship between our 'Philosophy of Freedom' Self that each of us essentially is and the truest spiritual possibilities of money, sex and power. As Plato was the first to note, and Spinoza the second, 'All things excellent are as difficult as they are rare.' [7]

Notes

[1] Jean (Roxanne) Lanier, 'From Having to Being: Toward Sexual Enlightenment,' in Georg Feuerstein, ed., *Enlightened Sexuality: Essays on Body-Positive Spirituality* (Freedom, CA: The Crossing Press, 1989), p. 17.

[2] For a thorough and insightful account of the interplay of spirit and shadow in daily life from the perspective of a transpersonal psychologist steeped in Asian and western spiritual teachings, see Frances Vaughan, *Shadows of the Sacred: Seeing through Spiritual Illusions* (Wheaton, IL: Quest Books, 1995)

[3] Robert A. McDermott, *The Essential Steiner* (SF: Harper San Francisco, 1984) p. 415.

[4] Rudolf Steiner, *Intuitive Thinking as a Spiritual Path: A Philosophy of*

Freedom, trans. Michael Lipson (NY: Anthroposophic Press, 1995)
    5. Rudolf Steiner, *How to Know HigherWorlds: A Modern Path of Initiation*, trans. Christopher Bamford, afterword Arthur Zajonc (NY: Anthroposophic Press, 1994)
    6. For idolatry, see Owen Barfield, *Saving the Appearances: A Study in Idolatry* (NY: Harcourt, Brace & World, 1957)
    7. Plato, *Laws*; Spinoza, *Ethics*.

4
The Bell Ringing verse
Robert McDermott

A verse is spoken each morning in Waldorf classrooms all over the world. Students begin the day with recitation which creates harmony and community in the classroom and the repetition builds strength in students. Although the verse is not discussed in class, it is important that the teacher has a deep understanding of it. Verses can accompany activities in the home as well, and create an atmosphere of togetherness and reverence. A grace before meals, a poem, prayer or verse at bedtime can become a family ritual.

The following is Robert McDermott's meditation on the Bell Ringing verse by Rudolf Steiner. Robert was neither a Waldorf student nor teacher, but is the parent of a student who attended a Waldorf school. He offers his meditation on this verse in the hope that it might encourage others to work with it themselves.

The verse was written by Rudolf Steiner for an eight year old student identified as R.G. The translation printed here uses gender inclusive language. Another translation 'At the Ringing of the Bells,' is printed in Rudolf Steiner, *Truth-Wrought-Words and Other Verses*, trans. Arvia MacKaye Ege (NY Anthroposophical Press, 1979) p.13

The Bell Ringing verse

To wonder at beauty
Stand guard over truth
Look up to the noble
Decide for the good
This leads us truly
To purpose in living,
To right in our doing,

To peace in our feeling
To light in our thinking.
And teaches us trust
In the working of God,
In all that there is,
In the width of the world,
In the depth of the soul.

To wonder at beauty

Aristotle explained that the love of wisdom begins in wonder; so does beauty. By wisdom and beauty we come to love the human, the Earth and the Spirit. Beauty is as deep as the soul and as wide as the world. John Keats wrote: 'A thing of beauty is a joy forever.' Beauty lives in the fairy tale, in the rhythms of words and music, in the play of colors, in the secrets of nature, in the loving of persons, in silence.

Stand guard over truth

In a world gone clever, truth needs protection. We don't consider truth very often, or very well. We consider what works, what will fly. Why do we need truth when we manage so well with seems, sort of, and virtual? Imitation passes for the original in thinking as well as in art. We guard countries, possessions and persons in jail. To guard truth involves knowing where the real, including one's real self, begins and leaves off. Which of my thoughts and actions spring from myself, and which have been supplied by image doctors? If I so resolve, I can stand guard over the truth of my being, and guard against a counterfeit self created stealthily by social convention and my own unwakefullness.

Look up to the noble

Where is the noble after the deceptions of the Vietnam War and Watergate, after the psychology of co-dependency, projection, and the profit motive? Now that we know so well the Wizard of Oz, and have seen behind the veil of the altar and the throne, whom can we and our children admire? Perhaps it is still not too late for children and adults to find the noble in the sacrifice of parents and teachers, and the persistent search of children for ideals in action. Even though the love of parents and teachers for children never makes the evening news, such love happens every day. Daily heroism should be sufficient but we seem to need as well the extraordinary exemplar. Fortunately, exemplars are available in every culture and for each stage of life.

Steiner recommended fairy tales for young children, followed by myths and legends, and then history and biography—each as suitable resources for noble and health-giving images. The Bhagavadgita says: 'A great soul is difficult to find.' Great souls and noble ideals are found only by seekers. Thousands were in the presence of Jesus but did not see Him because they weren't seeking. Jesus said: 'Seek and you shall find.' It takes trust, effort, and helpful adults for children to find the noble within, and beyond.

Decide for the good

Goodness requires action. Black Elk had a magnificent dream, and he knew that it wasn't fully real until he acted on it in the world. The good is at risk for lack of attention, conviction and determination. The motto of Hampshire College says: *non satis scire*—'To know is not enough.' The Mother of the Sri Aurobindo Ashram said: 'No more words. Action.' Though action is also insufficient; it is free and spiritually-based choosing that makes the difference. Accidental and unconscious performance of the good is less than doing the good deliberately. Non-choosing may work out, but the good issues from choosing. Rudolf Steiner not only leaves his readers free to decide for themselves what right might be in each case, but he knew that one's own decision is the only way to achieve the right.

The act of choosing is an essential part of the good in all areas, including artistic work and interpersonal relationships. Not choosing is also a choice. The inner and outer are not joined automatically, or easily, but by an integration of thinking, feeling and willing which is active and spiritually free.

This leads us truly to purpose in living

Most of us have to create meanings by our individuality, relationships, and special activities. The opportunity to chose one's life-work is recent in human history. In the ancient past, family circumstances fixed one's life-work. In the present time, a person chooses a life-work from a confusing array of choices. This life-defining task can be as much a problem, and a crisis, as an opportunity. As Marx wisely said (we needn't discard his true insights along with his failures), in capitalist societies meanings and purposes are typically not to be found in one's job. This requires inner resources. When children complain of 'having nothing to do,' and when adults fall into addictive behaviors, such inner strengths are blocked or underdeveloped. Vocation was a useful word, for it pointed to the reality of a wiser self able to detect the rightful lure of one's destiny.

To right in our doing

We are led to the right by our relation to the good. Right is the part of good which is made manifest by moral choice. We are in a quandary concerning competing values and claims to justice (e.g., imprisonment, euthanasia, abortion) because the right is rooted in realities too deep for ordinary thinking. It took Plato a lifetime of meditative reflection to realize that justice is the individual and social harmony of truth, love and beauty within The Good. Plato and Aristotle rightly understood that it is only possible to do what is right by a just relation to the whole.

In traditional cultures, the right was established by a dominant concept such as the Chinese *tao*, or the Indian *dharma*, both of which have a double meaning—teaching and way. The dominant thinkers of modern western culture teach that no one knows the true teaching or the true way. In this time of systemic alienation, we need help discerning and doing the right. If we seek, we will receive the help of the spiritual world manifested by higher beings, as well as by the spiritual striving of families, teachers and friends. The very American words of John F. Kennedy's inaugural address express a modern western understanding of the law of karma concerning right doing: 'We know that on earth God's work is truly our own.' Buddhist teachers recommend and exemplify *upaya*, skillful means, or right in our doing.

To peace in our feeling

At the birth of the Messiah, the angels offered glory to God and peace on earth. Peace, like happiness, cannot be attained directly, but follows from good will. Incredibly, people of good will abound in countries and communities living in pain and terror. We look with amazement at the depth of peace exhibited by Native Americans and African Americans in the United States; pro-democracy advocates in China, Burma and many countries in Latin America; Blacks in South Africa; hundreds of millions of peaceful women and children around the world who are victims of violence. It is from the communities of the suffering that the prophets of peace have come. Seamus Heaney, the Irish poet and Nobel Laureate, has told us that the suffering peoples are creating the most powerful and most honest literature in our time.

The Twentieth Century has witnessed 250 million deaths from wars, and has been blessed by peaceful persons of good will, including Mahatma Gandhi, Simone Weil, Martin Luther King, Jr., Dorothy Day, Thich Nhat Han, His Holiness the Dalai Lama, Archbishop Tutu, Nelson Mandela, Aung Sau Suu Khy. A study of the lives and works of such individuals shows that peace issues from a commitment to beauty, truth, nobility and goodness. As Gandhi showed, peace never comes from violence or from weakness; it comes from truth-force, or courageous love.

To light in our thinking

The god Prometheus brought light to humanity in the double form of fire and knowledge. The Buddha brought enlightenment; His Holiness the Dalai Lama refers to the Bodhisattva vow as a 'flash of lightening in the dark of night.' Christ called Himself the Light of the World—and He came into a dark world which did not comprehend Him. St. Augustine taught that salvation comes from knowledge by illumination. Many strive for bright ideas, and those who succeed are called brilliant. The ideas themselves live in the light, and the light is one with beauty, truth and goodness. Isolated ideas can appear bright at first but if they are not grounded in reality, in the Light of the World, they fade.

The relationship between light and thinking must be real, but also mysterious. Light and thinking are dying in our time; they share God's life and ours, but only if we are awake to their presence. This line could read, 'to life in our thinking,' or more exactly, 'to God's life in our free spiritual thinking,' or 'to Logos-thinking.' Thinking is alive, light and Logos-filled to the extent that it is awake, free and loving, to the extent that by our act of thinking we are relating to interiors, to the spiritual in whatever we know. While dead (and deadly) thinking is the opposite of love, light- and life-filled thinking issues from our love of the divine that inheres in the universe.

Spinoza's 'amor intellectualis' (love of God) is a profound double-entendre: to the extent that we love God it is by God's love of us. It is true that the love by which I love God is the love by which God's love turns back to Itself. It is the same with thinking: The Light by which I think is the Light by which God the Logos illumines all things that have come into the world. To think a truly bright idea is to jump from reality that I am to a reality I embrace, as spark to spark, and light to light. To think truly is to live and move and have one's being as one with the Light of the World.

And teaches us trust in the working of God

Media and education warn against trust. Higher education in the modern West is especially opposed to trust in God. Too many prophets have led hapless followers to absurdities and atrocities. Cemeteries are filled with trusting believers. Knaves and rogues abound, as do their victims. God seems to be no exception: many who trust in God's providence die of cancer and accidents as readily and as cruelly as rapists.

Trust in the working of God is not an isolated deed, but a hard won orientation and grounding. It is more like faith or confidence than belief: we believe that such-and-such is the case, but we trust, have confidence or faith in something or someone. Jesus taught trust: 'Consider the lilies of the field...' Emerson taught trust in one's own truth. This is difficult in a world of second-hand knowledge and quick solutions. Trust must be learned, and relearned. The report from Nietzsche at the end of the nineteenth century that 'God is dead' has been repeated by thinkers throughout the twentieth century. Has God abandoned the modern western psyche, or is God dead only to those who are dead to God's presence? It is easier to trust that the divine is everywhere than that it is somewhere in particular. Wherever and however God is, God's presence shines with beauty, truth, goodness and love.

In all that there is

In complexity and extent, the all increases daily. The great task of the present and future is the deepening of relationships between individuals and groups, between one group and others, between the human and the rest of the cosmos, between thinking, feeling and willing, between spirit and matter. How can we make real in experience what we know by theory—that there are no loose ends? To experience the all, we need to meet ugliness, falsehood and evil as well as beauty, truth and goodness. Rudolf Steiner reminds us of a legend in which Jesus' followers expressed disgust at the sight and smell of a decaying dog, but Jesus countered by admiring the dog's teeth. Antipathies distort reality and prevent deep relationships. Reality is a seamless garment which our biases and analyses rend in pieces. To know the All, we need to replace critical with sympathetic thinking. As analysis and argument divide, sympathy and imagination unite.

In the width of the world

From outer space the earth is a blue marble. Carl Sagan knows the cosmos by intellectual knowledge, Brian Swimme by affectionate knowledge. By her devotion to a cell's complexity and mystery, Barbara McClintock revealed the intimate relationship between the microscopic and the macrocosmic. Boundaries recently thought to be inviolate are now known to be arbitrary. How wide is the world? How wide is our view of the world? Consciousness is extended by the rush of cultural, scientific and technological innovations. The globalization of arts and business, travel and media, relentlessly expand, but do not necessarily deepen, our relation to the universe.

In the depth of the soul

Rudolf Steiner found ways by which we can attain knowledge of higher (or deeper) worlds, or spiritual realities, by relating the spiritual in the individual to the spiritual in the universe. The relationship between depth of the soul and the depth of the universe produces knowledge without diminishing mystery.

The depth of the soul actively receives health-giving feelings; images and archetypes come from fairy tales, myths and the exercise of imagination. From the depth of the soul issue both words and silence. Words are often helpful but hardly adequate. Even the words of Rudolf Steiner, of His Holiness the Dalai Lama, and of other spiritual teachers, are but pointers to a stillness in the depth of the soul and in the depths of the universe.

A bell ringing is a pointer to a community made possible by the sacrifice of parents and teachers, and of their parents and teachers; and the sacrifice of His Holiness the Dalai Lama, exemplar and embodiment of wisdom and compassion; and the sacrifices of Rudolf Steiner, a teacher of teachers whose spiritual research made possible the Waldorf insights into human development, learning and cultural renewal. Such sacrifices have created communities capable of receiving children in reverence, educating them in love, and sending them forth in freedom. It is for children that the bell rings.

Lee Sturgeon-Day

Born in Britain in 1941, educated in England, and later (as a high school drop-out) in Italy and France. After a year in the Far East my first 'solid' job was personal assistant to Sir John Betjeman (Britain's Poet Laureate) for three years, when, among other fascinating and eccentric folk, I met my first anthroposophist, (lovely, but definitely into something pretty weird!). Later experiences include: secretarial work, food research and writing, managing a London coffee-house, farming, lighting rock concerts, and flamethrowing in a circus, in between writing bad novels, living again in Italy, and traveling to Persia and other Middle Eastern countries. Since taking up anthroposophy (now I'm the weirdo?), career changes have included: professional counseling, adult education (biography work), founding Lifeways for Healing Education in Detroit, parenting a son (Adam), and writing a book (*A Slice of Life*). I moved to Sacramento, California for a Waldorf high school and, among other connections, have been joyfully reunited with Japan (through the Japanese Program at Rudolf Steiner College), which I left so reluctantly over 30 years ago.

Now (50 years on from World War 2) we stand at the end of the century on another battlefield. As Dr. Bernard Lievegoed called it in his last testament, a *Battle for the Soul*; for true human development into the future as free individuals and as members of a world community. For all the support I've received on my journey, my hope is to offer something back to the many 'warrior' souls I encounter in any, every, walk of life. My first loves were words and friends. They still are: the meetings, the conversations, and the strength, courage, inspiration, humor and hope we can give each other for the days and years ahead. I am sure this book of personal sharing on many life themes will be an important contribution (iron rations?) for readers and writers alike, and I'm very glad to be part of this enterprise.

5
Mrs Bun and Master Bun, the baker's son— some reflections on single parenting

A few years ago I was invited to talk at a conference on family life. 'But I don't know anything about family life,' I replied.

Family—for me—comprised a father, mother, boy, girl, like the 'Happy Families' card game I played as a child: Mr Bun the Baker, Mrs Bun the Baker's Wife, and no point scored till you had collected Master and Miss Bun as well. My own little duo—one mother, one son—clearly fell short of this ideal, and didn't really count as a proper family.

Despite abounding variety of family groupings in our times, I think many parents, single or otherwise, measure their particular family against entrenched stereotypes. And the single parent may suffer particularly. When the father of my child remarried and inherited other children, it was suggested that my son should join him: 'So he can be raised in a *proper* family,'—implying the lack of a father and other siblings was *improper*, inadequate, possibly damaging.

Our stereotypes are rooted in archetypal images which have gradually materialized as cultural norms. In our predominantly Judaeo-Christian culture, we have the Holy Family: flawless Madonna, adoring Father, Divine Child. This now, in the West, has also come to include a daughter, nice home, glossy car and fully-functioning washing machine. Though we know very well that few families really have shiny-haired, tireless Moms, handsome, devoted Dads, and winsome kids whose rare aberrations are merely opportunities to discover the right brand of cereal or soap powder, few of us are immune to the power of these images. Don't we all—in dark moments—believe it is others who have *proper* families, and that our own is somehow off track?

In his book, *Marriage—Dead or Alive?*[1], Dr Guggenbuhl-Craig suggests we turn to Greek mythology for some alternative imagery. Here we find everything: rape, adultery, abandonment, incest; unwed mothers, single fathers, step and half-siblings; children spawned by gods and beasts, reared by passing strangers. Little that happens in our world today cannot be found in these tales. Yet although they may shift and broaden our perspectives, we are not ancient Greeks, we live in different times, with different imperatives. We need to discern the particular challenges and opportunities that our age is bringing us, and find appropriate inspiration to guide us into the future.

The 'necessary chaos' of our times

Rudolf Steiner describes our era in the following words:

> In such a time as ours, man must behold all sorts of things that are arising out of chaos. Chaos is necessary. We are living at a time in which man must pass through those impelling forces in the course of evolution that set him upon his own feet and permeate him with individual consciousness.[2]

It is clear that we are living through chaotic times. In this century—at least in the West—we have seen the crumbling of forms and traditions— both religious and secular—that confined and supported us in our communities. Through the breach in these walls, a wave has swept us into a world of new realities. Our new freedoms have created all kinds of relationships that did not exist before; we've had no practice at them, can draw on no previous wisdom for guidance. At the same time, it seems, we have also lost certain inner, instinctual capacities that equally have set limits and guided our behavior. Go into any bookstore and see the size of the 'How To' shelves. It appears we need to learn everything from scratch: how to breathe, eat, walk, talk; how to find a mate, keep one, dispose of one; how to parent, how to keep young, how to age, how to die. In short, how to go about the business of being human quite independently of any inborn abilities. This is also utterly new!

The first reality we have to accept for ourselves, and affirm for others, is that we are groundbreakers. We are moving into uncharted territory, both individually and collectively. We cannot expect it to be easy, nor that we will attain our goals overnight. If we are attempting to stand on our own feet as individuals, lacking either inner or outer supports, then we will be like children learning to walk. We will stagger, reel and fall—again and again and again. In this process we may develop muscles and capacities. And unless we see this for what it is—an entirely new step in evolution—we will be prey to two great illusions: firstly that somewhere in our past we failed, went wrong, and are now reaping the consequences of our own, and others' past actions—which can paralyze our efforts in the here and now. Where we are in our lives, with what we have inherited, is a creative opportunity for the future, not solely a cause for shame and blame.

The second great deception, skillfully marketed both materially and psycho-spiritually, is that there is an instant solution to our current predicaments. This is the culture of multiple-choice (one right answer, the rest wrong), the 'pursuit of happiness' (which includes health and wealth), and the quick-fix of any condition that falls short of it. Whether we are encouraged to upgrade our car or carpeting, or attend a weekend workshop for personal transformation, the message is the same: once we discover our secret 'right' answer, we can live in bliss from here on out. Both illusions, past and future, are the banana skins or, as one friend puts it, the 'vaudeville hooks' that pull our feet from under us, and prevent us standing in the present with the hopefulness, resolve and courage to work and create with the raw material each of us is given by our destinies.

True development, 'Individuation' (to quote Carl Jung), 'is a long and arduous path of moral suffering'; we need to turn our eyes from the deceptive allure of the TV ads, perhaps invoke the lovely words of the St. Francis prayer: 'Teach me, Oh Lord, to fight and not to heed the wounds, to labor and not to seek reward...'. We need to know and accept that the fruits of our struggles should not be measured by instant results, visible success; for, in the words of Marge Piercy, the poet:

> This is how we are going to live for a long time: not always,
> for every gardener knows that after the digging, after the planting,
> after the long season of tending and growth, the harvest comes.[3]

A new path of 'initiation'

It is striking too, that Steiner points to a new path of development for modern man and woman. It is no longer appropriate for a select few to retreat to 'mystery centers', be initiated into self-knowledge and knowledge of the world, and then return to guide the rest of us. Being in the world is today's path of 'initiation,' and is potentially taken by all. We acquire such knowledge in the hurly-burly of daily life, through our encounters with others, in the supermarket, at the office, by the kitchen sink. What mother does not truly know this? The levels of consciousness, the capacity for presence of mind and action, required to cope with myriad, continually shifting demands, are quite extraordinary! I know one who can simultaneously stir a pot with her elbow, bandage a bleeding knee, field a phone call, and respond to such questions as: 'Why isn't God married?' Becoming a shaman in a week at some desert retreat (all meals provided), is a breeze compared to her round-the-clock, Herculean labors. And is she not, truly, at the end of the day, more spiritually evolved?

Creating 'unique' families

If the imperative of our times is to permeate ourselves with an increasingly individualized consciousness, then each of us will be striving to free ourselves from collective traditions and instinctual responses. We can see ourselves and our relationships as unique creative expressions of the particular resources and circumstances available to each of us. We will need to explore and work with the norms and forms we have inherited from our past, and stand within today. And we must learn to perceive and relate to the individual strengths and weaknesses of those with whom we are building community. Thus my single-parenting should and will be different from all others. Though I share with others certain archetypal patterns, as plants in their development follow similar laws, we will each be working with different materials to fashion our families. (Two single parents covered many themes and issues in the previous *Lifeways* book, which I highly recommend.) My own thoughts and experiences may encourage others on their own journey of discovery and creation; but they are emphatically not a 'How To' treatise, and may well be read as a 'How Not To' one!

Parsifal—a legend for our times [4]

One story that inspires and strengthens me in my struggle to reject cultural stereotypes and repeated feelings of failure and inadequacy, is that of Parsifal, which Steiner indicates as a legend particularly relevant for our times. While I know this tells, in mighty pictures, of the path to be trodden by every modern man and woman, I avidly appropriated certain images to support my life as a single mother of a single son. Parsifal begins his life with an absent father and a mother who taught him nothing of value for his life ahead. One of the two lessons he learned from her: 'Kiss the ladies,' proved disastrous advice when he first left home around age 13!

Did my own son intuit this when, aged four or five, he told me his good behavior was learned from others, not from me? 'When I go out I look at grown-ups' faces, I see what makes them happy. I don't like them when they're sad.'

Parsifal learns through often bitter life experience. He makes mistake upon mistake. Each fresh trial calls for a fresh response, calling upon capacities he has not exercised before. This tells us we will never feel (or be) prepared beforehand for the task. Again, my son articulated this truth for me when, age six, he wisely commented: 'By the time you know about six-year-olds, Mom, I'll be seven!' I need frequently to recall the words of one of my training therapists: 'The greatest gift we can give our children is the experience that we, their parents, are trying. That we have the guts to try, fail and try again. This will give them the strength and courage they need in the struggles they will face in their own lives.'

We are not educated today to trust and create within a living process, but rather to have a general formula which we then apply. But this is not the way of Parsifal. It is through a personal, existential process that he awakens, develops, and at last comes to the Holy Grail. It is striking that he does not do so alone, but with his previously unknown brother. This points to the truth that we need others on our journey, who are also often strangers.

New communities

Steiner speaks of this—the great Christian imperatives we have barely begun to realize, of forging new communities, no longer based on blood ties, and living increasingly the reality that we *are* our brother's keeper, and he (or she) is ours. The days of taking care of oneself and one's own (so often at the other's expense), and of the solo flight to power or perfection, still strenuously pursued in the West, must end. We must increasingly know ourselves as members of the whole human community and act within it with the sense that each of our lives and choices intimately affects the whole.

Whether or not we ascribe to this particular religious imagery, our biological families are no longer the primary community for many of us. When I began single-parenting, my nearest blood-kin was 800 miles away. I lived in a foreign city in a foreign country, mainly among strangers. Over the past years, I have come to see that a single parent and a single child have a particular opportunity to take up the twin challenges of individualizing, and building new communities. With only two of us engaged in the creation of our family, it is often easier to risk and experiment than it is with larger numbers. For lack of other family members, we are also both thrust into the wider community. My own son, age four, described his awareness of the latter reality when, detecting a note of sadness in his voice as he spoke of the baby sister he had lost through my miscarriage, I asked him: 'Do you wish you had a sister?'

'No,' he replied firmly, 'the whole world is my brother and my sister.'

Later, when he became aware of his emerging preferences for certain people, he amended this to: 'The whole world may be my family, but some people are more family than others!' I think we would agree that we all have a long way to go to realize this greater sense of human kinship.

The single parent and the single child each need relationships outside the home. We depend highly on others, and invariably move to build systems of friendship and support for ourselves. While single parents often band together, sharing care, it has been interesting to see over the years equally vital relationships with 'intact' families, childless couples and single people, and to watch my child develop friendships across age differences as he might well have done with blood siblings.

Single or 'shared' parenting?

A deep lesson of these experiences for me is that others are there for us, and many may educate my child far better than I. This has helped me surrender, by degrees, my omnipotent role. Although the sense of being fully responsible, of carrying all the burdens, is indeed a vital strengthener of our capacity for commitment, it can easily slide into possessive control. I am not necessarily the one who knows best, does best, or, in fact, the one my son always needs. If we have parented alone from an early period in our child's life, we have had little experience of negotiating choices and sharing care. We may find it hard to let go, and allow others to teach and guide our children, often more effectively and appropriately than we ourselves. Faith and trust are required of us, and an openness free of assumptions about the ways and forms in which such help may come. Distraught that my son lacked male figures in his life, doing 'manly' things, I was so busy moaning about this one day at the beach that I almost failed to notice he had attached himself to an elderly sculptor, who was teaching him how to carve a piece of driftwood, and row a boat. But, having noticed, I asked the man if he would apprentice my son from time to time. I believe the hours they spent together were mutually enjoyed. Likewise it has been a great privilege to care for other people's children—often those of single parents—and through this extend my own 'family.'

Oedipus complex and other horrors?

As we watch our child create relationships with other 'parent' figures, we will probably face the question of our own needs and dependencies. Particularly in the early years we may have little or no time to pursue other activities, other relationships ourselves. It is only natural that our child becomes our most intimate and consistent companion. Much pop psychology alludes to the inherent dangers, particularly in the mother-son relationship. Who has not heard of the Oedipus complex, of the dire and damaging consequences for a male child raised by a woman alone? Once, returning from a happy outing to the movie, *One Hundred and One Dalmatians*, followed by my son's favorite supper of Wendy's Chicken Nuggets, the evening paper flaunted banner headlines: 'Mother Dates Son! Single Women Use Sons as Surrogate Lovers!' Had I taken the first step in a downhill run towards his ruination?

It requires a tremendous inner honesty to distinguish where and how our own needs may be playing into the relationship in potentially harmful ways, and where we may be using our child to fill soul gaps. It also calls for sensing our child as a unique individual, not merely a generic young male; we must learn from each situation how to proceed, rather than allowing blanket theories to dictate our actions. When my son was 11, I became concerned with the fact that I still sometimes woke to find him snuggled up in bed with me. Well, we all know where that might lead! I asked him when he thought he might shed this habit, and he promptly told me he wouldn't need to sleep with me after he was 12. A few months after his 12th birthday, I found him snuggled up with me again.

'You know,' I told him, 'you won't be able to do this when you're fat and forty.'

'Yes, I know that,' he replied. 'So let's enjoy it while we can!' He popped in a few more times, but stopped well before his 13th birthday, marking this

transition with a large sign on his own door: 'NO ADULT MAY ENTER—
ESPECIALLY MOM!' A directive I have respected ever since.

*'James James Morrison Morrison Weatherby George Dupree
took great care of his mother, though he was only three'*
A.A. Milne [5]

It is generally true that the single child of a single parent enters the adult
world earlier than those with siblings in intact families. Much is made of the
burden we lay on our children through sharing our adult concerns. After all,
we often have no one else around at key moments in our lives. But while we
need to be sensitive to sharing in age-appropriate ways, we might also
imagine that our child may have chosen his situation because he is able to
make good use of the experience it brings. Again, it is a matter for individual
assessment. When my marriage ended, my son was four years old. I did my
best to hide my own grief, and attend solely to his. He found me under the
bedclothes one day and asked what was wrong. I told him I had a headache.
'You don't,' he said. 'You're sad because Dad left us.' He stayed a while,
tenderly stroking my head. When I shared with a friend how bad I felt about
letting him be my caretaker, she wisely replied that this might be his way of
learning that others had feelings, and to exercise his own caring capacities.
I have, over the years, watched these emerge in him, and once in a while he
has fiercely championed the cause of adult women, particularly single
mothers. I have to remind myself that we are individual spiritual beings,
using the medium of a mother-son relationship to fulfill certain goals in our
development together and apart, that go way beyond the parent-child roles.
Such an imagination can free us to perceive the particular resources we have
to offer each other. It may also help us sense what our individual child can
deal with at any particular life-phase.

The question of honesty between parent and child is also paramount.
Being honest does not mean a perpetual 'tell and show,' but it does mean
knowing that our children usually know what is going on and deserve the
truth from us, hopefully conveyed in ways each individual child can meet
and bear. My own son usually tells me, in no uncertain terms, what is
happening, and is often ahead of me. He has extraordinary insights into
human nature—quite painful in the case of my own. Yet I am deeply
grateful to him for lighting up my inner confusion on many occasions with
some blunt comment as to what is really going on:

'That's your problem, Mom. It's got nothing to do with me. So you'd better sort it out...' etc. If life is our path of initiation, it will often be other people who initiate us in self-knowledge, and none see and articulate their insights so clearly as our own children!

It was also pointed out to me by friends that my son is often capable of meeting situations that would flatten me psychologically, and that my anxieties were self-directed and had little to do with him. This was yet another reminder that we are dealing with individuals here, with individual capacities that transcend our chronological ages.

'Neurotic patterns' or 'creative resources?'

Each of us brings from our past many experiences to bear on parenting. Many psychologists today focus strongly on the neurotic patterns that afflict us, and our tendency to replicate the familiar behaviors of childhood. I prefer to see our past as offering us creative resources—even in the most negative and painful histories. How we choose to work with the debit and credit of our early years distinguishes us as individuals. The purpose of exploring our past is to enable us to work consciously with the material it offers us.

My own first years were spent in Britain, in a wartime matriarchy. From this I learned that women were courageous, resourceful, and able to carry the work usually ascribed to men as well as their own. This obviously gave me the confidence that I could cope with single-parenting. My mother had survived, and so might I! I had, however, few positive pictures of a man's function in the scheme of things. The fighters only returned 'on leave,' to engender excitement and chaos. After what seemed like one long party, they left. Some, like my own father, did not return. I have needed to fill some critical gaps here, to learn from current experiences what I may reasonably expect of my son's participation in the life and work of our home, and never assume he will automatically live out the only patterns and images I first knew. When I flew off the handle recently (my anger simply a shield for the anxiety his brands of excitement and chaos provoked in me) he merely retorted: 'Cool it, Mom. I'm not grown-up yet. Don't you know this is just the way teenagers are supposed to be?'

Once we know our patterns, and the vulnerabilities they may trigger in us, we can shed our blanket assumptions and begin to respond to the individual person on an individual basis. The most difficult experience usually offers us the best opportunity to individualize; the loss, through death, of many male figures in my life, has pushed me to overcome my fears that my son might not survive. He is not one of a crowd of fragile males.

He is a distinct person with a unique destiny. Most of the people we admire in life have usually had to grapple with tough life experiences. Exploring our own, we will discover the potential buried within them for conscious self-development.

'Wilderness skills!'

In moving into this new territory of relationships, we need what I have come to call 'wilderness' skills. I'd like to share two I've found particularly valuable.

The first engages imagination. As the psychologist James Hillman points out, all our problems are due to a failure of imagination—which is a deep, and often untapped resource in all of us.

When my son, now a teenager, came home, he invariably charged in and began criticizing me, as I went about my blameless business. Despite knowing this to be typical adolescent behavior, I often felt wounded, and retaliated in kind. After one particularly explosive battle, I recaptured my experience and allowed it to form itself into an image, or metaphor. The picture that arose was of my son in a mediaeval castle, with slits in the stone walls through which he was hurling poisoned arrows. I, in a trench some distance away, was lauching cannon balls. Between us lay 'No-Man's-Land,' a large area where much weaponry was landing. I believed from this image that my son needed his walls, also the distance of 'No-Man's-Land,' yet his arrows were actually his way of maintaining contact with me. True or not this helped me enormously in relating to the new phase of increased separation between us.

I also carried this picture into sleep. The life of sleep is the other powerful resource we have at our disposal. We all know how differently things appear after a night or two. We can consciously activate and draw from this world through the way we prepare ourselves to enter it. Picturing others, and our relationships, in the evening, can engender creative impulses in the days that follow. There is a wonderful Intercessory Prayer for others, too, that I highly recommend.[6] Focusing on the other increases our objective interest and concern, and frees us from merely reactive responses to the way they impact upon us. Love is, as Rilke puts it, the ability to 'see the other whole and clear and perfect against the sky', not simply as a figure obtruding into our personal landscape. And love is surely what we are striving to cultivate in all our relationships.

Letting go

The act of truly letting go of our children, allowing them to claim their separate identities and individual destinies, is one that proceeds in stages. It is a particular challenge for both the single parent and the single child. Both are aware that each has no other kin as close. For the mother it can be especially painful. She has already—even if self-chosen—lost her mate, may even mistrust her capacity for relations with men. She has no other child. Might this male flesh of her flesh walk away without a backward glance? The child can feel a deep responsibility to the parent he will leave alone.

Our task as women, and mothers, is to encourage our male child out into the world, the world of men, and this can be hard when there is no father present to act as a guide and support. We have both to maintain the nest for him, and help him fly from it. We need to trust that male figures will be there for our sons, in all kinds of guises, to help them accomplish their rite of passage into manhood. We also need to believe we do have the strength to bear the loss their departure from us brings. One of the gifts for a 'fatherless' child is that he often has a wide variety of male role models in his life. This may help him discover and choose his own values and ideal of manhood more freely, from assorted experiences and images. Each woman needs to face her particular vulnerability in her own way, whatever it takes to do so. We may have more resources than we know, for hopefully we have already learned to create a self-sustaining life as an adult, rather than being someone else's better, or worse half! We must be able to allow our children to go forth in freedom. Having done this, we will have accomplished a tremendous act in the development of the capacity to stand fully upon our own feet.

One of the deep mysteries of life and our relationships is that those based on genuine love and freedom continue to bind us together spiritually and eternally, however separate we may be in space and time. Connections maintained from guilt, need, or loveless duty, do not survive or flourish. Our child's departure from the home is the ultimate challenge and test of our capacities to go beyond blood ties and to honor each other as free individuals.

A wonderful picture is given us in the St. John's Gospel story of the Marriage of Cana. While Jesus is busy in the crowd, his disciples tell him his mother is there, implying He should turn his attention to her. When Mary is brought to Him, He says: 'Woman—what have I to do with thee?' This is sometimes taken as a somewhat blunt rejection of His biological family. I think it indicates an extraordinary new moment in their relationship, a quite genuine question of what these two individuals may have to do with one another, apart from and beyond the mother-son bond.

In meeting this issue myself, with my son, I experience us taking it step by step. I am now able to assure him honestly that, while I will certainly miss him—I love him and love his company—his absence, partial or total, frees me up for other things. I certainly ask and expect no 'repayment' for the years of care and sacrifice. I was therefore rather astonished recently, at supper one night, when he reached over to wipe some crumbs from my mouth, and said: 'I guess, when you're 90, I'll be brushing crumbs off from all over you.' I asked if he felt I expected him to take care of me in my old age.

'No,' he replied. 'But it's just what I would do.' Well—we have a few years yet to see if this is the case. Meanwhile, I hope we are establishing a relationship in which any future caring for me is a free decision on his part.

'Creating out of nothing'

I once asked my mother, who had a pretty loveless childhood, how she was able to love us, her own children, so fully and freely. She replied that she had learned to 'create out of nothing.' In one of Steiner's most wonderful lectures, he speaks of this as our greatest human capacity. He shows that we are always in relation with something or someone in the world. In any such moment we are bound to the situation by necessity. But our freedom lies in how we choose to respond to it, how we think, feel or do what we will. And he calls these responses of ours 'creating out of nothingness.' He adds that, in Christian esotericism, this was known as 'creating out of relationships,' or 'creating out of the Holy Spirit.'

It is worth bearing this in mind as we strive to meet the challenge of all our life relationships. We actually have the freedom to respond to them in any way we choose. I think many of us single parents have struggled with all kinds of negative feelings—despair, shame, bitterness, fear—to win through to the sense that we do, like all others, have a proper family. It is not the four square 'Happy Family' of my childhood card game. It may often appear quite strange to others, even to ourselves. But if we are pledged to create a community that can contain, reflect and support the free development of its uniquely individual members, it will be no less fruitful than those that include Mr. and Miss Bun too!

Steiner concludes his lecture with a final picture I think we must know to be true, when he says that our free responses to these life relationships are the actual substance out of which our future world will be made: our joys, struggles, hopes, fears and deeds. In striving to break new ground in our times, we will also be clearing a path for those who follow us.

Notes

1. A. Guggenbuhl-Craig. *Marriage—Dead or Alive?*
2. R. Steiner. 'Specters of the Old Testament in the Nationalism of the Present.' *The Challenge of Our Times.*
3. Marge Piercy. *The Seven of Pentacles.*
4. Wolfram von Eschenbach. *Parsifal.*
5. A.A. Milne. *Christopher Robin Poems.*
6. A. Bittleston. Intercessory Prayer. *Prayer and Meditations* (Floris Books, Edinburgh).
7. R. Steiner, 'Evolution, Involution and Creation out of Nothingness', *The Being of Man and His Future Evolution* (Rudolf Steiner Press).

Melissa Lyons

As I sit here to write a few lines about myself, I am frustrated with not knowing what to say. Most of all, I see myself as being very much in the middle of the search for an identity and roots in the world, even though I am thirty-three years old and have followed my interests in the past.

As a child, I loved learning and discovering patterns in the world. I was very active and spent a lot of time tumbling and jumping around in gymnastics. I delighted in the study of languages and in college I found my way to Tokyo, Japan, where I embarked on an intensive study of the Japanese language and culture. It was clear that I needed to explore this world which was in many ways entirely different from what I knew. After college, I returned to Tokyo and then, after various jobs (translating, waitressing, selling advertising) in Tokyo and a few American cities, I ended up in New York City working on Wall Street for a Japanese investment bank. After a few years there, I knew that the financial world wasn't for me, and I found my way to the Orientation Year at Sunbridge College in my late twenties. Here, I discovered eurythmy, and was amazed! Everything that had originally been exciting to me—language, sound, movement—was there, in one. I am currently in my third year of training at the School of Eurythmy in Spring Valley, New York. I would never have thought that one day I would be seriously studying an art!

I originally wrote this chapter for a class given by Christopher and Signe Schaefer on 'the Individual and the Twentieth Century' in the Orientation Year at Sunbridge College. It interests me how we are growing up these days, how all the changes that have occurred in the family structure in the last thirty to forty years have affected who we are. I am also eager to hear about the experiences of others in this realm.

6

Fragmentation and wholeness in single parent households: an adult-child's perspective

It is difficult to focus on any one phenomenon symptomatic of our times without seeing how it ultimately relates to other issues of equal importance. It does not take long to recognize that there are connections between most of the larger issues facing us in the second half of the twentieth century—the disintegration of family, economic instability, education as a disservice, environmental degradation, mental illness, spiritual and physical poverty, dominance of technology, lack of beauty, etc... None of these issues has a single cause, nor a single solution. All of these problems lead one to similar basic questions about the very mode of our consciousness and our manner of thinking about ourselves, one another, and the world at large.

One such issue that has arisen in the last three decades is that of children being raised by a single parent. In most cases, the parent is the mother.

I was raised, along with my brother and sister, solely by my mother. This was in the sixties and seventies. At that time I rarely encountered other children at school who were growing up in single parent households. However, in the last ten to fifteen years, this has become increasingly typical. I recently heard that one in three children are cared for by only one parent; in some areas the percentage is even higher. Because I have the experience of growing up in a single parent home, I often find myself wondering about the experiences of others in similar circumstances, and about how such an experience might form the lives of all involved, both parents and children. How would it affect children's development? Is there perhaps some deeper meaning underlying single parent households, which might only be grasped over time, a life-time perhaps, if not more?

Caution is needed when talking about 'single parent households'. That one parent is raising the family may be the only common characteristic of the families this description includes. Each parent, each child, each family has its own history and personality. And so the living reality for each is fundamentally unique; the number of stories is as great as the number of individuals involved. I can only write of my own experience and of my interpretation of what that experience meant to me, in the hope that it may shed some light on the issue of children being raised in single parent households, as a phenomenon of our times.

My father left our family in 1968, when my brother, I, and my sister were six, four, and two years old, respectively. My father always lived in places far away from our home and rarely made contact with anyone in my immediate family. At the time of the divorce, my mother was twenty-four years old. She started to work at a store in the mall and eventually supported our family by working as the manager of a women's clothing store. One of her goals as a single mother was to do all she could to avoid receiving welfare support.

Ever since, in my teens, I became more conscious of our situation as a family, I have been thinking about why our situation was the way it was, and how it affected my siblings and myself, and my mother. In the last few years I have come to realize that our experience was one not only of fragmentation and loss but also of a striving towards integration and wholeness.

Fragmentation and loss

The experience of fragmentation and loss is an inherent part of the life of a family in which the mother or father, as a single parent, is working full time in order to support the family. The parent often lacks the time and energy to give attention to the children and gain an understanding of the unique characteristics and temperament of each child. I remember longing deeply for my mother to know each of us children as an individual. I think that this knowing would have encouraged each of us to strive to know ourselves. As a child, I would often try to get my mother to talk about how each of us was different from the other. I sensed in myself and in my brother and sister a desire to be nurtured more, and a longing to have someone pay attention to our habits, tendencies, and moods. Because this did not happen often, all of us lived with an underlying feeling of being neglected, or unnoticed.

When children are not given enough attention, they rarely develop a sense of calm, which makes it difficult for them to become aware that they are capable of achieving their destiny. This often results in nervousness. Energy is directed towards doing what one can to quickly grab or seize the attention of the parent, relatives, and teachers. I think that children are conscious on some level of both the superficial and manipulative nature of their tricks and tactics to make others notice them, no matter how briefly. They can, as a result, feel isolated and more distant from a search for truth and sincerity in their relationships with themselves and other people.

Another factor contributing to the experience of fragmentation is that, in a single parent home, almost everything is done in a hurry. The pace of daily life is frenzied. Things are not done with much enjoyment, but to simply get them done. In my family, there was rarely a beginning, middle or end to any action, discussion, or expression of feeling. Cleaning, eating, shopping, talking, going to church, were performed as if we were all in an ongoing state of panic. It was rare that someone listened to another with the steady calm needed to hear the content of a story or an idea and thereby grant the experience of reality to the speaker. To be heard, one had to speak quickly and in clipped phrases to penetrate the pervasive cloud of noise formed by the business and frenzy of the day. All this made time feel like it existed in chunks or blocks; rare were the occasions when time flowed and streamed through the family's sharing of thoughts or deeds.

Another tendency in a single parent household which adds to a sense of loss and fragmentation, is that a child who needs special care and attention is often neglected, because the parent lacks time and energy. The siblings usually see that this child is suffering in some way. For example, in my family, my sister needed extra attention in her school work. My mother often could not find the patience and presence of mind needed to help with homework, and my sister gradually lost touch with her ability to concentrate on schoolwork, developing only a dim trust in her ability to learn. My brother and I, as well as my mother, were saddened by my sister's struggle and could feel her anguish.

An obvious factor contributing to the sense of fragmentation and loss is the constant awareness of the other parent's absence. An emptiness, the feeling of a void or vacancy, pervades the atmosphere of the home. The occasional mention of the absent parent reminds the children that the family has been split, torn apart. I think that each child feels this break, this void, in his or her being. I remember thinking that my father's presence would have had a calming, ordering effect on the habits and consciousness of the family. I also remember seeing in the behaviour and emotion of my brother hints of a longing for the presence of a father. A child can live for years thinking that imbalances in the family could be mended if the missing parent were present. The pain stemming from this absence lives in children's hearts and minds.

As well as their own pain, children are also usually very aware of the pain and sacrifices of the parent who is caring for them every day. They are not oblivious to the limitations this places on the development of the parent as an individual. The child can see that a mother, for example, is under pressure to focus on the family and has little chance to explore aspects of herself and life in general, that would enrich her life and 'help her along' in the world. It can even seem to the child that the mother's own well-being is threatened; the mother seems somehow to be losing the precious opportunity to get to know herself. The children might go so far as to think that they and their need for care are the main causes of the parent's loss of the chance for personal development. Feelings of guilt and responsibility arise.

I remember feeling most guilty for taking time and energy from my mother when she lost her temper or showed signs of anxiety and frustration. The worried and tired look on her face when paying for groceries, for example, would make me feel sorry and somehow responsible. Children will also imagine the loneliness of each parent. Their loneliness sinks deep into the hearts of children. But they also experience their impotency to heal it, for they know that the parent is lonely for the company of other adults, not for that of children. To this day my siblings and I long for our mother to find a way to heal her years of living in loneliness.

Others who have experienced similar situations could no doubt add much to my descriptions. But besides anxiety, fragmentation and loss, I would like to show that the same circumstances can also lead to a dynamic in the family that engenders a sense of wholeness and integration.

Wholeness and integration

The most basic level on which a sense of wholeness is experienced is that one recognizes the capacity of the family to stay together and survive. The realization that 'It can be done! We're trying, together!' awakens one to an appreciation of the value of the effort itself. A great determination to do whatever is necessary to hold the family together can be witnessed in the parent daily. My mother was a great heroine to me because she was always getting things done and was still able to show interest in matters outside the home, such as national politics. The endless striving and resilience of the parent affirms and nurtures the striving and resilience of the children. Children then develop a sense of trust that life holds meaning. Sometimes, what the parent accomplishes seems due more to a miracle than honest effort. But children soon perceive how things actually get done in the home. They see the perseverance of the parent in the performance of concrete, practical tasks. They see the connection of real work and effort with the health and well-being of themselves and the family as a whole. I remember hearing the sounds of my mother already working in the kitchen long before I woke up for school. Or I would see her rush around on her fifteen minute breaks at the mall to go buy something one of us needed for the next day at school. In her actions I witnessed daily the connection between effort and accomplishment.

Another aspect of the activity in a single parent home that can give a sense of wholeness is the rhythm a parent creates because of the need to be economical with time. Most single parents have much to do in little time. The organized daily schedule, to which the family is more or less strictly held, can provide children with a sense of rhythm and its relation to 'getting things done.' Yes, this rhythm often becomes a frenetic pace, but life's activities are punctuated and given vitality by the parent's swift and rhythmic orchestration of the daily tasks. The experience of daily rhythms, no matter how rigid or loose according to circumstances, can enliven the children's own movement through the day.

I believe that most children, in one way or another, experience the pathos of the situation of their mother or father who is raising them. I use the word pathos here to mean 'that quality, in a real situation, which evokes sympathy and a sense of sorrow or pity' (Webster's *New World Dictionary*). This is aroused in the child by a knowledge that the parent has made great sacrifices, which leads to his or her well-being and growth and that of the family as a whole. Through this realization, the child might further understand how growth demands sacrifice, and how life is connected to death. The child sees something die in the parent, and perhaps her siblings and herself as well, as a result of the family situation. But the child is also aware of growth, a cohesiveness, stemming from what is sacrificed or temporarily stunted. The necessity of giving something up for the benefit of the growth of something else, is directly experienced everyday. The child may not come to this knowledge consciously in a way that immediately leads to a healthy understanding, but the experience of the connection between growth and decay may help to form a foundation for a sound appreciation of life's demands.

By experiencing and perhaps understanding this connection, all
members of a single parent family may identify with one another's
experiences of deprivation or sacrifice and thereby help carry, if not heal,
the pain. One can see how experiences are shared, passed around, and held
by the whole family. The family is supported by this mutual, often silent
recognition and sharing of one another's experiences of sacrifice and
growth. In this way, all have the chance to begin to learn how wholeness
and health are achieved through the acknowledgement of the
interdependence of everyone in the family.

Another manner in which a child may experience a sense of integration
and wholeness is in witnessing the parent's blending of masculine and
feminine qualities. I witnessed in my mother the uniting of both feminine
and masculine characteristics and behaviour. There was no way for me to
strictly define the roles of the female and male according to feminine and
masculine traits, respectively, based on what I learned from living with my
mother. I saw her embody feminine qualities when the occasion demanded
a feminine approach, or call on her more masculine traits when they were
more appropriate. My siblings and I benefitted from watching our mother
act according to the demands of the situation at hand, without restricting
herself to only those qualities thought to be feminine and therefore suited
to women only. I think that she did this more out of necessity than any
inclination towards feminism. I imagine that many other children raised by
one parent who chose to work in and outside the home have been given the
opportunity to witness the intricate though functional blending of
masculine and feminine qualities in their parent. This can no doubt help
them contribute to society a more balanced, gender-free awareness of
masculine and feminine qualities.

These are of course only some of the ways in which children raised in
single parent homes can gain inspiration towards wholeness. I would also
like to mention that many experiences of fragmentation, and inspirations
towards wholeness exist equally in unbroken homes, expecially in recent
times when both the mother and father work outside the home and time is
thought to be a precious commodity.

As I write, I am brought to ask: What is the destiny of both the parents and
children living in single parent households? What do they need to learn
from the experiences inherent in such circumstances in our times? Is the
world calling in some way for the insights and capacities that might be
gained from these circumstances? After all, the number of children raised
by one parent is escalating. I often wonder how both children and parents

are faring as the economy worsens and the ability of people to cope weakens. It would be unfortunate for the issue of single parent families to be oversimplified either by a tendency to demoralize single parents, or to glamorize their predicament. The beginning of my own understanding of my family experience lies in looking closely at the experience itself and reflecting on what actually happened and is still happening. Then, I begin to see hints of meaning underlying it all. And then maybe I, and others too, can use this understanding to better understand our destinies as individuals, and maybe also the destiny of our times.

King Graver

I was born in 1944 and raised in a small town in central Wisconsin, not too far from a combination of Lake Wobegon and Ozzie and Harriet. My favorite places as a child were my side yard and later 'the swamp' where endless summer hours were spent playing Mike Fink, catching carp and telling stories. I went to high school because I had to and College because everyone else did. It wasn't until after the Army that I realized I had pretty much wasted my College time and that I really did want to learn. I did my graduate work at the University of Oregon in the same field, Industrial Psychology and Organizational Behavior, that my father did his. What is interesting is that it wasn't until somewhere in the middle of this writing that I was even aware of the fact that I had followed his path.

After selling industrial chemicals and equipment for 18 years, I found that I needed to do something else. During that time, my avocation had been Kimberton Waldorf School where our daughters attended. Serving on almost every committee one can think of, and as Board Chair for a number of years, it became clear to me that there was something in Waldorf Education which was important (I mean really important) and which had the potential to be the source of a healing that I think is needed in the world. Through my involvement in the school, I slowly began to learn more about anthroposophy and through that, events in my life began to seem different when looked at under this new light. All this lead to a career change in 1995 where I gave up the world of business and industry for the world of education to become the Administrator at Kimberton Waldorf School.

While at a course at Sunbridge College in Spring Valley, NY, I was asked if I would write a chapter on fathering for this book. One of the things that's interesting about fathering is that the longer you look at the subject, the larger it gets; like a heap of rising bread dough. It took almost two years to the month for me to finish something to which I had said, 'Sure, I'll write on fathering. Have a draft to you in a couple months.' Right!

What a trip! Each time I thought I was finished, I'd end up punching it down again, only to have it rise a few months later. In the main, this happened because the process of writing (which I had never done before) forced me to look deeply into my own childhood, my relationship with my father and my relationship to my children.

A number of us have recently started a Waldorf Fathering Group at the school to consider how we, as fathers, relate to the education of our children. It would be my hope that other fathers reading this article might also consider it a starting point and gather together with others through schools, places of worship or jobs to share their experiences and perceptions of fathering. It is in that sharing that the journey can begin.

7
Fathering

I have found that I cannot look at my experience as a father without looking more deeply at my experience as a son. I was born in 1944 and raised in a small midwestern town. My mother died when I was born and my father remarried when I was about 18 months old. My new mother brought to me a sister who is two years older. The vast majority of households in the postwar 40's and 50's were composed, like mine, of a breadwinner father and a home-with-the-children mother. While my first 21 years started with the 'Ozzie and Harriet era', the period ended with graduation from college in 1966, when young people were actively searching to find new relationships between responsibility and freedom, family and independence, self and community.

As fathers, if we wish to develop our relationship with our children, it is not simply a matter of finding a bit of extra time here and there. It begins with consciously engaging in a process of rediscovering who we have been, and are becoming. The task before us as fathers is far greater than the raising of 'proper and successful' children. It has to do with serving as a guide. It has to do with being more conscious of our actions and intentions, our beliefs and values. It is easy to talk about doing things with our children so they can be our buddies. It is much more difficult to realize that it is more 'who we are' than 'what we do' that is so fully taken in by our children.

Coming together as fathers to really speak openly and deeply with each other about inner experiences is new for most men. The times we live in, with the wide diversity of family forms, are calling on us to actively experiment with ways in which a sharing can take place based on our individual experiences. Whether it be beating drums in the woods, or meeting together at school, or having a beer after work, if we truly take up the fathering task, we are obliged to look more deeply at the questions inherent in that aspect of our lives.

My recollection of my father is of a man who, like most others, was devoted to and incredibly conscientious about his work life. I now see that he was, in the role defined by the culture of the times, the ideal provider, whose task it was to give to his family those things which were not possible in his youth, owing to the Depression and the war years. He did very well indeed, and while I never felt that we were rich, I do not recall a sense of wanting. To do this providing, however, he had to work long and hard. Even though he was clearly devoted to our family, there was a certain detachment. I understand now that at that particular time in history, fathering was actually defined for most men as being the economic provider and a man's success was judged by how well he did that. That is how my experience as a father began.

One might assume that my mother was the more influential parent, being the one more 'present.' I had assumed this to be the case until I really began to look at my childhood. On reflection, it is my father who now stands out as the one from whom most of my life's commandments have been garnered.

I was married at age 25, and last summer my wife and I celebrated our 25th wedding anniversary. We have two wonderful daughters who have brought us untold opportunities to learn about ourselves. Now, at ages 18 and 21, as they begin to find their way in the world, my fathering role has changed considerably from the early years. Our family pendulum has swung between harmony and conflict, well-being and pain, laughter and tears, vacation and the daily grind. At any specific moment, it is hard to keep a relationship to the larger picture. Only on reflection have I begun to understand the interplay that has been present between my daughters' lives and mine: how they have really taught me while, at the same time, I was guiding them. I recently heard that in Danish and Hebrew, the word for teacher and the word for student is the same. It is that reciprocal nature of the relationship that can make it painful sometimes when we are confronted with ourselves in our children.

The study of our own lives carries the potential for providing significant insights into the source of some of our thoughts, feelings and actions. It has the possibility of shedding light on aspects of our lives which have been covered over since childhood. This active and willful bringing of our own biography to a heightened consciousness, then has a second potential. For me, it was an awareness that just as I, as a child, took in aspects of who my own father was, my own children have taken in what I am. An exercise I did recently was to simply list those 'commandments' I grew up with. 'You must clean your plate.' 'Don't cry over split milk.' 'Boys never...' 'If you can't say anything nice, don't say anything at all.' It was first a struggle for me to even identify what these commandments were, but the real eye-opener came when I began to understand their source. I discovered that these commandments were really carried in some way as inner qualities by my father. Though sometimes trite, they represented the 'values' that were, for better or worse, passed on to me.

Through my father, for example, I came to understand, 'A job worth doing is worth doing well.' Quite naturally, of course, I rebelled against that idea as a child and spent most of my effort trying to figure out the easy way rather than doing my best. In school I was the classic underachiever. 'Gets along well with fellow students but should really work harder on his studies' became the perennial comment on my report cards. It actually was not until I started graduate school, after three years in the army, that this idea of doing one's best came alive in me. (The notable exception was the cart I built when I was a kid, drawn by our mighty, self-propelling Jacobsen lawnmower. It was and still is, in my mind, the work of a master craftsman. It lasted a whole summer with only minor maintenance and was in use almost daily carrying me and my buddies around our neighborhood.) I obviously did not recognize it at the time, but what began to happen was that those things I chose to do were done with great care.

Now, having discovered something about how that commandment came to life in me, how it moved from father to son, I am better able to relate to how those commandments I am carrying (knowingly or not) are brought into the lives of my children. While both the girls are bright and capable, the younger one (just beginning college) has yet to catch fire in terms of school work and the older one (in her senior year in college) really has begun to do that. What I perceived as 'not working up to capacity' has, at times, been very frustrating because I had not seen the larger picture. I saw only the product of their efforts, knew their greater potential and would say things like, 'If only you would try harder...' How silly! Had I responded to that? Didn't I, eventually, bring to life in myself the notion of doing one's best? Certainly! But I did it on my own terms and our girls will too. I do not need to drive the lesson home, but I do need to find ways to help them experience the inner satisfaction I have found in a job well done.

Perhaps I did not exhibit pride in accomplishment in a recognizable way, but it appears to me now that if we are 'in tune' with our children and look for moments when they do show pride in accomplishment or satisfaction with a job well done, there is a real need to recognize and support the effort and the feeling. Forget about the product. Children do not have the skills to draw perfect pictures (whatever that means), but they do draw and they are proud of the things they discover in the process. I can easily imagine myself, when presented with the latest in a series of refrigerator art, asking 'What is it?' rather than being excited, together with my daughter, about how much fun it was to do, or how pretty the colors were; or simply being so happy that she was happy that the picture deserved a 'special' place on the fridge.

Being a dad takes patience. I had always thought about this in the context of the child who eats too slowly or fools around instead of going right to bed. The books all tell us to be calm yet strong. We certainly do not want to lose control. Children are going to break things, move more slowly at times than we would, spill things, bang up the car, and on, and on. That is the nature of growing up and, as parents, we need to find our own way to deal with these daily crises. This seems to be an outward patience, and it is needed; but what I have recently discovered is something of a different nature.

The other kind of patience, actually an inner quality, is a kind of faith. It has to do with being aware of a larger picture. To be sensitive to the meaning of the larger picture as it relates to our children, we must be more conscious of ourselves: the shortcomings we overcame (or didn't), how we did that (or didn't), what was important for us to hear from our fathers, how we discovered those things manifesting in ourselves, etc. I have seen in my children that when they identify something that they really want to do and set about doing it, they do just fine. When it is something imposed from the outside, they may have trouble summoning up desire. Which posture would be the most helpful to them: a mini-lecture on the value of doing your best, or perhaps trying to take an inner posture towards what they are doing that might help light the fire in them? When they accomplish something on their own, no matter the significance, do I praise the effort enough? Do I nourish a sense of satisfaction, or am I quick to point out that if they had put as much effort into their last school project as they did making the doll house with their friends, they would have been better off?

For me, the question of fathering is really one of identifying those qualities I think will be important for my children to be able to call on in their future, while trying to live my life in such a way that those qualities are actually visible in me. When the time comes, the children will have had the seed planted and can nourish it, grow it and reap the fruits. Fathering, then, is as much about self-development as it is about the specific relationship between a man and his children. My father, at least as I recall, did not spend much time doing things with me but who he was has formed some of the underlying values in my life. Dedication, steadfastness, true interest in others, conscientiousness: these are all things which were not so much spoken as felt.

Robert McGammon in his bestseller, *A Boy's Life*, states it quite well:

> When I was twelve, the world was my magic lantern, and by its green spirit glow I saw the past, the present and into the future. You probably did too, you just can't recall it. See, this is my opinion: we all start out knowing magic. We are born with whirlwinds, forest fires and comets inside us. We are able to sing to the birds, read the clouds and see our destiny in grains of sand. Then we get the magic educated right out of our souls. We get it churched out, spanked out, washed out and combed out. We get put on the straight and narrow and told to be responsible. Told to act our age. Told to grow up, for God's sake. And you know why we were told that? Because the people doing the telling were afraid of our wildness and youth, and because the magic we knew made them ashamed and sad of what they'd allowed to wither and die in themselves.

The child's sense of magic is real. Mine, I am afraid, had become comatose. To be really present, must we not find again the magic in our own souls? It is not in our heads, it is in our hearts! Why do we so often want our children to be like us, to think like us? They are children and we are adults. Childhood should be filled with joy and wonder and discovery. Does that mean that adult life is not? It has been a question for me of rediscovering what that really means and I will give two examples.

The first one provides a concrete picture of shattering the magic. For a child, a miniature golf course can be a magical fairy land, a place where imagination can spring to life. During our family vacation, we were all playing the game and what was I doing? I was teaching them how to hold the club and hit the ball. There is not anything wrong with a bit of instruction, but to turn this magical place into a physics or geometry lab and to then get really frustrated with them because they 'couldn't do it right'... What was I thinking?

I had forgotten that the miniature golf course I went to when I was a child was a bit like actually being the giant in a fairy tale: a setting with little forests and waterfalls, windmills and castles with drawbridges that went up and down, and holes in the ground where the ball disappeared, only to pop up somewhere else quite unexpectedly. It was about discovery and fun and the excitement of getting the ball through the clown's mouth. It was about imagining stories; and there I was, thinking I was going to get them on the

PMGA Tour. I had forgotten that it did not matter what the score was or how accomplished the children became at golf. What did matter was that their sense of magic was sustained by me remembering my own sense of magic.

From a second example, I can easily see how my children received the impression that adulthood was going to be a real drag. All too often, I now realize, I would come home from work tired, frustrated, full of negatives, worrying about money, complaining about customers, etc. Why would a child want to grow up and face an adult life like that? I was unconscious of the fact that conversations with my wife were being listened to in great detail by the children. I had not realized the depth to which they took in the content and, perhaps more importantly, interpreted what was said and formed inner pictures about life from the tone, from between the lines. Children interpret out of their own experience and capacities. They do not yet have the ability to think through what it is that they are hearing. What we say is their whole truth which they do not necessarily question.

I remember as a child that some of the adult conversations were about frustration that my father had at work. But the overriding impression I now have is that he was quite proud of the contribution he made to the company and really enjoyed doing what he did, despite the frustrations. In a recent conversation with my youngest daughter, she said that she always felt sad for me because she thought I hated my work. She asked if I ever smiled or laughed at work. I was stunned. Where had that come from? Well, as we continued to talk, she very clearly brought back to me snippets of conversations that led her to her conclusion that work life for me was intolerable gloom. I had been unconscious about what I was saying, how I was saying it, and what the effect on the children might be. I had forgotten to talk about all those things I found exciting, satisfying and wonderful. The magic had gone away.

As I have written and rewritten this article, each time I near the end, the question I face is, 'How do I end something when I feel like I'm just beginning?' Perhaps the important thing is to have begun, because who knows where we might end up? In talking to other fathers, each has expressed a real desire to have opportunities to talk and interact with other fathers. Perhaps, if you share that desire, you could create that space for such conversation in your community. It does not have to be a big formal thing. Maybe it is nothing more than taking the children out for a walk with other fathers and kids. That is a real beginning.

I discovered that it's important to find ways to uncover what the children are picking up. Had my daughter and I not had that conversation and the chance to talk it through, I would never have known what image I had unwittingly passed to her. I also learned that it's never too late. The impression I had left was brought out into the light and corrected (or at least I've been able to bring other elements that fill in the picture for her). Remember though, she's 18. I couldn't have done it in the same way if she were eight.

This example also moves to the question of finding a balance between work life and home life. The issue, at least as I have frequently heard it, is typically framed in the context of time management. There came a time for me, however, when I asked the question of whether or not my family life and work life were in balance with my inner life, not just with each other. For many the answer seems to be to 'turn off' the work life at the end of the day and 'turn on' the family life. Although this may be an answer, I began to feel a need to identify what my core questions were in life and then find a way to deal with these as part of a vocation. This, it seemed to me, was a way to bring balance of inner life and outer life.

My family and I had a conversation about such a job change and I was surprised and very pleased at the reaction of the children. They were incredibly supportive even though it would mean a reduction in income, and they were more than willing to pitch in. They expressed wanting me to be happy and to do something I might really love to do.

Reflecting on this question of balancing work and family life led me in a direction I hadn't expected. Because I like history, I began to wonder about how we got to where we are as a society. What was the picture of the balance of work and family life like over the course of American history? I read a book titled *Fatherhood in America—A History* by Robert Griswold. In it, he offers a detailed picture of historical events in the development of family life, from about the time of the American Revolution, and of the changing role of the father. He looks at changes that have come upon us from economic necessity, church doctrine, the legal system, ethnic backgrounds and class differences.

With the beginning of the change from a 'corporate household', where the work was done primarily in the home shop, through the time of the Industrial Revolution, there was a major change in the relationship of fathers to their children. Once the father left home to do his work, the connection between fathers and their children grew weaker. This sounded painfully familiar to me. Indeed, in our time it's no longer just the father who leaves the house for the work place but in many families, the mother as well.

I began to wonder about those individual fathers who actually lived in that time. Did they feel themselves to be part of a long evolutionary process which, as we look back at it, profoundly changed American society? Did even one dad, maybe a harness maker, look around and ask, 'What will it mean for future generations if I leave my home shop and go to work in the factory?' Did he talk to his neighbor, the blacksmith, about it? I suspect that just like most of us today, he was 'too busy' with his day-to-day life to be aware of the significant difference his action and the actions of most of the fathers would make, not just in their time but 200 years later. Posed like this, the question may sound a bit ridiculous, but how can we come to an understanding of the future for our children unless we try to come to terms with our collective actions and their consequences?

That one father, the harnessmaker, did make a difference. Not only to his family, but his decision, however arrived at and for what ever reason, affected his grandchildren and their families, great grandchildren and all their families, and so on, to our present day. What we do and who we are, individually and collectively, have very real effects on tomorrow—to a large extent through what we teach our children, one dad at a time. We all make a difference. The point is not only that we make a difference but that the level of consciousness in which we go about our daily activity really matters.

A new consciousness requires that we develop the capacity to see the world not just as a sequence of literal events, but that we take interest in searching for meaning in a longer evolutionary picture. While this may appear at first glance to be rather esoteric, I hope that it can be seen quite concretely. If, as I have tried to say, we do influence our children, their future and therefore the future itself, I would go back to one of the thoughts which began this chapter. If it is true that to fully engage in the role of being a father to our children, we must engage in a process of who we have been and are becoming, then we need a framework within which to do that. It seems to me that this search for a touchstone can be seen all around us.

In our culture, we blame our condition on our economy, our legal system, our insatiable appetite for 'things', feminism, the male psyche, the Church, the Republicans, the Democrats and even the disinterested. We often feel that what is happening reflects something 'out there' that has gone wrong and 'they' should fix it. The 'they' which we seem to look to is the Government, but what can the Government really do? I believe our culture is a reflection of our own human evolution and what we do gives a picture of what we believe to be of value.

The traditional nuclear family of the not too distant past is rapidly vanishing. The nature of fathering, even as we experienced it as sons, is also becoming a thing of the past. Remember that in the 50's, it was the father's defined role to provide the house; and the mother's to transform it into a home. That was true for about 85% of the families in the United States. Today, only about 7% of the families are configured in that traditional way. The rest are arranged in a wide variety of relationships ranging from two parents working outside the home, to the single parent household, to same-sex parents, to extended families, to various combinations of siblings, half and step-siblings sharing multiple homes. We see the majority of mothers moving into the work place, and are just beginning to see men make the choice to be 'house-husbands'.

Given all this, it certainly appears to me that the rather comfortable model of our youth (remember, I'm 50 something) is gone and that in its place we have a certain discomfort about which way to turn; which framework to base our search on, if we want to search at all. But if we as fathers can begin to come together and truly share what is, in one sense, a step into the unknown, perhaps we can begin to discover the insights we need in our relationships with our children.

Elizabeth Sheen

I was born in London in 1938 to a family of professional musicians, which led to a childhood rich with artistic experiences and which led me to dance. Movement is still a passion of mine: eurythmy, folk dancing, ballroom or just moving round the room to a favourite piece of music.

I married in 1962 and was introduced to Waldorf Education and anthroposophy by my husband. There were, and are, struggles and great joys arising from the challenges that came with meeting this philosophy. But through the wonderful people that I have had the pleasure of meeting and knowing through anthroposophy, I found a meaning and direction to my life.

I chose to be at home when bringing up our four children, though I continued to sing semi-professionally throughout those years. I am now struggling somewhat with all that comes to meet me at this time in my life. When I offered to write an article on caring for one's elderly parents, I had to include all the other difficulties which I was facing; children leaving home, grandchildren across the Atlantic, the menopause, aging, and trying to redefine myself and find the next step forward. I am always so sanguine and enthusiastic at the thought of putting it all down in writing but when I begin then I discover, once more, how difficult it is! I tend to write as I speak, which isn't always a good thing, as I tend to speak before I think! My first draft turned out to be very negative, as I dwelt on the problems and lost sight of the other side of the coin. Having to rewrite sections was incredibly hard, and I found that I really didn't like what I had written some months earlier. Things change all the time and what is relevant one day, may not be the next. But I have persevered and hope that some of what I have said will touch a chord with someone, somewhere.

Over the years it has been wonderful to meet many people for whom the first *Lifeways* has been such a support.

8
Midlife changes

How strange it is to be in my middle fifties and be a mother, grandmother, wife, sister and child. So many hats to wear and if you're sanguine, as I am, you sometimes put on the wrong hat. I am my aging parents' child, and yet I begin also to be their mother as, in some respects, they enter second childhood. What a muddle it can seem: 'Who am I? Here we go again; I thought I had sorted that one out, but no it keeps coming back.' Oh to be 'oneself' and yet, what is that? What is it that helps to make us what we are? Surely all the people whom we love and who love us: our parents, grandparents, aunts, uncles, siblings, Godparents in our early years, then later husbands, wives, children and finally, grandchildren. So I have come to a new place where I must strive to find balance with my aging parents. They still see and experience me as their child, and yet as an adult I am needed in a mothering role. (Also as a friend and adviser to help with decisions, which are often painful and difficult.)

At the same time, I also find myself in another period of change; yes, THE change! Changes are not new, I have been experiencing them all my life; how would I grow inwardly without them? But this one is quite a challenge. At first, I found the sleepless nights the most difficult, as more and more unwanted thoughts flew around my head like demented May-bugs; or small snippets of songs or symphonies repeated ad nauseum that would not be replaced by others that I tried to put in their place. But slowly, over the months, I've tried to be more open and relaxed at these times and to try and listen more closely to what can come to me in the wee, small hours.

I have had one or two really special thoughts which I write down and mull over the next day. For instance, one evening I sang a duet from Mozart's Magic Flute where Papageno and Pamina sing of the joys of love. On waking that night around 3am, wet through and burning from a hot flush, the thought came to me that Pamina and Tamino had to go through trials of fire and water before they took the next step in their lives together, so maybe I, too, am experiencing my own trials of initiation. This thought gave me such peace. Remarkably, since having these thoughts, the sweats and wakefulness have lessened.

I am also experiencing the pain of loss now that all four of my children have finally left home. For 28 years I have been a mother and chose to stay at home, for better or for worse. Now they are standing on their own feet— and of course I feel very glad, but did they all have to go abroad?! (So many thousands of miles away, leaving the connection a tenuous one, by phone or, rarely these days, a letter.) So it happens that my grandchildren are also far away and one's arms feel empty and useless.

> All that remains to the mother in modern consumer society is the role of scapegoat: pyschoanalysis uses huge amounts of money and time to persuade sons and daughters to foist their problems on to the absent mother, who has no opportunity to utter a word in her own defence. Hostility to the mother in our societies is an index of mental health. Mothers whose hearts yearn for their children are told that they have over-identified with their mothering role, that they were possessive or over-protective...In societies where this is not the case, where a mother's love and nearness are considered among the sweetest sweets of existence, seeing one's daughters become mothers is a joyous experience.
>
> In traditional societies, the aging mother has mothering functions to perform in the families of her grown-up children, caring for the birthing woman, mothering the older children when their mother is involved with the new-born.
>
> The patterns of black female role behaviour rarely result in depression in middle-age. Often the 'grannie' or 'auntie' lives with the family and cares for the children while the mother works; thus the older woman suffers no maternal role loss.
>
> *The Change* by Germaine Greer (p.74)

These trials and changes always seem to come all at once at the same time: the loss of children, the menopause, one's parents becoming dependent or dying, the realization that one's youth has really gone and will never be regained, coming to terms with stiffening joints, greying hair and wrinkles.

At menopause as never before, a woman comes face to face with her own mortality. A part of her is dying. Nothing she can do will bring her ovaries back to life. The grief of menopause affects every woman, consciously or otherwise. The feeling that one's day has passed its noon and the shadows are lengthening, that Summer is long gone and the days are growing ever shorter and bleaker, is a just one and should be respected. At the turning point the descent into night is felt as rapid: only when the stress of the climacteric is over can the aging woman realize that autumn can be long, golden, milder and warmer than Summer and is the most productive season of the year... When the fifty year old woman says to herself 'Now is the best time of all' she means it all the more because she known it is not for ever.

'This thou perceivest, which makes thy love more strong
To love that well, which thou must leave ere long'

Shakespeare *Sonnet 73*

The Change by Germaine Greer (p.142)

'Pull yourself together'—'You're so lucky to have a home, family, friends, husband, etc.,'—'Things could be worse'—'Do something.' It is not easy at this time to regain one's self respect, especially if you do not have a career to replace the hectic life of homemaker. I found it very difficult to cope with being at home with many hours to fill. Thanks to support from friends and family, I have started to build up a life by rekindling an old passion for crafts, but it takes discipline to organize my days fruitfully, and I still get distracted by domestic duties, running errands; in short, doing things for other people and feeling guilty when I say 'no'!

Your husband, if you have one, is wondering what on earth is going on! 'Who is this weepy, moody, resentful, sick person?' 'Why can't life go on as before?' 'Oh no, have I got to do something here?' 'Have I got to get involved with FEELINGS, and stuff that I would prefer not to talk about at all?' If the relationship is going to go somewhere from here, then, yes, he has got to be involved and helped to understand what's going on. But please, NOT the same response to everything—'Oh don't worry; I expect it is just the Menopause'!

Grief. Once involved in the hidden drama of the climacteric the aging woman should retreat into her own spiritual world and come to terms with herself. She should not be jolted out of it or bullied or ridiculed. To be patient she must be allowed to be quiet. ...All mothers weep for their children's childhood, for the disappearance of those small magical people, who understood so well how to give love and how to take it. It is at least as sad for a woman to know that 'the love affair' with her babies will never come again as never to have known it, especially now that a grandmother's physical hunger for her grandchildren is a thing of no importance.

Our culture has very little tolerance of grief. We are forbidden to mourn even the death of those nearest and dearest. A woman whose child dies is not allowed to sit with other women crying and keening. A woman whose parent dies is not allowed to veil her head and withdraw from human intercourse in order to understand what has happened to her... The most heartening thing that writers can find to say about the menopause is that there need be 'no change', as if human life was anything but change!

The Change by Germaine Greer (p.310)

Many of us, while coping with such things, are also involved in some way with our aging parents: either in a nurturing and caring capacity or in coming to terms with the loss of one or both of them. Again, so many questions have presented themselves to me over this period: responsibility and duty, resentment and guilt, tolerance or lack of it...

What are our responsibilities and where do they lie? Because we have received something, does it therefore follow that we must give in return, or is parental love given unconditionally? Will I expect my children to come home and care for me? Is it a generation question? Not long ago, and still prevalent in some countries, the youngest daughter was expected to stay at home and not get married so that she could look after her parents. A lovely book was published recently, *Like Water for Chocolate* by Laura Esquivel, which humorously examines this. Of course, there are instances where daughters or sons wish to be care-givers, and if this is out of pure love and not duty, then that is a wonderful thing.

If, however, it is expected of us, resentment can set in because choices have to be made between parents, and husbands and children. Who is one's immediate family, the former or the latter? I once forgot a sick child at home because I became absorbed in a crisis with my parents. And so follows guilt; guilty feelings towards both parties, whichever one I am not with! I can remember driving past my parents' house on several occasions, not wanting to go in. I still feel that way if a few days pass by and I have not made the effort to visit or call. Where do these feelings of guilt come from? I suppose it has to do with being selfish; where does one draw the line between selfishness and looking after oneself? I often want to do what makes me happy and avoid the tasks and chores that I find irksome. Of course, a lot of the time it is not irksome but a great joy and pleasure to be with my parents.

It really is a juggling act, trying to please all. As a mother I find it particularly hard to change from caring for others to looking after myself. My nurturing instinct wants to help everyone, yet if I do the same for myself, I feel selfish and guilty!

Another cause of guilt is lack of tolerance. Why is it more difficult for me to accept strange and annoying habits in my parents than those in my husband? I wonder if this is to do with having to face up to, and accept, that they *are* getting old, and these habits and behaviour simply underline that fact. It is also much easier for me to talk to my husband without offending him, and although I have sometimes plucked up courage and tried to tackle these things with my parents, it does not seem to have any lasting effect!

I hope that by struggling with these feelings and trying to control them, I will become more tolerant. I do try to imagine what I will be like when I am in my 70s and 80s! I have already made a few promises to myself and to my husband that I hope I will remember, in order that he, and those who may have to care for me, will not have to suffer too much.

So, here I am, still sweating slightly, trying to keep balanced as I face an exciting new beginning in one sphere, juggle all the daily tasks, learn to say no, please myself occasionally, and continue across the miles to support my family. As for my one remaining parent, I hope to develop my tolerance and to carry on helping where I can, without resentment but with love and joy.

Nancy Jewel Poer

When I was in my thirties and asking the question, 'Okay, what am I here for anyway?', the answer shaped itself in two soul stirring words: 'spiritual midwifery.' They still shimmer on the horizon of my struggles and striving. Few gifts exceed being witness to the light of another, those moments when spirit shines through mortality. Little wonder I came to teaching and aiding at thresholds of birth and death where one can touch the all-embracing rhythms of human existence.

With our six children, and those I've taught, it was the flourishing of soul and spirit that interested me. I thrilled to the sparkle of mighty beings in tiny bodies and sought to support them in self mastery so they could later bestow their gifts on a needy world. We also had some great and glorious fun together. My published art prints are for all the children.

My mother was an enthusiastic anthroposophist and pioneer, and I follow her. I love the innovative founding years of things, have begun three Waldorf Kindergartens, taught at all grade levels, initiated community home-death work, helped to found Rudolf Steiner College in 1976 and still teach there. Waldorf Education, Early Childhood, Motherhood and Parenting, Spiritual Destiny of America, Virtual Reality and Children, and Thresholds of Birth and Death are themes I lecture on across the country.

Home is White Feather Ranch in the Sierra foothills where I live with my husband of forty-two years. We've travelled the highs and lows of marriage and, as pilots, share a love of flying, parachute jumping together for our thirtieth anniversary. Our commitment to parenting was deepened by the death of our firstborn infant; our wonderful children and grandchildren are our fulfillment. Contentment comes with driving the old pickup with a load of compost or lumber, feeding the cattle, and sharing stars and sunsets with the many friends who come from around the world. Here at the ranch we work to provide a place where people can regain their connection to the earth, to each other, and to the spiritual work ahead. It is a privilege to join others in this book in encouraging families everywhere through these difficult and exciting times.

9
Our families and the threshold of death: our contemporary views on death and dying

Our birth is but a sleep and a forgetting:
The Soul that rises with us, our life's Star,
Hath had elsewhere its setting,
And cometh from afar...

Wordsworth, *Ode To Immortality*

'Our life's Star'...this lovely phrase that rings so deep and true. Intimations of immortality we once knew but have forgotten as a modern culture. We've forgotten the spiritual realms from which we came and our 'birthing' at the thresholds of earthly life.

Our first birth, into physical life, is nurtured and mother-given. But death is also a birth...a birth back into our spiritual existence. In death, we must labor to give birth to ourselves! For death is the release of our immortal soul-spiritual essence back into universal being. Homecoming. It is so interesting how often death is spoken of as 'going home'. Elderly individuals who have been in nursing homes for years will suddenly one day square their shoulders, rally with far seeing eyes and announce, 'I'm going home.' Then they die. The spirit slips from earth bound flesh and crosses into invisible soul-spiritual realms.

Ours is a world of Western materialism. With the physical empirical thinking that marks our age, we have been conditioned against believing in anything we cannot see, touch or measure. Death is often experienced as a grim finality. But this was not the common consciousness of humanity in times past, when the laws of the physical world did not lay claim to soul and spirit existence as well. In previous ages death was a natural part of life, and spiritual existence an unquestioned reality.

For example, the humble birth ritual of the African bushman with its heart-moving truths can stir even a modern soul. Solemnly, the parents take their newborn child and lift it up in offering to the stars, to the heavenly source from which it came, recognizing with gratitude that life springs from the universe. They know that life on earth is a gift bordered by time, and that in the end we shall return to God, to our home in the stars. With this encompassing wisdom they rise each day and greet God in sun and wind and every living thing, knowing as sure as a heart beat that we are an integral part of it all. We live on earth to do our dance, to give our transformative gifts to each other and the planet, and then go home to the universe.

As modern humanity we live far more as individuals with self-centered consciousness and less as citizens of the great universe. Our self-centered awareness intensifies our progress as individualities, but leaves us far more critical of ourselves, others, and life's painful realities. Without an abiding faith in a cosmic embracing reality beyond our earthly persona, one can hardly have a healthy view of death and dying.

We live in a world experiencing cruel and pervasive death through war, crime, famine, plagues and increasingly random, senseless self destructive violence. It is a deep challenge not to succumb to apathy and helplessness, anger or paralyzing fear. All fears have at their core the ultimate deepest fear in life...the fear of death. With an encompassing spiritual view that includes immortality—a continuing existence of the individual human spirit—death can be put into perspective.

As small children we stand close to the spiritual realities of life; but as we grow in self consciousness we feel more and more isolated. By adolescence, childhood innocence and spiritual knowing are left behind. For teenagers, flowing with the vital juices of physical life (a time of natural omnipotence), death is shocking, out of season, dismaying and fascinating. For some, faced with the soulless decadence of much of modern life, it may seem a way out. We need ever more spiritual support for our young people. And for many adults, culturally conditioned in restrictive materialistic world views, there is scarcely any healing compensation for all the pain of existence.

How can we make a personal stand in the face of all this? We cannot eradicate outer wars, but can we breathe rightness and reason into this inevitable experience of losing loved ones through death? This experience touches us all. How can we bring support to our loved ones in a way that truly gives a dignity to death? Life gives us unavoidable opportunities to help us face this threshold with greater consciousness. The task is to engender a deeper transformative insight which can move beyond the barriers of physical death to greater awareness of universal life. When individuals around a death are able to blend hopeful courage and loving care with the sorrow and loss, it is an uplifting deed for everyone.

New revelations from near-death experiences

An exciting result of our modern technological age, is that we have the life saving techniques to bring people back to life who formerly would have died. Through them our modern nihilism is soundly refuted! These individuals, now some eight million world-wide, of all ages, religions and ethnic backgrounds, have documented near-death experiences.

They are often able to describe the people and events around their 'apparently' dead body as well as experiences in the spiritual world of existence. Not only is the actual moment of death without pain, but it is experienced as a birth and an awakening. Most people encounter a Being of celestial light radiating the greatest compassion, wisdom and universal love. There are many books currently published which relate these stories.

Today, no discussion on death and dying can really be complete without gratitude to Dr. Elizabeth Kübler-Ross, whose courageous pioneering work has transformed our cultural viewpoint on death in the last twenty-five years. She brings out the spiritual truths from her practical experience of aiding thousands at death's threshold. She encourages family involvement, home death when possible, and has written many books on the subject; it is her conviction that both children and the dying can tell us universal truths.

From the mouths of babes

Most small children dreamily remember the spiritual world from which they came. Still star-spangled and angel-kissed, they inwardly know it is a reality. Their fears of death, or acceptance of it, are largely instilled over time by adults around them. They can logically fear abandonment, fear that no one will be there to care for them and give them love. They can have fear of burial. Older children may fear they have been a cause of a relative's death. All these concerns can be alleviated by spiritual awareness, courage, and caring through sorrow, if the adults around them can develop these qualities.

From the 'mouths of babes' still close to the source, we can receive the timeless truths of our full human existence, earthly, heavenly.

When our dear Grandma died at our home, we held a wake for her during the three days following. During these three days the one who has died is experiencing a panorama of his or her life and is adjusting to spiritual existence. It is most helpful if prayers, spiritual reading and thoughts from family and friends accompany those who have died to aid them in the transition. Remembering usually comes quite naturally: stories and loving moments come about in family-sharing after the death, and honoring of the life at the funeral services. Yet we can also accompany the departed soul more consciously, with prayers and support throughout this special time.

A young mother with a two year old came to pay her respects during our three day vigil after Grandma's death. The mother had never looked upon a body and was frankly apprehensive. She felt it important to honor Grandma, but she did not want to give her young son harsh impressions, so she left him in the car in the driveway. As two year olds will, he did not stay put, but came dashing into the room and rushed to the casket, grabbed the handle and tried to rock it. The reverent mother flushed, embarrassed. I laughed and said, 'It's fine, surely it is Grandma's cradle to carry her home.' The child bounced around the room, investigating crystals, pictures and flowers. As the mother prepared to leave, she picked up the exuberant boy. Now for the first time he could see the body lying in the casket. He gave it only a cursory disinterested glance and then looking upward above the body, with a radiant face he waved his chubby finger and joyfully chortled, 'Bye, bye!' The mother was astonished and I delighted. There was no question the young child experienced the surrounding spiritual being of Grandma in the room!

When I asked a small son how he was doing with Grandma's death, he cheerfully replied, 'Oh, Grandma's just up in heaven looking down on her little old bones.'

'We only own our spirits,' a seven year old announced to me. 'Our bodies came from God. When we go to heaven they go back to God and then he gives us new ones.'

Another girl, also seven when her father died, reassured her mother, 'Daddy has finished his tasks on earth and has taken them to heaven as gifts.'

Such statements are not wishful thinking in children. They arise from the deepest wisdom, a time of life when our souls can still be connected with spiritual oneness. They know with eternal wisdom that life follows death as surely as God is love and summer follows winter.

The family and death

My husband and I were determined that the experience of the ending of life could have as much care and meaning for our six children as one would give the welcoming of a baby. With that resolve, we nursed our bedridden elders for over three years, so they could die at home with us. We eventually supported many others to bring loved ones home to die, or to care for them with richer awareness. We felt this part of family life was just as important a lesson for our children as any course they would take in school. Certainly it was not easy. But fulfilling? Without question.

As grandmother and grandfather progressed through strokes and paralysis to full nursing care, it was confining work for us. For many families giving such nursing care is impossible—situations vary widely. But most families could have more beneficial involvment with their dying ones than they realize. We have had many community-supported home deaths, wakes and funeral services without involving professional funeral homes. This is legal when all state requirements are met.

Becoming more open to spiritual and eternal truths shared through supporting the dying, can give a great sense of gratitude and completion.

Just as individuals differ, so deaths are different. Each one has a style. Some go out with a sigh and a smile, others a shout. Some with a sudden accident in the prime of life, others after a long path of suffering. Spiritually, our first task is to be open to a sense of timing for each individual, that the death time is part of their bigger life 'plan'. From this we can find a certain comfort amidst our shocking loss and grief, sensing that somehow they 'knew what they were doing.'

We can then stand at the bed-side through a loved one's coma or labored breathing, honoring their 'deed' of dying, their process to give birth to themselves. It is then that the gifts of a lifetime are given back to the universe. The individual is working toward that moment, to make a transition to spirit being. We can carry a sense of this and know that our loving touch, our prayers and thoughts of encouragement can be perceived by their soul and spirit during all the process, regardless of their outer condition.

It's hard to do. We have to overcome our sensibilities, our pain, and physical repugnance of the process. It is so very understandable when people say they do not want to be around the dying but 'remember them the way they were' in earthly health and fullness, rather than weak, confused and emaciated.

Birth into the physical existence is a blooming process. With every passing day the baby becomes more rosy, round and plump and sparkly-eyed. With their charming smiles and laughter, our joy and satisfaction in their emerging beauty and personality grows too.

Birth back to the spiritual is hardly as satisfying to our senses. We have known someone as attractive, active and robust. Now they lose vitality, flesh is sallow and weakened. The spirit is moving out. Can we see *through* this outer debilitation to the true reality of the process? While the body dies, the spiritual individuality prepares to bloom.

An experience with my paralyzed father sings through time for me years after his death, as bright and new as the morning sun. My Dad, always so strong, able, capable, protective, and guiding, was felled by a stroke and lay in bed technically as helpless as a new born babe. Yet one morning I came into his room warmed with rosy light shining through the sheer magenta curtains. He lay there, a crooked grin on his face, peacefully staring into memories and gruffly queried, 'Who are you?' I laughed and said, 'I'm your daughter, Pappy.' He warmed and knew me. No other words were spoken, but in that irradiating timeless moment the waves of love we had known forever filled every corner of that room...and far beyond...that warming love that knows no barriers, that nothing can ever, ever take away from one's heart.

My father had not diminished one iota in the powerful caring presence of his true individuality. This precious knowing was an apex moment in our relationship. I knew this outer condition was *his* process and *his* way of going, the way he needed to finish up and shed a body so well used for over ninety years. Surely I could respect that. He had had a real grip on life and it was going to take some doing to let it go! We both honored the process and all the family grew with it.

The last days when he was dying, the family assembled in the room, taking turns holding his hand, praying and singing. The ten year old grandson played exuberantly outside his window, romping with the dog. The last day he dashed in declaring , 'I love you, Pappy, have a good time in heaven!' and was out to play again. He gave voice as clear and natural as spring air to the rightness of this family deed. Our relationship to the dying and those across the threshold is one of the heart.

Grandma's gift at death

Grandma Mary Edna was an archetype. She twinkled. Her eyes were small and merry brown. She had a cascade of double and triple chins which the grandchildren called her 'wattles' She patiently tolerated chubby fingers cuddling them with affectionate fascination. She endlessly baked bread and cookies for the children. One grandchild accused her of getting fat because she was so dismayed when the child outgrew her lap. Neighbor children wanted to adopt Grandma for their own.

When she broke her hip at 92, still a homemaker for her youngest paraplegic grandchild, we knew we needed to care for her at home. As I arranged hospital bed, potty chair, pads and washrags I mentioned to my husband it was like fixing a layette for a baby. 'No, it isn't!' he replied vehemently, it only being scant years since we emerged from fifteen years of diapers. But as we drove her home from the hospital with our fourteen year old twin girls cuddled protectively on either side of her and driving ever so slowly over the bumps, he gave me a sideways glance and said, 'You're right. You're right!'

So she began her five month stay with us until she died. Later, we would care for my father for nearly two years. It was not easy for the children to see beloved grandparents change to people of few words and physical helplessness. But through all the ups and downs breathed a steady goodness and rightness to the whole process. The girls would tease wheelchair-ridden Grandma with a fake spider till she squealed, a game they both relished. Gently brushing and stroking her silvery hair, they smoothed it to a soft fineness. All the children would save a choice tidbit at the dinner table for her, or with rippling strength in young arms, sons and daughters wheeled their elders out on to the back lawn to be in the afternoon sun. It was good. Because of these experiences we have found all our children have a warm understanding for the elderly in all states, and carry an empowering knowledge of what to do when confronted with their death.

The night Grandma died, the priest came and gave her communion. The family all gathered around her bed in the candlelit room. There was a majesty to the moment. Tenderly the priest spoke, 'Grandma, this is the substance to make us inclined to love...' She spent the evening taking long rasping breaths, especially hard for the children to bear. They tendered prayers and good-byes and it was not easy. I sang her a favorite song, 'Swing Low Sweet Chariot'. She was in hard but good labor. When would it be?

Exhausted, I needed sleep. My husband, her oldest grandchild, slept in the room with her. About one in the morning a white owl hooted loudly and circled the house. Most of the family later remembered hearing that call during their sleep. It was a marvelous moonlit, windswept winter night. Then my husband called for me from the bottom of the stairs and I flew down, scarcely touching the steps.

Grandma's eyes were 'far seeing' into realms across the threshold. My husband supported her with his powerful arms from behind and I embraced her to complete the circle. With our last words ringing ardently around her, 'Grandma, we love you', she left her old body. We laid her gently on the bed. She had made it!

We sat in awe, our hearts full and opened to the wonder. It was totally quiet. The peace...the incredible peace. The shell of the body, empty beyond emptiness...the atmosphere full to overflowing. Now nothing to do. She no longer needed blankets or warmth, or slippers or water...or touch.

After a time we called the children, one by one. They came downstairs into the room now graced and holy. A gangly teenage son remarked, 'This isn't spooky at all'. We huddled and hugged. Then we all went out in the clean winter night on the back lawn, looking up to the glittering stars. There was an excitement to it. We chattered and shivered and stamped our feet in the chill winter wind and talked of the wonderful owl. Together we exulted our bon voyage of hope, sadness, gratitude and joy to our beloved Grandma into the wind and the night.

Her casket had been made by our eldest son. Together over Christmas we had all finished it together, rubbing it with a rich oil that brought the wood to a gleam. As we now prepared it in the back yard with fragrant pine boughs and lined it with magenta curtains from her room, a son asked 'But what will the neighbors think?' 'They will think we really care,' I replied with conviction. Perhaps not entirely so but the way it ought to be.

We had her body there at home in the same pink sunlit room where she died. Grandma had cared for people all her life. Somehow it seemed she would choose no other role in death. Well over a hundred men, women, and children had their first experience of death there at our old home. Not in a hushed and somber mortuary, but in the midst of life in a lively old three-story family home. Close by was the kitchen. People laughed, visited, shared coffee and abundant food prepared and brought by caring friends. Outside the children were swinging on the rope swing, playing in the sandbox, the chickens crowing and scratching. Teenagers were on the phone, the back door slammed between comings and goings. People would go into her room alone or in groups, just to be there. In a way it seemed like Grandma was a queen holding court, a royal funeral ceremony, the passing of the kingdom.

Such an honoring of dying can be, for both children and adults, a soul counterforce against the onslaught of countless ugly, and fearful death images from the media. Gratitude for the wholesomeness of that experience with Grandma was expressed by family after family that came in those days. That did not mean it was not an awesome and difficult experience for some. But it was death...as part of life...a natural part of life. We saw it as Grandma still taking care of everyone.

Here are some of the words written by those pilgrims to her bedside, friends who came to sit alone there for a quiet hour, in the three days and nights...

'Thank you, Grandma, for the blessing you have given...and to the children. Help me carry, in some way the joy of your spirit and love of the children.'

'As I sit here, I feel the strength and peacefulness that you leave to all of us.'

'I will take with me today an encouragment for others that life is beautiful...'

'Thank you, for sharing your strength with me...'

'May we always see you in the flight of the white owl, the softness, the purity, the freedom and joy...We love you dearly...'

'It is my birthday. How wonderful to live with Grandma on this special day...Grandma's passing is a light to the new day and new way. May we all be so blessed.'

'Grandma has given me a special gift and continues to be an inspiration in the spiritual worlds which lie before me. Thank you, Grandma.'

And eighteen-month old Cedar, a frequent visitor and friend, did dances around the room and sang a song of joy, 'La, la, la, la la.'

Grief and transformation

There is no doubt we must acknowledge our grief. Grief must have its flow, its day and days. Sometimes it takes some years for the separation to heal. Yet if grief is prolonged unduly, it encapsulates and isolates; isolates individuals from one another on earth and from the one who has died. Rudolf Steiner writes that it is our gratitude for having been a part of a loved one's life, our appreciative remembrance of loving moments that open the connections to loved ones across the threshold. If our soul is always wrapped in our sorrow they cannot reach to us. If we can open our soul in gratitude and love for what we have shared in life and for their continuing spiritual evolution, they can then become close and immediate.

They are quietly ever present and can help with our lives even though we are often unaware. That this is a reality is borne out through countless personal experiences. Throughout the world people report 'appearances' of those who have died with reassurances that they are 'Okay'. One devout man appeared to his wife shortly after his death and shortly before hers with the assurances 'It's wonderful!'

Rudolf Steiner gives the following verses to strengthen the soul against the fears that come with death and loss.

Against fear

> May the events that seek me
> Come unto me;
> May I receive them
> With a quiet mind
> Through the Father's ground of peace
> On which we walk.
>
> May the people who seek me
> Come unto me;
> May I receive them
> With an understanding heart
> Through Christ's stream of love
> In which we live.
>
> May the spirits which seek me
> Come unto me;
> May I receive them
> With a clear soul
> Through the healing Spirit's light
> By which we see.

Verse for one who has died

Into the fields of Spirit will I send
The faithful love we found on Earth,
Uniting soul with soul
And thou wilt find my loving thought
When from the Spirit lands of light
Thou hither turn thy seeking soul
To find what thou dost seek in me.

Or the following:

Upward to thee strives the love of my soul
Upward to thee flows the stream of my love!
May they sustain thee
May they enfold thee
In heights of Hope,
In spheres of Love.

Home death and legal issues

There can be a great sense of comfort and completion in being able to give full support to another at the end of life's journey. In many cases it is not practical or possible to have total responsibility, and professionals are necessary. But where the strength and the will to do so is there in family and friends, there are broad possibilities for giving care which most people do not realize.

First of all, it *is* legal to care for your own loved ones at death. Rarely is embalming required, at least not in the first days. This is not widely known. Embalming prevents deterioration as strong preservatives are used. In certain cases it is advisable. Yet the separation of soul, spirit and vital forces from the body is a process, and it takes place in the three days following physical death. Many religious philosophies recognize this spiritual reality. The death of the physical body is the first stage in the transition of life, memories, soul and spirit moving on to other aspects of existence.

If the environment is cool, not only can the body be kept but amazing transformation can take place, a kind of glow, an essence of beauty. I have seen individuals who were nearly 90 years at death look 35 on the second to third day. For coolness, dry ice may be used in a special way. There are various books available on state legal requirements as well as on home care of those who have died. (See *Notes.*)

When a death has occurred at home and there has been no regular medical care by a physician, an autopsy may be required to determine cause of death. It is therefore advisable to have a home death plan agreed with a doctor, who will be responsible for signing the death certificate.

Funeral homes take care of all the paper work when involved. Understandably, home death rituals are not given much support by the industry as they run counter to its customs and incomes. Some will be supportive, but any involvement will also involve a standard minimum fee.

For me every death is as unique as the individual who has died; hopefully it will be appropriate for that individual and his or her family. Therefore, the circumstances, whether handled at home or by professionals, need to be considered for what is practical, beautiful and spiritually supportive...the right art form for that particular situation. This includes embalming or not, cremation, setting and family involvement, etc.

One of the most rewarding deaths I was involved in, was one where I never had direct care for the body. I just gave advice to the daughter of a woman dying in a nursing home. The daughter, whom I will call Ann, had had a difficult and harsh relationship with her mother. Yet she was determined to give support, resolution and forgiveness in death that was not possible in life. Given directives, she was able to transport her mother's body to her home and care for her.

I had told her not to necessarily expect understanding from those involved but to have the courage to carry it through. Surprisingly, her sister chose to be included in the care. Ann was most concerned about her mother's neighbors whom she had invited to the vigil. Imagine her fulfillment when an elderly couple came to the home, beautifully and artistically arranged and, near to tears, declared that they wished someone would do this for them.

Triumphantly, Ann called me after her deed of the three days. Through her joy I sensed that a lifetime of hurt had received incredible healing for both mother and daughter through this act of love, courage and ceremony.

It is so hard to fully appreciate the gifts of these days around death, as we are often deep in shock, grief, and details of the situation. But in between these realities, an open heart will tell us the angels have come blessedly close to welcome a loved one home.

Death and community

I muse over my involvement in many community deaths over the years, recalling toddlers chirping in the rooms of invalids and patting ancient hands, or patient ministers and workers there to read and comfort through the days. Often friends and family have carried all aspects of caring for the one who has died. I remember the loving hands of friends transporting a tiny body from the coroner, several wood craftsmen coming together to build a casket, after a child's sudden death. A worker turned the midnight clock to the wall announcing 'We work on other time' as they created through the night. The beautiful casket was later filled by other caring hands with lovely silks and cloth, sweet smelling branches. Others washed and dressed the body. Meals were prepared, the family was hugged.

The poignant story is told and retold; vigils are arranged by friends. Through the night beside a candle-lit casket, prayers and readings are offered to warm the crossing of the soul into heaven and a new orientation of being. Midwifery energy.

The three days after death are carefully honored as the soul is experiencing its new existence. Before the casket is finally closed and blessed, the remains may be covered with a veil and gently strewn with the petals of flowers brought by friends. Loved ones and friends can find a van and transport the casket on to its journeys, funeral and beyond. So it can be. The void of loss calls to be warmed by love and care as families adjust to new dimensions of being. Every death has its special unfolding. There is no single right way, but involvement gives support and sharing and begins the process of healing.

Children's deaths are the hardest of all. Yet these deaths are community-altering as few life events can be. While parents of the children suffer the continuing poignancy of the promise unfulfilled in earthly life, they can shimmer with spiritual halos as the child's spirit continuously works through them with a vibrant connection to the higher worlds and their deeper possibilities in life. At the funeral service the child, with the might of an angel, orchestrates from across the threshold, bringing souls together at the foot of the cross of death. Here community is formed. All pretence is dropped, masks put away, pettiness banished. Sorrow and wonder bring forth compassion as clean and fresh as the child's innocence. Opening hearts flow with shared human caring, rarely experienced. Community is real.

Rudolf Steiner writes that 'the funeral is one of the most important places for humanity to come together... to meet where the spiritual so surely touches into our earthly existence.'

If we can find the courage to face this most fearful of all thresholds with a deeper consciousness, we can begin to experience the possibility of resurrection beyond pain, loss and suffering. We can know what the ancients and children know, death is a transition and a new beginning.

As we are quietly experiencing dying and death, we can also know life on ever richer levels. Having faced death we can truly live! In seeing the body we *know* the spirit we knew is no longer within. Right after death, new and powerful thoughts can arise in the presence of a heaven expanding spirit, be it adult or child, and most especially if they carry a core of spiritual devotion and awareness. They give gifts to us all.

Our birth is but a sleep and a forgetting...our death is an awakening and remembering...of our true being! We should seek to find knowledge of the spirit, stories to strengthen our faith, listen to the children, nature, dreams and the songs of those who are wise and close to nature. Life is filled with beginnings and endings, with leaving the old and finding the new. Trust in the cycles, that life is natural and good and right and worthy of celebration with each threshold transcended. This is the courage and trust we need to live for ourselves, for our children...to live in the world today. In death is the gift of life.

Notes

Life After Life, Raymond Moody
To Live Until We Say Goodbye; On Death and Dying, Elizabeth Kubler Ross
Return from Tomorrow, George Ritchie
Where Are You?, Schelling
Who Dies?, Stephen Levine
Embraced by the Light, Betty Eadie
Death, The End is the Beginning, Evelyn Francis Capel
Earthly Death, Cosmic Life, Rudolf Steiner
Though You Die, Stanley Drake
Caring For Your Own Dead, Carlson (legal requirements in all states)
Home Death and Caring For Your Own, Nancy Poer

Waltraud Woods and Aicha Woods

Waltraud Woods, Aicha holding Daemien, Gisela Schleicher (Grandma)

Waltraud Schleicher Woods

It is January 11, 1996 and, with Aicha's support, I have just finished writing a small part of the story of a young life and death. I realize there is much more to tell. Waldorf education plays a major part and I will continue to work.

My own life followed a path using guidelines offered to me as a child. I was born into a family where mother and father had begun to work out of anthroposophy a decade before my birth. They recognized the importance for their children of the human, natural and built environment in their formative years. With the help of generous friends they made it possible for me and my sister to attend Waldorf schools through the 12th grade. I thrived in the constant interplay between artistic and intellectual work.

As a young woman I first found my way to ceramics, using my hands to shape and mold. I then chose to continue with studies in Architecture, the molding of the interior and exterior physical environment. I found it is the one field where the human, artistic and technical can be given coherence. Following my degree I had the opportunity to pursue studies in Europe. I then moved to Paris and lived there for ten years working with many colleagues on projects in different countries.

Aicha and Shadrach were born very close together, she in Paris and he in New York. Shadrach's father died when the children were very young. I was most fortunate that my mother and the Waldorf school were there to shelter and guide them while I began teaching architecture courses. During these past years I have worked on planning guidelines for a University, attempting to always foster a greater awareness of the needs of all the people in a dense urban complex.

My son Shadrach died on Mt. Snow on January 11, 1992. Aicha, with her family, has now found her path, as Shadrach also had chosen to do, by becoming an architect.

I was prompted, surely by Shadrach, to write about him because I feel I must find a language for his death, for dying. I must find a way out of my own silence. There is also a real need to talk to each other about death, to talk about how we can each come to an understanding of what we go through together. Shadrach's young friends showed me how willing they were to share the intimate experience they each felt.

I continue to hold Shadrach, and all of them, in my thoughts.

Aicha S. Woods

February 15, 1996. My brother Shadrach would have celebrated his twenty-sixth birthday today. I can picture him here in New Haven, contemplating the view from the seventh floor of the Art and Architecture building; he finds a certain comfort in the slate roofs and Gothic masonry turrets of the Yale campus. At his drafting table in the studio, Shad approaches design projects with a careful consideration of materials and structure, and a clear conviction of ethics in architecture. He is quick to share a laugh with his colleagues in studio, and readily joins an impromtu round of hacky-sack in the 'pit.' He would have revelled in the high drifts of snow left by the recent blizzard.

Shad planned to pursue a masters in architecture. I always imagined that he would go to graduate school first, and establish his career as an architect here on the East Coast. My own plans were vague; I thought I would hang out in the Bay Area until I had figured out just what I wanted to do. Instead it was I who filled out the application packets sent for by my brother. In my portfolio, I included a pictograph of Shadrach's story—I sent him ahead.

This is my story. I am currently in the second year of the M.Arch program at Yale. I approach studio projects very differently than my brother might have, although every now and then when I am stuck, I try to imagine how he might have solved a problem.

I am the mother of a five-year-old boy. My son Daemien's birth and Shad's death occurred within thirteen months. I do not know how I could have come to terms with Shad's death without my son, who gurgled patiently through teary rough drafts of Shadrach's story. We talk about Uncle Shadrach daily—he is sometimes blamed for broken toys. Every night Daemien and I sing together:

(To the tune of 'She'll be coming 'Round the Mountain')

Good Night, Daemien, Good Night,
With your Angel bide the night,
And bring love to Uncle Shadrach, way up in the stars,
And come down with the morning light.

Angels hearken to my childhood. I was about Daemien's age when our Daddy died and went to heaven. Throughout my childhood angels were present: the sense that Daddy and Omama were looking down upon my brother and me; my own guardian angel whom Grandma told me about; the recurring angels in the Waldorf School curriculum.

While in many ways I have mixed feelings about Waldorf education, I value immensely the rich collection of stories and images that I have access to from my childhood. As the third generation in an 'anthropop' family, this is my cultural heritage.

Finally, stories are healing, they are acts of love. As I reread the final draft of the story my mother and I have been working on, I was touched by the way her story cradles my own.

10
Shadrach

He sings to me
And calls my name
 From somewhere up there
Over there, from somewhere here
 From the depths of our minds.[1]

Yup'ik Eskimo Song

Wednesday morning: Shadrach, you and my angel have been working together again. I missed slamming into that car by inches. I do not think that anyone else realized how close I really came to that back bumper. I know you were there.

I look forward to my ride in the car on Friday evenings and again on Monday morning. I am away from everything which would distract me in the usual everyday routine. I know the route, and I enjoy observing the change of the seasons along the Merritt Parkway.

Shadrach, I think of you at the wheel, Grandma next to you completely relaxed. I am in the back seat, looking across your broad shoulders at the steadiness of your hand on the wheel, never really feeling the car speed up or slow down. You drove, enveloped in the security of your surroundings. I get into my car, feel that peace of mind and then spend an hour and a half, sometimes two hours, quietly waiting for your presence, thinking of things which I know would have interested you in your young life, also knowing that you would be interested in all that I can share with you. A deep concentration comes over me and I find I can dwell completely on one thought for some time without constantly interrupting myself with peripheral ideas. You are there, because I will it. But I also believe you are there because you are finding it a place of being for you, a moment of connection.

After you died, as I approached Spring Valley, I often did not know how I could stand going home, knowing that I would not be calling you, hearing you say, 'What's up?' and talking about vacation plans. Now, many months later, I know that you are always there if I can only make the quiet resting place in my heart.

My Shadrach, there are many times when I despair at my own feelings. I was angry at you. Why did you go to bed so late? I could not wake you the next morning to help me with something I had planned. And what was it that got you so angry that for days I could not understand if it was something I had done? Why do I recall these tensions which we sometimes experienced?

What were you telling me that day in January, which is in my thoughts so often that it seems like a year must have passed in those hours? Tennison had come, and you and she were going skiing; it had been postponed a number of times, and now there were only a few days of vacation left. You did not have gloves and a hat. I was irritated because you were leaving when sister/daughter, nephew/grandson, brother/son were home together for such a short time, and I loved having you all there together. You and Tennison had taken Daemien on a walk that morning in the pack on your back. You had been so loving and gentle. We knew that he was very special to you; your friends told of your joy at the birth of this nephew in California and your wanting to go and see him that first Christmas of his life.

And then you were ready, and Aicha and I needed to do something before Daemien awoke from his nap. We were a little impatient to get you off on your trip. Maybe both of you were lingering. All I can remember is you giving me a special hug and saying, 'Goodbye Mom,' which you, at other times, passed over and said only, 'So long.'

Saturday, 11 January 1992

The air was cold outside, but there was bright sunshine flooding the kitchen. Daemien was already sitting on the tall stool so that he could watch everything on the high counter. The waffle iron steamed, my hands were dusted with flour. When the phone rang, I hesitated a moment, thinking that someone else would answer it.

But it was I, thanks to my angel, who heard the gentle woman's voice announce the vast change to all our lives: a child is dead.

As the young doctor hesitantly told me the details of the events which had just occurred, the brilliant blue sky was over me, the sunlight gleamed on the snow covered slope. I felt the cool air brush my face as I sped downhill, I saw the dark trees, and my lungs ached with indrawn breath. I needed to be told a number of times to understand the finality of all those words. My 'Shadrach is dead' brought the outstretched arms of Grandma, Aicha and Daemien. In that small kitchen, we rocked together in our embrace of love. Father and son, taken from us, but brought together again; the little boy child with the snow white hair; the golden dreadlocks; the son who ran with the wind, the smiling young man. I reached out to my mother, my daughter, my grandson.

Was I to run to the spot where the sun still gleamed on the ski tracks in the snow? Was I to go to the morgue? Was I to go to the inquest? Was I to ride all those miles with the cold body? Was I needed to bring the broken bones of our man child home?

Then I realized that we were not alone, Shadrach was with us. Much later, Aicha asked, 'What made you realize this? Did you, at the time, or are you just writing this in retrospect?' Shadrach was there with us during those first moments of learning of his death. He showed me the slope, he made me feel the wind. I experienced his elation. Only later, did my heart writhe with his pain.

One moment you hug me and say, Goodbye, Mom,
And the next moment, I remember,
The soft gentle childish voice tells me you are gone, gone, gone.
Away, not to return as you had always done before.
I could not even call you back.
The hours, days, months and years, as they pass,
Are filled with unspoken conversation between a mother and her
child.
But I think we did speak in gestures,
And knew each other well,
And felt the bond of confidence.
You, at that one incredible, glowing moment,
Were so filled with energy and life...
I screamed and screamed, in desperate silence, my son, my son,
How can it happen once again to me,
A part of that vessel of the tenderest love,
Torn out, another piece of me ripped from my soul.
At that moment Aicha and Damien began
The slow and painful filling of the void.
Just as Aicha and Shadracki had done 18 years earlier
When father Shadrach died.
I turned to them.

There were so many others to comfort us, who needed our comfort. The
others, lovely, loving Tennison, who held the dying Shadrach in her arms,
and Toby and Harry. They needed love. They needed to be brought home.
I turned to my friend, Jim, as I had often done with questions in my heart.
I did not fully realize that he and Rhondi lived very close to Mt. Snow. In
their kind embrace they gathered Tennison, Toby and Harry and brought
them on that long winter journey home to us.

I turned to Gisela W. who was always at my side in thought. By chance she
was nearby, and she came to help us understand what Shadrach needed from
us and to open up our grief. Signe, mother with a girl-child and a boy-child,
sister and brother to Aicha and Shadrach, cradled my mother's despair.
Aicha, with the blue-eyed Daemien in her arms, was my guiding light. I
turned to them whenever I felt myself swirled into chaos. I found a note on
my pillow that night. Aicha wrote, 'Come sleep in my bed if you like.' It was
a call from the heart. I am still filled with sadness because I do not know why
I did not go and hold her. Instead, I had withdrawn into my grief.

Aicha and I laughed and cried, as many, many others did, for those three days and during these past years.
This is the story she tells to Daemien.

The Boy and The Dove

Once upon a time, there was a boy who lived with his grandmother and his mother and his sister. He wrote a poem that went like this:

With the morning sun comes the dove,
Her white wings glistening yellow and gold,
She rests herself on a branch of the lone tree,
Across the cold lot comes the boy.
His black boots scraping the black tar;
He reaches the tree and stops.
The world is quiet and the boy gazes at the dove.
The dove transfixes the boy
And the boy is unable to go on.
As the dove flies from the tree,
His curving lips rise.[2]

Well, the boy grew up, and his sister grew up, and after a while they went different ways, but they would come together again every Christmas, at home where the grandmother lived. And one winter, around Christmas time, the boy went to meet with different men who had known his father. They were all quite taken by the tall young man who came to them, with his wide shoulders, with his gentle, sincere manner, his searching eyes. They said he reminded them of his father, who was also named Shadrach. This Christmas there was a baby in the house. Everyday, the young Shadrach took the baby on his strong back and went walking until the baby slept. Then the young man decided to go to the mountains with his girlfriend, Tennison, to get some peace, some fresh air and especially to ski; he was a very good skier. He said goodbye to the baby and the sister and the mother and the grandmother, and he turned around again to give his mother an extra hug goodbye. Then they drove away to the mountains in his funny little red, yellow and green truck.

After some time, he got to where he was going. He went up the mountain; it was a beautiful day. He went up the mountain, and when he got to the top, he could see far, far away, almost forever—it was that clear. He pointed his skis down and sailed through fresh white snow. He sailed down, swish, swoosh, graceful as a bird, except on the way down he met a tree. This was a mighty tree. So powerful was their embrace that the man's broad chest caved in. Gently, Tennison gathered him in her arms; she saw his spirit go. Now, the man must have had a lot of spirit in that chest because when it burst out, it churned up the sky something fierce. And the wind howled and bent trees a hundred miles away from the mountain. The mother, the grandmother, the sister and many other people who loved Shadrach saw the sky and knew something had happened, for clouds of all different shapes and colors raced across the sky in strange patterns. Then, for four days, the weather was all stormy, and for four days, many people came together, from near and from far. And they came together and told stories about Shadrach, the man and the boy. All the love with which Shadrach had filled the hearts of the people that came together. They shared food, and laughter, and they cried. And they shared stories, and cigarettes and pictures and songs and prayers. All this time the little baby was there, too, and he made people laugh and smile even while they were crying. After four days, the proper rites were performed. Shadrach's body was no longer the strong, athletic body it had been; it was shrunken and pale. His family took the body across the river and burned it. And then, the wind finally quieted, and the sun came out, and it was calm, as if Shadrach was finally released from his body, at peace, like the dove.

Then it was summertime—the summertime in New York is lush and green and hot. The little baby was walking now, and he played in the garden and in tubs of water. He kept the women laughing while they worked in the garden. The women weeded the garden, they planted flowers, they picked lettuce and peas and raspberries. This same season, many years ago, Shadrach's great-grandmother and his father died on the same day, within four hours of each other. This summer there is another gathering, this time to plant a tree. The people came together and planted two trees for young Shadrach: a weeping cherry and a Korean dogwood, both tender, delicate, beautiful trees. And the sister put some anger down on paper and buried it along with Shadrach's grey, sand-like ashes, under the dogwood tree. It went like this:

In my dreams I am always mad at you.
Last night I dreamt I was going on a bike trip.
5 minutes before I was going to leave
You borrowed my bike and broke it.

I yelled at you, called you a little shit —
Then I felt bad for being such a bully.
I guess if I had known you were leaving
I would have tried to stop you too.

*

When winter comes around again, the mood is different. There's fear, there's anticipation, I think, of Shadrach's death, again. Rituals are conducted in a frantic manner, platters of food are prepared. People are called to gather again. And they do, but the intensity, the spiritual and emotional intensity of the time before is not there. The rituals seem to be empty, and they seem to be hiding some unspoken feelings. There is one point of joy, though. The little boy is there for Christmas, and Christmas belongs to him. And the family can celebrate Christmas for the child. They decorate the tree with glass birds and unwrap the creche figurines. The mother gets up with the little boy in the morning, and they go on adventures to the grocery store and to the chickens up on the hill. This brings back memories for the mother of her own boy when he was that age. And this makes her happy and causes her bittersweet pain. But the little boy brings joy; he is light. And the women down here know that when that little boy smiles, his smile shines right back up to their good men in heaven.

*

The message from my mother on the answering machine is bubbly. She sounds as if she has a wonderful secret she can't wait to share. For so long now her voice has been tired, her messages tentative and sigh-ful. A year can crawl by slowly, and then all of a sudden it is time to get a new calendar and throw the old year out, or store it for the future. We couldn't throw away this past year even if we tried, so I will wrap it up carefully a few days at a time.

So quickly that space of primordial grief is buried in logistics. I never imagined how complicated a death could be, especially when it gets you by surprise. The day filled up with phone calls; where is the priest, she is on her way over, the doctor here is talking to the hospital there; no, we don't want an autopsy; can anyone recommend a funeral home? We compile a long list of people to call. The worst is calling family and friends. My brave mother is on automatic pilot as she dials the phone for the fiftieth time. Even as the first calls go out, platters of food appear in the kitchen. Women friends finish the morning dishes and put on fresh pots of coffee. A whole community mobilizes quietly around our home and carries us. Outside, the wind blows too strong for a January day. I can feel the violence of Shadrach's death in the weather; he is as shocked by it as we are. Grandma is the only one with a sense of clarity. She has an understanding of death. She knows that this is a crucial spiritual threshold for Shadrach, and that he needs guidance in crossing it. So she holds herself together, holds back her grief, so that she can help Shadrach with clear and deliberate prayer. I think she prays for her daughter, too. Grandma is strong, but that day she ages. She is at ease with Shadrach, but so many people make her nervous. 'Isn't it a terrible shock?' She repeats blankly to everyone who comes in the door. Later in her room, she tells me how much she hates the to-do and etiquette surrounding death. After her husband's funeral she went and hid so that she wouldn't have to hear condolences. 'The dead don't care about all that stuff. It's silly.' Daemien, the baby, gurgles happily. He is extra angelic amid drawn, red-eyed faces. He tolerates his mother's frequent outbursts of sobbing and doesn't complain when she forgets his lunch. Daemien is happy to see so many people. He makes them laugh.

We women didn't know that our Shadrach was a hero until he died. In the days following his death, people come to our house and gave us pieces of Shadrach we had never known before. We are amazed by the impressions he left on the world. Friends come from thousands of miles away to share their version of Shadrach. At night, we gather in the living room, overflowing with people. My mother welcomes everyone, her voice low, steady, dreamlike. She announces the plans, the fragile structure of our immediate existence: what we are going to read tonight; the funeral will be Wednesday; it will be good if people parked in the commuter lot. Then she invites people to share. At first it is awkward. Then somebody ventures, 'On the way over tonight, I was thinking about Shadrach, you know, how he has—how he had, this way of making you feel O.K. about who you are, no matter what...'

'Shadrach was someone I always aspired to be like, so sure of himself...'

The eulogies continue late into the night. Warmth is generated by voices and the silent moments in between. An incredible human spirit is felt by all present: we love together. Many of us have never met. All this time a funny thing goes on in my mind; I can only remember Shadrach's most annoying traits, like the temper tantrums he had when he was little, and how he would retreat to the bathroom with the newspaper when it was time to clear the table and stay there until the dishes were all washed.

We read, 'Let not your heart be troubled: ye believe in God, believe also in me. In my Father's house there are many mansions: if it were not so, I would have told you. I go to prepare a place for you, I will come again, and receive you unto myself; that where I am, there ye may be also. And whither I go ye know and the way ye know...' I imagine Shadrach wandering around in a great mansion; his daddy is up there to welcome him, to show him around. This is comforting knowledge because it must be awfully confusing to be wrenched from life so abruptly. I believe in heaven because my mother told us that is where our daddy went. Shadrach went looking for his father just before he died. He wrote letters and made appointments with uncharacteristic determination. He went to people who knew his father, and they talked about architecture. Now Shadrach can talk about architecture up there in those great mansions.

Shadrach's body is arriving at our house any minute now. I am absolutely terrified. My mother has been gone all morning, making arrangements at the funeral home. Tennison is with me, she is calm. She tells me about Shadrach's death, how she felt him leave his body as he lay in her arms, how she closed his eyelids when his eyes went blank. They come late with the body. The mortician confesses to my mother, 'Gosh, he was such a big guy we really had a hard time getting him into the casket. I mean we had to try several times.' Tennison and I suppress our giggles. Finally, they have everything prepared, and my mother calls me behind the curtained partition. I go in with my eyes averted from the open casket. We stand in a circle with Gisela, the priest, and we pray. Then the moment I dread arrives. First, my mother and Grandma go to the casket and stand quietly. When they turn around, my mother looks relieved; she looks strong and peaceful. I balk and burst into violent sobs, 'Don't make me see my brother dead; I don't want him to be dead!' My mother holds me to her. She speaks to me softly. Her sweater gets wet with my tears and snot. Then she leads me to the casket. There is a body in there alright, but it isn't my brother at all! It is a pale corpse with a neatly trimmed beard, with a mouth that has an unnatural curve, and a piece of cardboard stuffed under its shirt where a chest used to be. The only resemblance to Shadrach are the eyebrows. I am profoundly relieved.

When people come to the house there is a hush. I can feel their apprehension when they realize what is behind the curtain, so I reassure them, 'Oh, don't worry, it's not really Shadrach in there, you'll see.' We live with Shadrach's body for a few days. More people come to the house. At one point the entire lacrosse team from Shadrach's college comes filing in. My mother and I are so touched we give each one of them tearful hugs. They come back in the evening and share Shadrach with us, their version of Shad, the dreadlock rebel with an earring, who blew them away with his athletic grace and his sense of honor. He opened their minds; they opened their hearts, and they opened my mind.

We women are slightly amused by the heroic legends surrounding Shadrach. Yes, we loved him dearly, but damn was it hard to get him to help out around the house, even harder to get him to communicate with us. 'I guess we kind of overwhelmed him, didn't we?' My mother and I have taken up smoking again. It is our excuse to sneak out to smoke with cousin Becci, too. In fact, I sneak out at every opportunity. I can no longer hold my composure and be properly mournful.

A year later my mother and I are still at it. One night she said to me, 'You know, I felt Shadrach come to me last night. I was sitting here in this chair, smoking a cigarette, and he was right here in the room with me. Isn't it funny that he should come when I'm in the basement, smoking?'

'Well, Mom, he sure isn't going to approach you while you are washing the dishes or doing laundry!' Shadrach always disappeared quickly when my mother was in a 'Big Hectic,' as we called it. This Christmas, a year later, my mother is in one constant 'Big Hectic.' She goes about her household rituals with a grim faced determination, at a pace that leaves no room for idle talk or laughter. I fear that she will break down any minute; she expends herself at an unhealthy rate. Even during our smoke breaks, her mind is racing on, planning out every detail of the day. When I leave New York, my shoulders are rock hard. It takes Bill three days to knead out all the tension I've accumulated. I regret that I didn't feel my mother's neck, massage her shoulders, make a soothing gesture. I only accused her of making all the rest of us uncomfortable. So I am delighted to hear her voice on the answering machine. When I call her back she asks, 'How are you and Shadrach doing?'

'Well, I guess we are doing just fine. How 'bout yourself?'

'Shadrach and I have come to terms. I finally just let him go. It's OK now.'

Thank you, Shad for giving mother back to us. I hear her old self for the first time in over a year. Outside the air is calm. I can imagine Shadrach's white dove taking flight.

                                                    ★

Shadrach, my heart aches sometimes when I pronounce your name. What was it that suddenly made it possible for me to see a path leading to you? I wish I could remember the very moment, earlier this year. Was it in the month of March on the anniversary of your conception? Since that moment, I am able to break through the thicket of grief into the clearing, into the sunlit place where I can discern the spiritual path on which we can meet.

There are moments when I am absorbed in the passage of time, the sequence of events. How is it possible to understand all that one thinks, feels and experiences? The moment of an event reveals so little to us. Maybe we must wait patiently, and some day a meaning will arise in us. But I think, let me understand it a little more clearly now, before the preoccupation of the everyday conceals the events from my view. So I go back, I go over, I review. I say to myself, it is through pain that I do this. But I am also looking towards the future. I retrace the events. It is a way of comprehending your unique destiny.

Shadracki, Shadracki, there was a memorial service for you conducted by Gisela W. in March, following the January of your death. I sat there a few minutes before it began, thinking about the Christian Community and how it has been such a part of our family life. I was christened at the age of six and confirmed at fourteen with friends, some of whom I still know. Many years later, in Paris, Aicha was christened, the words spoken in French. Then, at the age of two, you became the fifth in the Woods family to be christened, Shadrach. You insisted on walking, holding tight to Daddy's hand, down the aisle in the chapel, towards all the flickering candle lights on the altar. Your fair hair glistened and your eyes were filled with wonder at the stillness of the moment. For a number of years, you still remained Shadracki.

Gisela W., then just arrived to take on the congregation in New York, gave me strength during the long nights of Daddy's dying. She was beside me and helped me understand the moment of the crossing of the threshold, the death which was a birth into the spiritual world.

And once again, at your funeral, the modulation of my breathing was restored by Gisela's calm being. I was able to pass from darkness, gasping for air, into the radiant light which surrounded those young friends who carried your body to cremation.

Sitting there, in inner silence, I gradually became intensely aware of you. I saw your broad shouldered figure from the back. My view was from above and behind you. You, tall and completely at ease, turned with a smile to the figure next to you. As I became aware of the direction of your gaze I realized that it was father Shadrach standing at your side. Father Shadrach, also smiling that familiar smile, turned to look into your eyes, making a gesture of greeting to a loved one. Then I became aware that this was a gesture of bringing together, of gathering, of welcoming to well remembered surroundings. Clearly, the light now fell on a number of figures standing in an arch, ready, prepared, embracing the father and the son. And you, knowing that you were part of this group, were happy to be returned to their welcome. Each of you were prepared to take the next step, to take up the next task, to carry out what was needed. You, who had completed one phase with satisfaction, with praise, were being welcomed back into their midst to start anew. And there was father Shadrach, waiting for this moment.

You were lent to me, and all the time I thought you were mine. And I cannot help grieving for myself.

I must find a way to listen for you. You are calling out to me. The call can reach me only when I can leave my inner space completely receptive. I hold your image in my mind. Then I know that I have made room for your presence when you are ready to come to me.

You are no longer the person who was a tangible part of our lives. You are now, once again, the pure essence of yourself. You are as you were at the moment of birth, but now, also transformed by all that you have experienced on the earth. You have returned to the heavenly 'there' from where you came to us, taking with you a part of our hearts.

Let me not grieve for myself because I can now anticipate that I will always know you, Shadrach, that it was not just for this moment, but for all time. I need to develop more thoughts regarding your death, Shadrach, death, as it appears to young people; to understand how we, who love you, can be so near and yet not be aware of your presence.

Grandma knows what it is that you are searching for in us. Through her calm, clear concentration on thoughts of you, she has shown me how to move from self-consuming grief to an openness of the heart. Saturdays, before the bustle of the day, she quietly takes out her reading. Sitting in her chair by the window, she asks me softly if I want to join her. I see you need us to give you the 'time of day.' Yet I am, at first, unable to break away from the kitchen sink, the pile of laundry, to withdraw myself from the world around. But Grandma waits patiently for me to settle down. Then comes a mantra for you, in her voice. She reads a passage from the Bible, the resurrection, a quiet moment, the two of us in thought of you.

I look at a photograph of you and think, 'I want to know that young man.' Then, sometimes, I realize I do not quite recognize the mood, and therefore, do not experience you that way. There are other photos taken of you when I was not present which show you to be in a familiar mood. It is wonderful to look at these pictures of you, to take in that instant of your joy. I am now thinking of the photo of you and Michael dancing on the terrace at Bowdoin. Looking at you in this mood of being at one with yourself and your surroundings helps me picture you in my thoughts for a long time.

You are there coming off the Lacrosse field, Chet standing next to you.

Your face is flushed, your wide smile greeting Pete. You were elated, and there were the friends whose open faces said, 'Well done!'

To carry thoughts of you in all that you held dear, in all that you were striving towards, in all that was an achievement for you, is to give your life its full meaning.

I have become aware of how you, Shadrach, were so completely open to others. The words your friends shared give me a glimpse of you. There was a quality about you that had to do with being there completely for everyone. You affected so many people's lives and are now in their thoughts because you truly took an interest in each person. You listened and observed with an open ear and heart.

Chet sent me an eagle feather. He found it on the ground next to where he was sitting. From his rock chair, he had a wide view of the Colorado mountains rising all around. He watched the graceful, curved wings of an American eagle soaring up into the sky. You kept him company during his many solitary hours wandering in forests and on steep slopes.

Karin told me she wanted to dedicate her first exhibition in New York to you. Portraits of children are her theme. She has been filled with an incredible amount of artistic energy these past few years, and it continues to strengthen her. I believe that you, in the shock of your death, have left us all with a strong resolve to accomplish many things. You and Karin sheltered a deep love and respect. You carried the ideal of each other in your thoughts and hearts. Shadrach, you are supporting her in her life's work.

There you shimmered on the surface of the wood, part of the texture of the grain. Your glowing young child's face surrounded by a cap of gold-white hair. Karin has used a photo taken of you around Christmas, before you became three years old. Karin says that many people have assumed it to be a photo of her. The same aura is there. It is both of you. There are many other childhood faces which Karin has gathered for her portraits on wood. To me, of course, your face changes constantly, a smile lights up, and you are so pleased to be part of what Karin is doing.

★

There was an incredible moment when I finally opened the black plastic bag which was brought home from Vermont in Shadrach's yellow truck. I had asked that it be left in the basement and knew that it was there, and that I would have to open it when I was by myself. I no longer remember exactly when that was. I do know that at that moment it felt like I became a witness to the accident. Looking at these particular, familiar clothes, I was overwhelmed as I became aware that not every piece was there to make up and cover the totality of my son. 'Missing in action' came to mind.

'Cloth is a kind of memory. When a person is absent or dies, cloth can absorb his or her absent presence. At such moments of crisis, these trivial matters, matters of matter, seem to loom disproportionately large. What are we to do with the clothes of the dead'[3]

After Shadrach died, I felt there was an offering to give his friends. They gave their thoughts and words which enveloped him, but a piece of remembered clothing bore a special imprint. To offer the clothes was giving comfort to these children in their distress. They felt their brother's touch.
   Some of the pieces also bore the marks of courage. I still imagine Aicha wearing Shadrach's red Green Meadow Lacrosse jacket as she faces elation and trials in her life in Berkeley. I have never seen her in it, but it comforts me to know that she wears it proudly. I also think of Keith, in Colorado, exalting in the clear air of the sun drenched ski slopes. He uses Shadrach's other ski clothes and equipment with pride.

'Bodies come and go; the clothes which have received these bodies survive. They circulate...they are transmitted from parent to child, from sister to brother, from lover to lover, from friend to friend...the question was...what to do...with all the ways he had occupied space.'[4]

Signe's birthday. She suggests we each bring with us a gift, the 'essence of seed.' It is a very comforting exercise to have an idea around which one weaves one's thoughts. I have constantly held Shadrach in my thoughts these last long months. Perhaps because I could not avoid it. My heart aches when I pronounce his name. Long concentration still brings tears. Now it feels good to concentrate on a 'seed picture' for a short span of time.
   Seed time: a time of new growth or development.
   Signe sent us these words after Shadrach's death:

You were become a man
We all felt it
those days of Christmas.
You came often through our door
smiling and strong
clearer
as if with new resolve.

I thought
and even went as far as saying
'What joy to know this fine young man
And know I'll know him long,
and watch his life unfold.'
...

Seedling: a young plant that is grown from seed. A source or a beginning: a germ.

To move from endings to beginnings has been my wish. I could not bear to have your deaths, the two Shadrachs, remain a harvest song forever. I know that you had each laid the germ of renewal in my heart.

Colin and Lois told us that they are expecting a child in January of next year. They wanted to know if it would be alright to call a boy child Zachary Shadrach. They felt the world could use many Shadrachs.

Another step has now been taken, and I am being moved from the present into the future.

⋆

Doves come early in the morning, perch on the tree or railing and look around. They fluff up their feathers, settle down, and quietly observe with bright eyes. When the bird food is there, they come and peck sedately, not in the nervous rush of blue jays.

Loving doves, keep coming to the feeder. You are our link in nature with Shadrach, who observed you so carefully.

Notes

[1.] Suzanne Jasper, *The Call of the Story*, PARABOLA, Spring 1994, Vol XIX, No. 1, p.89

[2.] Poem by Shadrach Woods

[3.] Peter Stallybrass, *Worn Worlds: Clothes, Mourning and the Life of Things*, The Yale Review (Vol. 81, No.2).

[4.] Ibid.

Joan Almon

I was born in 1944 in Wilmington, Delaware, a community discovered by my parents five years earlier after fleeing from Nazi Germany. Wilmington was a pleasant town for growing up, with good schools, peaceful streets, and beautiful countryside around it. By high school, however, I was chomping at the bit for larger horizons and fell in love with New York, its vibrant streets and incredible museums and theaters. For my college years, however, I chose a small town with lots of charm and a large University where I could pick and choose my friends freely. Those four years in Ann Arbor at the University of Michigan stand out as a time of intense learning and self-discovery. It was the 1960's and the campus was alive with social unrest. An inner flame was awakened in me for social justice, and this flame was further activated by my studies in Sociology.

After College I moved to New York, seeking whatever work I could find in areas of social development. I was fortunate to find my first job in the office of Bayard Rustin, a major civil rights leader. Eventually I moved on to another group that helped sharecroppers in the south organize farming co-operatives. My years in New York came to an end when I travelled to California for a vacation and camped in Big Sur. I suddenly realized that there were deep parts of myself that were unexplored and undeveloped and that I needed to take some time off to 'find myself.' There followed two years in California with a great deal of travel and camping and a growing recognition that there was a spiritual world as well as a physical one.

In 1970 I returned east, settling in Baltimore, determined to find a way to weave the spiritual and the physical together in my life. Destiny began to speak more clearly, and after moving into a spiritually oriented community, I became one of the members who helped start an alternative nursery school. Within a few months we met Waldorf education, and as we brought different aspects into our pre-school, I was deeply moved by the response of the children. They were like little flowers opening to the Sun. I was determined to learn more about education and soon was studying anthroposophy.

That little kindergarten, begun in fall 1971, grew into the Waldorf School of Baltimore, and my own training developed over many years like a patchwork quilt. In 1976 I married and moved to the Washington, D.C. area, working in a large Waldorf kindergarten named Acorn Hill. In 1983 I became Chair of the newly formed Waldorf Kindergarten Association of North America and shortly after joined the Board of the International Waldorf Kindergarten Association. In 1989 I stopped kindergarten teaching in order to teach kindergarten trainings and travel to kindergartens. That work has taken me around the world and provided me with wonderful friends and rich experiences in every kind of social and economic setting. In 1992 I was asked to also take on a leadership role in the Anthroposophic Society in the United States and have found this to be the deepest and most challenging experience of my life.

11
The needs of the children of the 1990s: nurturing the creative spirit

I vividly recall from my college years during the early 1960s the enthusiasm in the psychology department for the work of B.F. Skinner. It was thought that behaviorism would save the day and would reach children in new and profound ways, bringing healing to many troubled children and getting healthy children off to a good start. I do not recall anyone speaking of the underlying view of the human being out of which behaviorism arose, but it was surely that the human being was basically an animal. True, we could stand upright, but we were still viewed as having a very close relationship to the animal kingdom. Behaviorism and laboratory research on animals were closely linked, and if experiments worked on rats, then it was assumed they would also work on children. No one was so forthright as to describe children as two-legged rats, but the notion of the human being as a 'naked ape' was much discussed.

In the early 1970s, when I began teaching young children and discovered Waldorf Education, these behavioral techniques were widely used in educational settings. I recall conversations with behaviorists as to why Waldorf education did not want to take a behavioral approach. It became clear that there was not only a fundamental difference in our understanding of education, but also—and more importantly—in our view of the human being. We wanted to educate children according to the classical sense of the word *educare*, meaning to draw out or lead forth. This approach assumes there is something of great value in the child which needs to be cultivated and drawn out. That is very different from the old idea of the child as a 'tabula rasa' or blank slate to be written upon; or the behaviorist approach of trading one set of behaviors for another, and presumably better, set.

Today one rarely hears of Skinner or his philosophy, yet its influence lingers on, and there is much debate taking place around the question of whether creativity in children is heightened or diminished when rewards are offered. Studies have yielded somewhat conflicting results, but generally it is felt that rewards have a positive influence only on short-term, superficial acts of creativity, while the deeper creative processes are hindered.

Although behaviorism lingers on, and with it the view of the human being as close kin to the animal, it has been largely replaced in the 1980s and 90s with a mechanistic view of the human being. We have long been told that our heart, an organ of incredible sensitivity and beauty, is nothing more than a pump; but this image was only the beginning of a growing view that the human being is basically a complex machine. The popularity of the computer and the powerful images associated with it have greatly influenced this view. Now one frequently hears the brain described in computer terms, and an assumption is growing that the computer is really much more powerful and efficient than the brain. The next step may be to ask: Why bother to think, why not let the computer do this for us?

What is missing in this view is a recognition of different levels of thinking, some of which may be quite mechanical while others call for tremendous activity on the part of the human spirit. Computers, for example, can process numbers much more quickly than human beings can, and with sufficient programming by thoughtful human beings they can appear to think. But in the end, the computer can only link existing bits into countless new possibilities. It cannot awaken in the night having had a 'Eureka' experience during which the mind leaps to a new level of insight. There are higher levels of our every-day thinking which are beyond the ability of any computer, and in addition there are higher forms of consciousness which Rudolf Steiner describes as Imagination, Inspiration, and Intuition, which are far beyond the ken of any machine. The current tragedy is that higher forms of thinking are not understood; it is all too easy to educate children only with lower forms of thinking in mind.

As the mechanistic view of the human being takes hold, we must ask ourselves what implication it has for educators, for families and especially for children. The education for the child of the cybernetic age is an education which places a computer on every desk and diminishes the task of the teacher. Such education is lauded as being the most efficient and cost-effective. When Chris Whittle first announced his intention of founding hundreds of for-profit schools, he described them as having one teacher for every 60 children, and the major thrust of instruction was to come from the child's computer. The teacher was there essentially to monitor the child's work.

It is easy to imagine such an approach to education. As computer programs become even more clever than they are now, they will allow for a tailor-made approach to learning. Children will have their own educational plans drawn up to cater for their individual strengths and weaknesses. It will be hard for parents and educators to argue that there is something wrong with this approach, for it will seem so logical and rational. Many will sense in their hearts that there is something wrong with the mechanistic approach to education, but may find themselves helpless unless a new image of the human being can be forged, along with an education that helps children become fully human.

Even when the modern child goes home he or she is not free to unfold in a purely human way, for in many families the computer has been whole-heartedly embraced, just as other forms of media have been in the past 40 years. It is becoming increasingly rare for American families to sit around the table and have the lively exchanges which were once common in pre-media days. Much of the home learning for today's children takes place in front of the screen, be it television or computer. We look to machines as educators both at home and in school, but we are blind to the fact that in the end a machine can only educate the machine-like in us. It is not within the capacity of a machine to experience and share love, creativity or morality; these can only be cultivated in the warmth and love between one human being and another. A child can learn to be an upright human being only from another upright human being.

To appreciate the life, spirit and creativity of the child means finding a whole new view of the human being. At first this appears to be a radical step and one that is greatly resisted, for if we begin to see the human being as having spirit as well as body and soul, then every facet of life must be reconsidered. At present, for instance, American education gives lip-service to the idea of a developmentally appropriate curriculum, but in fact arbitrarily assigns curriculum areas to whatever age it wants. The general guideline in teaching reading, mathematics and many other subjects seems to be 'the sooner the better,' and the result is a hurried curriculum as well as hurried children. If we can take into account the full nature of the child, however, then a feeling of reverence awakens in us for the child's creative spirit, and we feel called upon to create a curriculum that honors its unfolding. This leads to an entirely new approach to education, centred upon a deep concern for the child's growth and well-being. Let us now explore such an approach.

Striving towards a new understanding of the child

How wonderful it is to hold an infant and wonder about the new gifts which the child has brought to earth. To be in the presence of the newborn is like stepping into the fairy tale of Sleeping Beauty and watching the twelve wise women come forward to bestow their special gifts upon the child. But in Sleeping Beauty, all the good gifts could be undone by the thirteenth, who in her anger and rage decreed that in her fifteenth year the child would prick her finger on a spindle and fall down dead. When we think of the child as animal-like or machine-like, we play the role of this thirteenth wise woman who wished death upon the child without the possibility of transformation or metamorphosis.

Fortunately, in the fairy tale, the twelfth wise woman had not yet made her wish, and now came forward. The story says she could not take away the evil sentence, but could soften it; and she said: 'There shall be no death but a deep sleep of 100 years.' We are being asked to be the twelfth wise woman for today's children, taking away the sting of materialism, the denial of the spirit, which so threatens the creative spirit of childhood. We are being asked to soften the spell of modern life so that when the prick of consciousness comes in adolescence it does not bring death to the spirit but a deep sleep, like the butterfly sleeping in the cocoon, awaiting its transformation. Then the soul and spirit can be united at last.

All of this weaves around us when we gaze at a newborn child, and if we fail to recognize the spirit alive in each child we inadvertently begin to destroy it. Fortunately, during the past 20 years, more and more parents have begun to recognize the spirit inherent in their children. We see this in Waldorf education through the tremendous growth in the number of schools in North America: from about 12 in 1974 to 120 or more in 1994. Worldwide one sees a similar growth, especially in Eastern Europe where the newly emerging spirit hungers for an appropriate education.

A parent recently described to me what had drawn her to Waldorf education. She herself had gone through a process of spiritual awakening while pregnant with her first child. One night she dreamt of him as a radiant child, full of the forces of the sun. In her dream she watched him blossom and grow, but when he was six she saw him being imprisoned in a box which prevented further growth of his sun-like nature. She awoke trembling and resolved never to do such a thing to her child. She began then to search for an education which would allow her child to grow for a lifetime and beyond.

To receive each child with reverence is the first of the three golden rules which Rudolf Steiner offered to every Waldorf teacher, but it applies to every parent as well. When a child comes to earth we cannot help wondering where this child has come from. Where did the child dwell before entering the physical body? It is hard to imagine that this wondrous being began with physical conception, that he or she came into being through the interaction of mother and father alone. For those who gaze lovingly at the newborn there is a sense that a mystery of tremendous magnitude exists. Poets have sought to grasp this wonder, and the words of William Wordsworth stand out:

> Our birth is but a sleep and a forgetting;
> The Soul that rises with us, our life's Star,
> Hath had elsewhere its setting
> And cometh from afar;
> Not in entire forgetfulness,
> And not in utter nakedness,
> But trailing clouds of glory do we come
> From God who is our home:
> Heaven lies about us in our infancy! [1]

George MacDonald, the author of children's books and adult fantasies, whose work inspired C. S. Lewis and other great writers, also captures this mood in his poem called 'The Baby.'[2]

> Where did you come from, baby dear?
> Out of the everywhere into the here.
>
> Where did you get your eyes so blue?
> Out of the sky as I came through.
>
> What makes the light of them sparkle and spin?
> Some of the starry spikes left in......
>
> Where did you get that pearly ear?
> God spoke, and came out to hear.....

Although the journey to birth is a profound event, children are rarely able to speak of it, for it is hidden from conscious memory. An example of this was given by a four year old who whispered to her newborn sibling, 'Tell me about God. I'm forgetting.' Yet the memory lives somewhere within each child, and emerges in the form of drawings, especially of the rainbows which young children draw again and again. What do these rainbows signify? Might they be a memory in picture form of the rainbow bridge which every soul is said to cross on the way to earth? That was clearly the thought of a four year old who saw a rainbow in the sky and exclaimed to his mother, 'Oh look, Mommy, a baby is being born!'

The second of Rudolf Steiner's golden rules for working with children is to educate the child with love. Some children are easy to love, but others are difficult: those are the ones who challenge us to deepen and extend our capacity to love. For me, one such child was Alan, who entered my kindergarten many years ago. His mother had married at age 16, became pregnant and was widowed during pregnancy, her husband having died a drug-related death. She herself used drugs during pregnancy and in the months after birth. Her parent helped her raise the child whose life had such a difficult beginning.

Alan's mother was open with me about her background; but even if she had not been, my first meeting with Alan would have revealed a serious problem. We met when he was four. He walked straight towards me in the hall outside the kindergarten room and without a moment's hesitation kicked me in the shins! He was strong and it hurt, but fortunately it never occurred to me to turn him away. His was a difficult destiny, but he had a strength and a courage which one had to admire. He was not going to take his fate lying down, and he expressed this very clearly one day to a friend after hearing me recite the nursery rhyme of 'Humpty Dumpty,' with its wonderful picture of the fall.

Humpty Dumpty sat on the wall,
Humpty Dumpty had a great fall,
All the King's horses and all the King's men
Couldn't put Humpty together again.

'You know,' said Alan to his friend, 'I don't think Humpty Dumpty fell at all.' 'You don't?' said his friend, clearly shocked that anyone would ever doubt Mother Goose. 'No,' said Alan, quite firmly, 'I think he jumped!' I've often thought about Alan and that spirit within him that jumped into life despite all its difficulties. Did he stand on the far side of the rainbow bridge and preview all the tragedy that was going to happen to him when he landed on earth? Rather than turning back or simply falling into his fate, did he say, 'Oh, what the heck!' and jump anyway? When I think of the force of his little feet kicking me as he entered our kindergarten, it's easy to see that his first gesture into new situations was a jump and a kick. I last saw him when he was about 21. He was a wonderfully tall and handsome fellow who showed much promise but hadn't quite settled down yet. In a way he was still jumping and kicking. Sometimes people felt the pain of his kicks and turned their backs on him, but he was fortunate to have family and teachers who saw the courage behind the gesture and who were able to educate him with love.

The third golden rule which Rudolf Steiner offered was to let the child go forth in freedom. How are we to understand this? All too often the idea of freedom is applied too early, and children are given choice after choice at a very young age, long before they have the insights to make wise choices. Generally what they learn from this experience is that it is all right to make choices out of whim and willfulness, and the parents soon wonder why their child has become so dictatorial. Educating a child towards freedom requires a sensitive balance between holding the child within protective boundaries and at the same time encouraging steps towards independence.

There is no single formula to help a child towards freedom, and it is a matter of some complexity, for the situation varies from one culture to another. In a tribal or traditional culture, for example, there is less room for individuality and freedom than in a modern culture. One is expected to carry out the ideas and practices of the tradition, and the consequences can be severe if one seeks too much independence. In such cultures, or even in traditional religious groups in a modern culture, one can be banned or expelled from the community for showing too much freedom of thought or breaking with tradition.

In our times, however, the development of the free individual is of the greatest importance; we seek ways to help the child towards freedom yet with due regard for the social life around us. One of the problems facing educators and parents today is how to approach tradition and ritual, for young children are in need of a life suffused with beautiful traditions and rituals, yet one does not want to bind the child to a traditional kind of life. The key here is the word bind. Traditional life did bind children to family, religion and culture, and it was considered a tragedy if the child broke free. Modern life, if it is healthy, can offer young children the strength of family, religion and culture but in such a way that these are nourishing, not binding. The difference generally lies in the orientation of the parents and teachers and their hopes and expectations for the child. At the same time that Rudolf Steiner gave his three golden rules, he also warned adults not to make children into copies of themselves. He said that one should never use force or tyranny to perpetuate in the children that which dwells in us.

The children of each new generation bring something new to the earth, and it is especially important now when so much social and individual renewal is needed that we should not expect our children to perpetuate the past.

In *The Prophet*, Kahlil Gibran eloquently describes the need to let children go forth in freedom. In the section on children he says:

Your children are not your children.
They are the sons and daughters of Life's longing for itself...
You may give them your love but not your thoughts,
For they have their own thoughts.
You may house their bodies but not their souls,
For their souls dwell in the house of tomorrow, which you cannot visit,
not even in your dreams.
You may strive to be like them, but seek not to make them like you.
For life goes not backward nor tarries with yesterday.
You are the bows from which your children as living arrows are sent forth...[3]

These beautiful words describe the background for letting children go forth in freedom. But the actual deed of seeking freedom is one which the young person himself or herself must undertake by facing an abyss and crossing a threshold. Freedom is not easily attained as a matter of course. The process is more like that of the caterpillar spinning its cocoon of darkness, dissolving its old form and emerging in a new, more lifted and radiant way. This is transformative growth. The caterpillar, though, knows no other way, whereas a human being, in early adulthood or later, must find courage to take the necessary steps. The seeds for this courage, however, are planted in childhood, and the great fairy tales, myths and legends relate the story of human souls who take such steps into freedom. One can think of the Grimm's tale of The Seven Ravens where the sister travels to the Sun, Moon and Stars to find her brothers and free them of their enchantment. There is Odysseus on his mighty journey and Parzival on his quest, Joan of Arc facing her destiny with a high degree of courage, and many others, real and legendary. The world abounds with tales of heroes who break free and seek new ground for themselves and for humanity. To offer children such stories at appropriate ages is to plant seeds for the future, when as adolescents or young adults they will be faced with difficult choices. Then the stories of childhood come to mind again, and the young person may feel 'Ah ha, so that is what that story was all about!' With the memory an impulse towards courageous action arises, and this courage is much needed in our times.

It is shocking how few such stories today's children hear. Instead, they are offered modern super-heroes, Ninja Turtles, and Power Rangers—or whatever the latest gimmick is. These are grotesque distortions of the true heroes; they do not feed the soul and spirit of children with images that can grow and evolve with them, but instead, enter them as fixed images, which sit undigested like stones in their hearts.

Wherever one looks—at school, home or community—one sees barriers standing in the way of children's development. Today's children not only need the normal courage which children have always needed for growing and evolving as individuals, but an added element to overcome the problems of families in disarray, communities torn apart by violence or permeated with an apathy towards the well-being of their citizens, and schools which often seem more concerned with test scores and internal politics than with human lives. If society had deliberately intended to make the unfolding of the creative spirit as difficult as possible, it could not have accomplished much more than it has done through unawareness and ignorance. We have left our children with an unprecedented amount of work to do in overcoming these obstacles. There are ways to help them, however, and ways to improve the situation for future generations.

The needs of children today

What is it that children need from adults today if they are to grow up as healthy, creative human beings? As I have said, the children of this decade are faced with tremendous challenges, for their families, communities and societies are often undergoing high levels of stress. In addition, the children's own creative strength is eroded daily through immersion in a technological, media-oriented culture. But perhaps most debilitating is the fact that the adults around them—families, teachers and community members—look at them and see only a fragment of who they are. Their inner substance, their creative spirit is overlooked and denigrated. It is hard enough for an adult not to be recognized or affirmed at an inner level; it is disastrous for children. The self-fulfilling prophecy comes into play, and the child who has been thought of as animal-like tends to act like an animal, governed by passions and instinctual behaviors. The child who is viewed as a machine, tends to become dry and sclerotic, immensely clever but without heart or compassion. It is a fortunate child who is valued for all the human qualities which she or he embodies. Such children have the chance to unfold their full potential. Their minds can blossom with creative ideas, their hearts can respond to all that is around them on earth and in the heavens, and their limbs can be purposefully engaged in serving the world. Their individuality comes to fruition and the gifts which they brought with them on this journey to the earth can be freely offered.

People frequently ask if children are different today from 20 years ago. I have known a number of young children in the past ten years, for example, who have become vegetarians on their own, without encouragement from their parents who were not vegetarians. At age five, or even younger, these children have decided not to eat meat, usually out of love and concern for animals. Every generation has its own qualities, but this generation of children and young people seems to have brought a particularly strong concern for the earth. I am not now referring to the many children who have been prematurely awakened to the problems of the world which they then carry as an unhealthy burden and a sorrow. I am speaking of the ones who carry a concern for the world in a childlike way that is not too great a burden for their growing soul forces. They are basically happy children; they are happy to be on the earth and want to take care of it.

The last decade of this century is proving to be a very dramatic time for humanity. We are faced with enormous social choices, and at times we have fallen into the abyss of hatred and destruction, as in Bosnia or Rwanda. At other times, however, we have risen to new heights of social transformation as in the relatively peaceful ending of communism in eastern Europe and apartheid in South Africa. In the mid-1980s none of us could have anticipated the remarkable changes that would begin in 1989. They have appeared like a miracle and encouraged us to feel that new, healthier social forms are indeed possible.

Today's children have come to earth at a remarkable time. The earth itself is in need of healing and so are the social relations which unite us with one another. Today's technology helps facilitate communication and travel, but what good is that if human hearts are filled with anger and hatred? Something new is needed, and each new generation brings with it the gifts which the earth needs. One looks at today's children and wonders what gifts they have brought with them. Are they the gifts which the earth so sorely needs for its own healing and for overcoming human enmity? And if they have brought these gifts like seeds for a garden, will they find the opportunity to plant them in fertile soil or will they find only rocky, barren ground to receive them? It is a tragedy that today's children often find obstacle after obstacle that prevent their gifts from being received. It is a tragedy for the children and for us all.

In addition to speaking of the three golden rules of education—to receive the child in reverence, to educate the child in love and to let the child go forth in freedom—Rudolf Steiner also admonished us adults to be aware of the obstacles which hinder the development of the child, and to work energetically to remove those obstacles. Without our help the child cannot develop in a free and healthy way.

When we educate children, we need to recognize that each child brings something new with it from the cosmic world-order to earth. We must try to remove the obstacles that stand in the way of the child's body and soul development, and create an environment for the little one, in which his or her spirit can unfold in freedom.[4]

Today's children will reach maturity in the next century, the next millennium. We cannot be certain what their future holds or what their challenges will be. Our way of helping them is to remove the obstacles that hinder their development. The greatest of these obstacles is the denial of their spiritual being. With sufficient love, wisdom and courage we can find ways to help that inner being unfold. Then each child's creative spirit, the artist who dwells within, will be able to shine forth and help create new possibilities on the earth.

Notes

[1] William Wordsworth. 1958. 'Ode on Intimations of Immortality.' In *One Hundred and One Poems,* anthology compiled by Roy J. Cook, p. 61. Chicago: Reilly & Lee.

[2] George MacDonald. 1922. 'The Baby.' In *Journeys Through Bookland,* edited by Charles H. Sylvester, p. 11. Chicago: Bellow-Reeves, Co.

[3] Kahlil Gibran. 1973. *The Prophet.* London: William Heinemann Ltd.

[4] Rudolf Steiner. 1990. *Die geistig-seelischen Grundkräfte der Erziehungskunst,* p. 75. Dornach: Verlag. This volume appears in English as *Spiritual Ground of Education,* Spiritual Science Library, Blauvelt, NY, but this passage was translated for this paper by the author. At the end of lecture four one finds this quote and the three golden rules of education.

Susan Howard and Michael Howard

Susan Howard

I am grateful for a healthy childhood spent along the coast of Maine, where I grew up with strong life rhythms, hard-working parents with 'Maine Yankee' values, and a deep love for life on the edge of the Atlantic.

A high school foreign exchange program abruptly ended this childhood idyll at the age of 16, when I was plunged into political, social and personal upheaval in divided Berlin in the late sixties. This began a long relationship of attraction/repulsion with German culture, where I spent much of my student career and eventually, ten years later, met Waldorf education and Anthroposophy.

This encounter was the central turning point in my life. My initial skepticism about this new way of looking at education, at children, and at life, was transformed gradually into wholehearted enthusiasm through my involvement in the Waldorf kindergarten, which was to become my life's work.

I was a Waldorf kindergarten teacher and early childhood educator for 14 years before embarking with my husband on the journey of international adoption and parenting. After working for many years with parents in my role as teacher of young children, it has been a humbling and inspiring revelation to experience parenting from the 'other side'!

Michael Howard

I was born in Vancouver and raised in Canada, where already in my youth I was very artistically inclined. I studied wood carving in Quebec and bronze casting in Toronto before entering the Ontario College of Art, where I majored in sculpture.

At the age of 22 my interest in inner development led me to spend six months in India. Shortly thereafter I met the work of Rudolf Steiner, which led me to Emerson College in England in 1969. Through Steiner's insights I found a new direction for both my artistic work and my personal development.

Since that time my artistic work has been devoted to an exploration of the language of form as an expression of living spirit in the physical world. I have taught in Waldorf schools and adult education centers in England and America, and have spent the last ten years engaged in teaching and artistic research at Sunbridge College.

Both Susan and I feel profound gratitude for all that Anthroposophy and Waldorf education have contributed towards our journey as parents. We write this article as an expression of that gratitude and in a spirit of encouragement for others who are considering embarking upon such a journey.

12
International adoption: Will it work? Will it be good?

Once upon a time up in Heaven, there lived a little child in a beautiful Paradise garden. She had many friends there, and the animals and flowers all loved her very much. This garden was high up in the clouds, and she loved to take a piece of cloud in her hands and mold it into a little ball to toss up in the air and catch.

One day as she was playing, her cloud ball went high into the air. When it came down, it rolled away and she ran after it to catch it. It rolled all the way to the edge of the cloud garden, and when she reached for it, she looked over the edge and could see all the stars, the Sun, the Moon, and she could see all the way down to the Earth below.

Down there on the Earth, she saw a little house. Outside there was a woman picking berries and there was a man carving wood into beautiful sculptures. The woman was singing, 'Oh, how happy I would be if a child would come to me...'

As soon as she saw the man and woman, the little angel child wanted to go down to the earth to be their little daughter. So she went to her wise and loving Guardian Angel and told him her wish. 'It is a long journey,' said the Guardian Angel, 'I will go with you to the gate.' He led her to the edge of the Paradise garden, where the little star child said good-bye to her Angel. 'I will always be watching over you,' he said.

Then he helped her into a little cloud boat and set it afloat in the heavenly ocean. She sailed past the Sun and the Moon and all the twinkling stars, down, down, closer and closer to the Earth. Finally, the little boat sailed across to the Rainbow Bridge. She climbed out and went up the bridge, through all the colors— red, orange, yellow, green, blue, and purple, and then she slid down the other side— down, down, down—until she landed with a SPLASH! in the warm, brown water of a canal.

A kind and gentle lady with lovely brown eyes picked her up and held her in her arms. 'What a beautiful baby!' she exclaimed. But the baby girl was unhappy; she wanted to find the woman and the man she had seen from the edge of the cloud garden. The little girl cried and cried so much that the kind lady didn't know what to do. So she took the little girl to a wise old woman, who smiled and said, 'You can leave her with me. I will help her find her way.' Although the young, gentle lady loved the sad, little girl, she kissed her good-bye and gave her to the old woman, who cared for her and pondered how she could help the little child. As the days passed, the little baby girl grew more and more sad. Finally, the old woman prayed to God to help her. That night as she dreamed, the little girl's Guardian Angel spoke to her, 'This little child needs to find her mother and father, who live far, far away on the other side of the world. Take her to the Babies' Home—there, the kind people will take care of her and help find her mother and father.

So the next morning, the wise old woman did as the Angel had told her. She took the little baby girl to the Babies' Home until her mother and father could find her.

Far, far away, on the other side of the world, her mother and father were hoping and praying that their little child would come to them. 'How can we find her?' they wondered. That night, when they were sleeping, the little girl's Guardian Angel told them how. The next morning, they wrote a letter to the Babies' Home and asked if they could come for their daughter. The letter had to travel a long way around the world and over great oceans, but eventually, after a long wait, the answer came, 'Please come soon, your daughter is waiting for you.'

They quickly packed their bags—putting a little doll and a lollipop inside—and travelled a day and a night across the great ocean to the other side of the world to the Babies' Home.

There, they found their little daughter and were filled with love for her as they took her into their arms and hugged her. 'She is so beautiful!' they thought. 'What shall we call her? Let's call her Kiri Anna!' 'They know my name,' thought the little girl. And so she travelled with her mother and father a day and a night, across the great ocean to the other side of the world to the little house she had seen from the Paradise garden high up in the clouds.

Finally, she had found her earthly home where she knew her Guardian Angel would always watch over her. There, by a sparkling stream where many birds and squirrels, ducks and geese became her friends, she grew to be strong and to love all things.

★

Although it may sound like a fairy tale, this is a true story; it is our daughter's story as we tell it on her birthday. There were, of course, other truths, other levels of reality and experience.

There was the reality that before we were married we knew we could not have our own children; that is, we could not give birth to a child biologically. This hard fact did not have any bearing on the shared conviction that we were meant to mother and father. Adoption, and in particular international adoption, presented a natural course for us to follow.

Why international adoption? At the time, we were informed that adoption of an American child could easily take several years. As it turned out, pursuing an international adoption didn't go any more quickly, but at the time this information, plus the fact that we both had travelled extensively in Europe and Asia, made an international adoption feel right for us.

We learned of an agency based locally which specialized in international adoptions. With some trepidation we visited it and were delighted by the immediate air of understanding support; everyone we met had one or more adopted children from all corners of the earth. But our first blow was that we had to be married for a minimum of three years before even beginning the adoption process. Having married only a few months earlier, we left the agency with mixed emotions of elation, feeling that this was the right course for us, and deflation at the prospect of having to wait so long. This was our first taste of what became a familiar experience of 'agony and ecstasy'.

Three years later, our resolve had not wavered, and we returned to the agency to be assigned our fairy godmother, commonly called a social worker! Again we felt blessed to have such a down-to-earth and experienced person to guide us, to be in fact one of several midwives who selflessly facilitated the birth of our family. But suddenly we were overwhelmed with their questions, with destiny-shaping decisions to be made through checklists and forms.

...'Check one of the following: Would you accept a child with an operable/inoperable, moderate/life-threatening, heart/kidney/liver condition?'

What age child? What gender? From what culture? Korea, India, Brazil, Columbia, Philippines, Thailand...

How do we make such decisions? What are our motives? Well, we both love Thai cuisine and culture...how subjective! What will be the consequences of our choices? Is there any wisdom working through this all-too-human process? Who will our child be? And scariest of all, will it work? Will it be good?

If this was conception, adoption style, it was a very conscious process that provided ample opportunity for doubt and loss of resolve—months of endless application forms, essays on our child-rearing philosophies and religious beliefs; documentation of our salaries, our legal status, our educational backgrounds; endless documents to be notarized, certified, bound in seals and ribbons from State Department and embassies. Each step, each document seemed a Herculean challenge of assembling mountains of paper within impossible deadlines, only to hear nothing for days, weeks, months...WAITING! Waiting not for a mere nine months, but three times nine months. This seemed an interminable pregnancy.

At times, during the seemingly endless waiting, it felt as if the process would never end; the likelihood of this process resulting in a family seemed remote, and our initial intentions would seem unreal, our hoped-for child a mere figment of the imagination. But just at such moments of despair, special things happened which kept us going, events whose significance we might otherwise have missed because they were so subtle.

Just days after we completed our first long round of the bureaucratic application process, we left a Manhattan Cathedral filled with the sounds and images of a Christmas Eve nativity celebration and gazed up at the Christmas night stars. We were moved to wonder aloud whether our child had been born yet. Our thinking heads could not know, but when almost three years later we learned she had been born just one day before that Christmas Eve, we could recall the steady clarity of our feeling that evening and knew that our hearts had known something our heads could not.

And so we journeyed through our period of waiting. Each time our spirits flagged (fortunately we were rarely both down at the same time), something came to meet us. Sometimes it was something simple and matter-of-fact, such as experiencing other families with their adopted children whose physiological differences seemed insignificant beside the inner bond which clearly united them as a family. At other times, the gesture of assurance was more mysterious, such as the visitation of a tiny, wild bird of a species we could not identify, who suddenly appeared and befriended us in the wilds. He accompanied us with a gentle, steadfast presence which consoled us long after he was gone and helped us to feel that all would be well; if we but persevered, our child would be on her way.

And then one day (one of the few when we were not preoccupied with wondering when we would ever hear anything), we received a photograph and a sketchy biography of a two-and-a-half-year-old girl (we had been told that only boys came from Thailand, though we secretly hoped for a girl), and shortly afterwards instructions to be in Thailand in eleven days' time. And so the labor and delivery began. After so many months of waiting, suddenly an exciting but also agonizing drama developed. There ensued an almost nightmarish frenzy of trying to meet sudden demands for seemingly non-existent documents and nearly thwarted attempts to get an immigration visa in the all-too-short time period before we were to appear in Thailand. We wondered how the monotony of endless waiting had become, without warning, this intense rush into chaos!

Through the continued support of a diverse array of 'midwives' in the guise of helpful bureaucrats, social workers, and many strangers and friends who helped us through the painful hurdles of immigration, we suddenly found ourselves, documents in hand, on a twenty-four-hour journey halfway around the world. The trip seemed endless, with time to ponder the mysteries of destiny at work in such a complex process.

When a child is born of one's own flesh and blood, one can feel that it is not chance but some higher wisdom which has brought child and parents together. For better or worse some higher primordial force has played a hand in bringing about the child's arrival into one's life. With adoption, however, it can appear that for better or worse, it is hundreds of small decisions made for the most part by officials and bureaucrats one will never meet, which bring parents and children together. We had our child's photograph, but, who was inside that little body? How much of who she would one day become was already determined? How would we influence her development? How would she influence ours? Who would we become as a family?

We landed in Bangkok and were taken to the Babies' Home on the outskirts of Bangkok, where we were led to a waiting room with other adopting parents, waiting for our children to be brought to us. We watched expectantly as two children were brought in to meet their new parents, arms outstretched and faces filled with wonder. Suddenly we heard blood-curdling screams approaching down the corridor. A social worker turned to us with a concerned smile and asked, 'Has anyone told you about your child?' Our hearts pounded as she described our extremely unhappy child, socially withdrawn, uncommunicative and non-participating during her two years in the orphanage. The screams of protest in the corridor subsided as our little girl was led back to her group's cottage. We followed behind at a discreet distance, feeling utterly rejected and confused. Of all the trials along the way, this moment was the most agonizing of all.

We were offered some lunch, but we had little appetite. What had we gotten ourselves into? Would our daughter be socially handicapped for life? Would we have the strength and wisdom to help her? 'Perhaps they matched her with you because you are both teachers,' one of the other parents offered. This well-intended gesture did nothing to console us.

After her nap we were told simply to go and pick her up. This time, miraculously, in the familiar surroundings of her own cottage, she did not resist. And suddenly we were no longer in a nightmare; we were transported into a spaceless and timeless state of being. Our family was born.

We rocked gently back and forth on a swing, our daughter nestled in her mother's arms, her trembling little sobs subsiding as a monsoon shower poured down and passed away. As the sun came out, our little girl dared to peek out and take a lollipop from her mother. Two days later, it was hard to imagine we had not always been a family.

As we looked at the other adoptive families with their new children, we could neither imagine our daughter with any of the other parents nor could we imagine any other child as ours. This was the greatest mystery and blessing of all: in a moment, we became her parents and she our daughter in a manner and degree that could not have been the greater if she were our flesh and blood.

A week later, this child who rarely smiled, who was afraid of strangers and new situations, stepped into the chaos of New York's JFK airport with arms outstretched as if to embrace her new life and smiled a sparkling, triumphant smile that seemed to say, 'I have arrived! This is where I'm meant to be.'

How can we comprehend such a mystery ?

As we write, it is five years since our return home as a family; it seems like yesterday on the one hand and forever on the other that we took our little daughter into our arms in a faraway land. She has just entered Second Grade with great joy and enthusiasm, and is known for her sparkling smile and her friendly exuberance. She never ceases to amaze and delight us with her great sense of joy and pride in her life's journey.

We have the same hopes and anxieties for our daughter's future as any parents. And yet of course, we experience some that are unique to the path of adoption. It is just because we are in the middle of a life process that we are not qualified to address the issues we have not yet passed through ourselves. For example, the question of birth parents has not yet fully arisen for our daughter, and we do not know what complications will arise around her sense of identity as she enters puberty. However, we can round off our story thus far by outlining the thoughts and feelings which form the foundation upon which we build our life together as a family, including the particular dimension of being what is now commonly referred to as a multicultural family.

Rudolf Steiner is hardly the first to describe the human being as having three aspects: a soul and a spirit, in addition to the physical body. However, Steiner has imbued these ancient concepts with new meaning which can make them real for the daily life of modern individuals and bring clarity and confidence to the relationship between adoptive parents and child.

Traditionally, the biological parents were seen not only as the source from which the child received his or her physical body, but also as the providers for all the subsequent physical needs of food, clothing and shelter, until such time as the child grew to be capable of providing for herself. Most parents recognize that physical needs are only one aspect of what a child needs from them. We could use other terms, but in our case shall speak of the soul needs and the spiritual needs of the child which the parents must also provide for. Simply put, the soul need, as we see it, is to live in surroundings full of warmth, love, activity, and interest in the world and all people. Within such a warmth body of interest and care for the world, the child comes to know that he or she is recognized, supported and loved as a unique individuality.

It is only in seeing the unique spirit of their child that the parents have a basis for providing for their child's spiritual needs; for finding the particular developmental and cultural experiences which can help their child unfold his or her unique individual potential as a human being.

Traditionally, the biological or 'physical-body parents' automatically became what we shall call the 'soul parents' and 'spirit parents'. Today, it is possible, where life circumstances necessitate it, for these three forms of parenting to be assumed by different people. For example, it is generally recognized that having conceived a child, some parents lack the means or disposition to provide for the child's physical, soul, or spirit needs. However, it is just as possible today to find parents who are poor in physical means but rich in the soul life they can provide, as it is to find parents who are rich in physical means but poor in soul and spirit resources.

While adoptive parents are not the providers of the child's bodily constitution, they can nevertheless, provide for the subsequent needs of the child's physical body. But of even greater significance is the possibility of them being the child's soul and spirit parents. This possibility has as its basis something much more profound than the wishes and good intentions of the adopting parents. Rudolf Steiner describes in numerous books and lectures the interweaving of destiny we each have with many, many people over multiple lifetimes. Without knowing the particulars of our relationships in previous earthly incarnations, the fundamental thought that our relationships to others in this lifetime, whether brief or long-standing, easy or difficult, are built upon the quality of our relationships in previous lifetimes, awakens us to the profound significance of the roles we play in each others' lives.

With such thoughts, we have found clarity of purpose, courage, and strength of resolve in many challenging spheres of life, including adoption. The thought and more importantly the feeling that one has an ancient and intimate connection to an individual soul and spirit who is seeking earthly incarnation, can be meaningful to any prospective parent. When biological conception is no longer an option, adoption becomes more than a way to fulfill one's own need to be a parent. It is revealed as a mystery as profound as birth itself, if we feel—through all the bureaucracy and the seemingly subjective, arbitrary, and apparently chance decisions of the adoption process—that the child who will come to us is our child. We do not say that we are our child's biological parents, but our conviction that we are her soul and spirit parents, through our soul/spirit connection of earlier lifetimes, is as unshakable as the connection biological parents feel through their bodily relationship to their child.

It is a simple matter to use the so-called facts of modern science to argue that a child is nothing more nor less than a bundle of physical needs, some of which we call psychological. However, such scientific 'facts' alone cannot give us the insight and inner strength to understand and provide for the full spectrum of our children's needs. Could it not be that there exist other facts which science in its present form does not perceive or address? How could one better explain the look of recognition between a three-year-old girl and an adult couple of another culture than to say that as soul/spirit individualities they might already know each other well?

Within such a picture of life's inner realities, one can say that adoptive parents are indeed their child's 'real' parents, and that the adopted child is the adoptive parents' 'real' child. This does not mean that there will not be difficulties and conflicts among the family members. Such challenges too belong to, and indeed are karmically necessary for, the development of each individual involved. However, such a picture of life realities can free us as adoptive parents from feeling that our family is somehow artificially created and thus somehow less than fully 'real'.

We have no question that our daughter is truly our real daughter and that we are truly her real parents. Certainly for our family, we can say of international adoption: it DOES work! It IS good!

Robert W. Dandrew

Robert Dandrew, Dale Bennett (editor) and their family

Writing this essay was hell for me. I started out with a bang, writing every morning for a week while on vacation in the Adirondack mountains. I remember the smell of the instant coffee and cigarettes that accompanied me on that part of my journey. They were my friends, and I was using them to help me write the great American novel. It felt good; I was living a fantasy. It was only when I realized that I really didn't know what to say about my topic (about the fourth day of vacation) that I started to grow disinterested. So I procrastinated for the next year and a half.

Every month or so, one of the editors of *Lifeways* would ask me about my article. 'It's coming,' I would say. Once I was forced to print out of my laptop computer the fruits of all this writing I assured everyone I was doing. I had to hand over the incomplete first draft I had cranked out in the Adirondacks. The comments came back that it was 'good, but needs more development.' How those words pierced through my heart.

So, after several more months of letting everything else stand in the way of finishing my essay, I was confronted by the very intimidating scowls of the Lifeways ringleaders, telling me that I had to make good on my promise to deliver. These women were tough, and no manner of pleasantries could have gotten me out of their grips. I locked myself into a room and began the excruciating task of discovering exactly what my adoption means to me. It took me a few more months, but it was truly cathartic. I have to thank my beautiful wife, Dale Bennett, for encouraging me along.

They asked me to tell you a little something about me. I was born in 1961, adopted in 1962, graduated from high school in 1979, completed college in 1983 and married in 1985. My first job after college was in a university development office (fundraising, public relations, etc.). I've been doing development work ever since, and now I raise money for something I care deeply about. I'm the Director of Development at the Rudolf Steiner School in New York City.

13
Being adopted

My earliest memory is of me lying in a metal crib. A large window is to my left, with venetian blinds hung half-way down and sheer white curtains pulled to the sides. It is a sunny day, and I am listening to familiar sounds. After a while, an older woman with a white cap on her head comes to see me. She has been here before, many times, and she speaks to me in high tones with a smiling face. After a while she leaves, and I return to the familiar sounds.

It is my sense that this moment from my past took place between the point I left the hospital after birth and was placed in foster care. Details are sketchy and conflicting. I know that the bones in my ankles were determined to be problematical by the delivering physician, and I could not be placed in foster care immediately. I spent some time in a hospital and then at the Saint Lawrence County Orphanage in New York State.

Throughout my childhood and early adulthood, I have been visited by a recurring dream of my birth mother casting me into the world. In this dream, it is a dark night and my mother floats in the sky among many small stars. She spreads her legs and pulls me out from between them. She looks at me in her hands and then, stone faced, hurls me through space.

Adoption has shaped my life. Some children are born ill, some are born to accomplish things their parents could not, and others are born girls when their parents wanted boys. I was born to be adopted, and for most of my life I have only understood it as a horrible twist of fate. It has only been in recent years that I have been able to appreciate the ways in which my adoption has helped me.

Since I was very young, I was told that I was adopted. The story was that my birth parents, or 'natural parents' as the language was then, gave me up because they loved me and wanted me to have a good life that they were not able to provide. Around the age of seven, my adoptive father recounted the story the social worker shared with him before I was adopted. She explained that my parents were college students, both from good backgrounds, who found themselves expectant parents. They were not married and felt that they could not raise me. My natural mother named me Jodi Jon at birth and then turned me over to the social worker so that I could join a loving family. The social worker performed a careful search to find just the right new parents for me, who matched my natural parents 'in the most perfect way,' and that is how I arrived with my new parents.

My grandparents, aunts and uncles told me how fortunate I was to be adopted, and they were careful to reinforce the fact that I was just the same as their natural children. Even to my young ears, these words seemed scripted, as if they had all read a book on how to talk to adopted children. Years later, I discovered that they had. After my father died, I went through my parents' personal papers with my mother and found a guide for adoptive parents, prepared by the New York Department of Social Services. The guide offered suggestions for family and friends on how to make the adopted child feel comfortable. I also came across a colorful book about an adopted child that was read to me when I was young. This book tells the story of another lucky child who was 'wanted so much' by his loving new parents.

The message was made clear to me right away. My birth parents brought me into the world, but they were out of the picture. My identity was changed from Jodi Jon to Robert William (names my adoptive father and grandfather wanted) and I was to carry on with my new family and feel more loved and comfortable.

How strange this all was to me. Yes, I felt loved by my new parents, but I didn't want new parents. I didn't want to feel lucky or special. And although I was too young to know that my relatives were as uncomfortable about how to deal with my situation as I was, their words made me feel beholden to my adoptive parents and guilty for wondering about my birth parents.

My state was compounded by the fact that I had an older sister who was also adopted and a younger brother who was my parents' natural son. The three of us looked nothing like each other (the social worker's careful, scientific research on perfect matches clearly had some holes in it). My brother, who suffered from a rare kidney disease, received double attention because of his illness and the fact that he was the youngest. While my parents were rigid in their efforts to treat us equally, my grandmother was blatant in her favoritism toward my brother. Sometimes the pain of watching my brother receive a special gift from my grandmother (while having to force a smile and feel lucky) was unbearable.

Beyond the discrimination over my adoption, my childhood followed the route that most children's lives take. I had a nice home, a dog, a bicycle, neighborhood friends and family vacations. I managed to suppress most thoughts of my birth parents until one summer Sunday. After church, my father drove our family to the drug store for the Sunday paper. My brother and I ran into the store with him as usual to buy a bag of nuts. Inside the store, my father met a friend of his from school and called us children over to meet the man. My father introduced us as 'My adopted son, Robert, and our natural son, Vernon.'

This was the first time my father had referred to me as anything other than his son. This moment was a turning point in my life. Feeling that I could not confront this phantom of adoption with my parents, I knew then that I would continue to keep up a facade of normality. But I would also maintain a secret connection to this inner part of me that was so uncomfortable to everyone around me.

During my teenage years, typical feelings of inadequacy were exacerbated by the specter of adoption. Unlike most of my peers, I traced the source of my misfortune to the fact that I was given up at birth. I also distinguished that my pain was not simply because two people decided they did not want a child, but that I deserved to be given up. The fact that I was unworthy as a newborn served as the continuing reason for rejection and isolation in high school. If I was not accepted by a certain clique, I felt that these people were somehow in on the secret that my birth parents knew— that I was unworthy of their attention. The fact that my adoptive parents weren't comfortable with adoption only confirmed it all.

At the same time, however, this sense of disjunction provided me with a strong feeling of freedom. If I could not be accepted by my peers, I could easily retreat into the private world I built up during my childhood. Similarly, when I was disgusted with my family, it was a relief to remind myself that we were never connected to each other in the first place. (I once said to a fellow adoptee that we spend half our time wishing we were biologically related to our families and the other half thanking God we are not!).

Around the time I entered college and began to experience independence in a new way, I realized that the private world I had built up was not the strong core I thought it was. Yes, it provided me with space away from what I considered painful, but it didn't necessarily encourage reflection. On one level, this place provided me with the opportunity to hone my skills of observation. A child who feels disconnected from others can spend a great deal of time examining those from whom he feels separate. It is also true that this place allowed me to hide from sadness. In one afternoon, I could move from depression over being given up at birth to the full fantasy that I was never adopted.

I began to see that my place of private retreat provided both a clear space for observation and a hiding place. In this way, I realized that I was no different from anyone else. The only difference between me and those around me was that my place was built on the foundations of adoption. For others, the cornerstones could be cast from a variety of fortunes or misfortunes. Learning finally and fully that we all struggle was no small lesson for me. I began to see how some of what I considered to be negative aspects of my personality could have been caused not by my adoption, but by my reaction to it.

The years after college were spent pursuing my profession and in finding a mate to whom I felt as closely connected as I had to any other human being. The wonderful part about being in love was that I could experience a bond that seemed deeper than blood-ties.

My son was born a little more than a year after I was married. During the time my wife was carrying him, adoption was often on my mind. Here inside this womb was a precious baby, just as I was once. The only difference was that this baby was going to be kept by his parents. I struggled to understand how my birth parents, birth mother in particular, could give up their child. Knowing how strongly I felt about this growing fetus, and how deeply my wife felt, I determined that the decision to part with a child could only come from profound shallowness or deep anguish. Whatever the reason in my case, it was healing to know that I could forgive both.

Cradling my infant son in my arms for the first time, I was amazed to meet the first human being to whom I was biologically related. All of the things people say about babies that used to bother me now came back to me in a new way. 'He has his father's face;' 'There's no mistaking whose child he is.' Finally, things like this could be legitimately expressed! It was a comfort to know that the biological chain from which I felt severed after birth could now continue again, this time with me at the top.

However, my pleasure at my new-found natural link was not the climax I thought it would be. After years of thinking a biological connection would resolve things for me, I began to see it as essentially egotistical and somewhat animalistic. What stood before me as a more consuming thought was 'How do I become a parent?' While most people take for granted the words mother and father, adopted children struggle to find meaningful relationships to these words. Knowing that neither set of my parents handled the full range of their responsibilities in the way I wanted, would I have the innate skills to accomplish parenthood? Here again, was I feeling something unique to adopted people, or was I following a long line of parents of all backgrounds who experience first-time jitters?

Whatever the answer to my questions, there was no solution other than to look into the eyes of my child and know that I would do my utmost to nurture his development. This seemed to me to be the root of parenthood: to discover what is positive from one's own upbringing and free oneself from negative examples so that the best may be put in service of the child.

My birth parents, for whatever reason, decided they would not perform this role. My adoptive parents took on the responsibility. The popular thinking at the time of my adoption was that everything should be done 'as if the child were born to the adoptive parents.' It is precisely because of this that so much went wrong in my case. I was not born to my parents, and the false scenario that resulted left me with no other option than to believe that something was wrong.

Almost a decade ago, I took an interest in ideas of reincarnation and karma. I read the writings of various teachers and became fascinated with the notion that peoples' struggles and accomplishments were part of paths that stretched through numerous lifetimes. Of course, I assumed that my adoption broke whatever path I was on and that I was marooned in a cosmic dead end. My feelings about my upbringing, the deep sorrow I continued to suppress, kept me from any other understanding.

Life at that time was full and quite active. My daughter joined our family, and my wife and I built a new home. My professional career was in full swing. Our happy family environment was enhanced greatly when my wife's mother and her husband built a home next door. Our children had a big home with a forest to play in, and their doting grandparents were right next door. My wife was especially happy to have a close relationship with her mother after some stormy years prior.

In the midst of all of this, a friend of mine who was also adopted told me about a service for adoptees that she helped to establish, the New York State Adoption Registry. Within a few hours of hearing how this agency of the State Health Department provided 'non-identifying' information on birth parents and reunited those who applied to be reunited, I set out to pursue my birth parents. After waiting several months, I finally received the envelope containing information on my adoption. My report stated that my birth father was a 42-year old army sargeant with brown hair and blue eyes. He was a high school graduate and enjoyed golfing. He was caucasian, but his ethnic background was not reported. My birth mother left high school after the ninth grade and worked as a store clerk. She was 29 years old, with red hair and blue eyes. The reason stated for the adoption was that the father was unwilling to provide for the child so the mother felt it in the child's best interest to give him up.

Three things struck me about this report. First of all, if these facts were correct, my birth parents were not college students who made a mistake. Second, they both had blue eyes, while my eyes are brown. Third, the child's blood type reported at the bottom of the report did not match what I knew to be mine. I quickly wrote the agency and asked them to check their facts. They responded with a phone call confirming that the information was not from another person's record; the information was from my file. As far as New York State was concerned, this was my background.

The friend who referred me to the service explained how common it was in the early 1960s for social service agencies to gild the lily when presenting prospective adoptees to adoptors. Certainly, most people would want to believe that the children they are about to welcome into their lives are from 'good stock.' Unfortunately for me, I could not trust any aspect of the report, given major questions about eye color and blood type. My friend told me that I was one of thousands of adoptees in the same situation. For most of our nation's history, little care for details—or even the truth—has gone into adoption records, probably because the sense was that the information would remain useless after the child assumed his or her new identity.

My primary interests in filing with the agency were to find a physical description of my birth parents and to learn of their backgrounds. I also hoped that one or both of my parents might have learned about this mostly unknown and un-publicized service and registered to reconnect with me in the event I had requested the same. I had no illusions about a tearful reunion. I wanted to hear from their mouths why they chose to give me up, and I wanted to know what they looked like. This hopeful project left me disappointed on all fronts. I couldn't be sure who my birth parents were, and they hadn't registered to be reunited.

For the next year and a half, my family was very content together, and then my wife's mother died unexpectedly. For the first time in my life, I experienced deep pain over the loss of someone I loved. My mother-in-law was very demonstrative in her love for me and was very nurturing. When my father passed away a few years prior, things seemed pretty straightforward; he was gone, and that was that. I knew in my mother-in-law's case that her unconditional acceptance of me allowed for something different to grow between us. This experience reinforced for me how parental love comes out of deeds and not blood or legal ties. I came to know that what I craved all my life could indeed be supplied, even if in my case it did not come in the form I may have wanted from biological or adoptive parents.

My wife was certain that her mother's death was a passing from one stage of consciousness and preparing for a new incarnation. She deeply wanted to understand more of what this process might be and sought the advice of friends, one of whom recommended a person who had been helpful to her. My wife asked me to go with her to visit this man, who happened to be a priest of the Christian Community Church. It was here, in a conversation that was intended to focus on my mother-in-law, that a new door opened for me.

We talked for the better part of an afternoon about the intentions humans bring to each lifetime and how these are carried out or impeded. In my mother-in-law's case, we looked at difficult situations in her life and how she chose to take them on to help her in her development. At one point, he turned to me and asked, 'What are things you might have chosen before birth to help you in your development?' Embarrassed, I responded, 'Whatever I decided for myself was thrown off track because I was adopted.' His eyes swelled with surprise and then concern. 'But you chose to be adopted,' he said calmly. I sat there stunned for a few moments. Slowly, I said, 'I couldn't have chosen this.' 'Why not?' he said with a smile, 'Think about it.'

With these words, I entered a new chapter in my life. The next months were filled with a new kind of introspection that continues to this day. It was a great relief to think that my circumstance was not an accident. It was also an important key to understanding my life's path.

My birth parents gave me the gift of life and a physical body that continues to carry me well. My adoptive parents—whom I call with great certainty my parents—provided love and nurturing to the best of their abilities. The great differences between my parents and me, which I always saw as a by-product of our mismatching, could now be viewed in a new light. For example, their near-compulsive drive for hard work, which vexed me throughout my life, was also a check against my deep desire for easiness. Interestingly, when my parents were children, both were placed by their parents in the care of other adults. There are many ways in which my experiences can be seen in the light of their working through their karmic paths.

In pondering what life experiences led me to choose this path, I wonder if perhaps I was too dependent on other people. Or possibly, I had forsaken the love of someone important to me. Whatever the reason or set of reasons,

I entered this life needing something that we all need: self-reliance. It is this most important of traits that I know adoption helped me to gain. Standing firmly on ground that I have carved out for myself, I have been able to work and serve practically. I am not certain, given the traits and characteristics which I know to be essential parts of my being, that I would have been driven to discover myself in the way I have because of my adoption.

Families and other groups have always been the main source of nurturing for their members. It was only a few generations ago that a person's family provided primary education, economic support and spiritual development for each of its members. Today, we see the ties within these groups breaking down. Persons and organizations outside the home, from day-care providers to television networks, are offering much of what the family has traditionally provided—and frequently not as well. Rudolf Steiner saw this trend as part of a natural progression toward a time when individuals will become more conscious of, and assume greater responsibility for, their own development. Believing this to be the case, I see my adoption as preparation not only for this lifetime, but for those ahead.

David Sloan

Athletic competition was hard to avoid as the oldest of four boys growing up in Southern California during the sixties. Throughout my childhood I harbored dreams of becoming the next Sandy Koufax, until reality, quite literally, hit hard. As a 13-year-old pitcher, I managed to give up 12 runs in 1/3 of an inning. Such generosity does not usually lead to the major leagues. Thereafter my athletic aspirations diminished to more modest proportions— struggling to develop a reliable forehand in tennis, (some challenges take more than one lifetime to master), and trying vainly to make contact with my brother's legendary 'inside-out sinker' in our backyard wiffleball games.

Sports continued to play a defining role in my life for years, well after I met anthroposophy at 21, or my wife-to-be at 24, well after I began teaching at Green Meadow Waldorf School at 28, even after the last of our four children was born when I was 38. Thankfully, the competitive nature of my approach to sports (and probably every other aspect of my life) has undergone a transformation as I have had to confront, in my forties, the limitations of an aging physical body grown gravity-bound. Although I still experience the need to ground my life of teaching and endless meetings with physical activity, those activities have also taken on a different quality. Racquetball has gradually been supplanted by gardening, 'weekend warrior' basketball by cycling, rock-climbing by canoeing. One of my greatest joys in recent years has been sharing my love of the wilderness with students and, increasingly, with my own children. Hiking above timberlines, rafting down whitewater rivers, cross-country skiing in deep woods, offer the ideal combination for life lessons—strenuous physical challenges in nature's reassuring embrace.

My children are teaching me another lesson daily. It is a mixed blessing raising sports-minded children; every day their ascendency becomes more emphatic, more pronounced, often at their father's expense. I watch with both delight and a twinge of melancholy that I 'decrease' as they 'increase'—a truth that applies to all parents as we grow older. But I see expansive possibilities in the decreasing. I begin to understand, in a most visceral way, that as one's physical capacities diminish, inner capacities have the possibility of unfolding. We may lose leaves, but we gain sky.

14
Sports and our children

My youngest son calls impatiently from the backyard: 'C'mon, dad, you said you'd play! I've been waiting over 200 hours already!' He stands grandly in his oversized baseball uniform, the one with red piping on the jersey. He would trip over the voluminous gray wool pants had he not hiked the leggings up and cinched the waist with a belt.

On the bare spot designated as home plate, he pounds his plastic bat into the turf, adjust his cap, tugs his sagging pants up, and then spits disdainfully in the direction of the imaginary pitcher on the mound. He picks up the wiffle ball, tosses it in the air, and swings toward the plum tree standing directly behind second base, whereupon he dashes around the bases, odd-shaped pieces of wood pilfered from the kindling box. He ends his circuit with a triumphant whoop and a dust-raising slide into the plate. My youngest son is six years old and believes fervently in the power of fairies and home runs.

Meanwhile, outside the kitchen window I hear the incessant bounce of a basketball on asphalt, interrupted by the dramatic pause indicating a shot, followed by a scramble for the rebound by my two eldest sons. A moment later the older one yells, 'Come on, old man, time to meet your doom. Just you and me, one on one, King of the Court versus the Court Jester; Super Swish takes on Air Ball!'

I am tempted to ask him which of us is which, but I don't want to pour gasoline on the flames of his challenge. My eldest son is fifteen, as tall as I am, and growing more confident daily that the time is at hand when he will finally humiliate his father on the court—spinning, feinting, leaping, scoring at will, blocking every desperate shot his father heaves hoopward. I hear my second son giggling with relish at the prospect of witnessing such a slaughter.

Fortunately, my eight year old daughter comes to my aid like a guardian angel, calling up from the garage, 'Papa, will you go for a bike ride with me around the neighborhood?' I readily assent, postponing my inevitable comeuppance on the court and delaying the fulfillment of my promise to pitch to my budding Babe Ruth.

Yes, sports have assumed an increasingly central role in the fabric of our family life. A day does not pass in the spring, summer or fall without one spirited athletic contest or another taking place in our driveway or backyard. Our children's participation in after-school athletics has altered the entire balance of our lives as we scramble to get one to baseball practice and another to a summer league basketball game; while our daughter swims at the pond and the youngest is off playing tackle-with-no-pads football down the block with kids twice his size.

So pervasive has the preoccupation with sports become that we now have a 'gag rule' at suppertime, which precludes any mention of athletics during the meal, just to allow a bit of open time and space for another possible topic of interest to arise. This ban specifically applies to the reporting of all scores of all teams at any level, as well as the lodging of any grievances harbored against brothers or sister for unfair tactics used during the day; including the archetypal grievance and rebuttal: 'You cheated and you know it.' 'I did not. You're just a poor loser.'

Even with the ban, sports talk has a way of creeping into any seemingly unrelated conversation. When my youngest son heard that Clinton had won the Presidential election, he asked us, 'What team does he play for?'

From pastime to mania

Sports have crossed a certain line in our family, and in the culture at large, from pleasant pastime to mass mania. Whether one calls the phenomenon welcome or disturbing, a number of unsettling and difficult questions have arisen in our lives over the past decade or so:

• what lies behind the obsession Americans have for sports and fitness?
• what are the dangers as well as the benefits for our children as they engage in organized sports at earlier and earlier ages? Are there other options?
• how can we cultivate a sensible relationship to sports and physical activity, so that family life can be enhanced instead of imperiled?

To address the first question—the obsession is real, and pervasive. More adults than ever jog, bike, swim, serve, skate, lift, pitch, putt and rebound away their leisure time. For those who like to watch athletes sweat rather than to sweat themselves, the true glutton can literally view one sporting event after another twenty-four hours a day on television. Professional athletes are still idolized, but now they are known at least as much for the products they hawk and astronomical salaries they command as for their accomplishments in their respective sports. This trend represents a most unwelcome union— the cloud of commercialism has merged with the magnet of materialism to turn sports increasingly into a high stakes business.

A generation ago, we played for the love of the games themselves; and perhaps for the remotest of possibilities, that one day we might reach the pinnacle of athletic success—win the Olympic decathlon as Rafer Johnson did, pitch a no-hitter with the mastery of a Sandy Koufax or Nolan Ryan, dominate Wimbledon as Billy Jean King did, steamroll would-be tacklers in the manner of the indomitable Jim Brown. In other words we held fast to our dreams of attaining the glory that comes with becoming a champion. Nowadays fortune far exceeds fame as a driving force behind the sports mania. The allure of almost unimaginable financial reward turns children into 'investments' and parents into single-minded trainers and agents.

Yet there must be more to it than pure materialistic motives, because most people are realistic enough to recognize the long odds of actually rising into the professional ranks of any sport. Can we understand why millions of enthusiasts are attracted to sport, why it has become almost a kind of religion?

Spiritual longings

Writing in the first quarter of this century, Rudolf Steiner offered a provocative insight on just this point.

> Religion has lost the inner force to strengthen the physical in man...what man has lost in the sphere of religion he instinctively wants to acquire externally. Well, I am certainly not going to indulge in tirades against sport as such and I am convinced that it will develop further in a healthy manner. But it will play a different part in the future from what it does today when it has become a substitute for religion.[1]

In other words, it was possible in the past for one's religious life to work spiritually not only on one's soul but on one's physical body as well. This is no longer the case. According to Steiner, religion has lost the vitality to provide this spiritual nourishment on a fundamental, physical level. As a consequence, many people who still long for spiritual sustenance now seek it in purely physical pursuits, in sports.

Seventy years later, Steiner's observation appears truer than ever. The root meaning of religion has to do with reconnecting oneself to one's spiritual origins, and perhaps in the process connecting with those like-minded people whose aspirations parallel ours. Isn't the experience of being a fan, a sports enthusiast, outwardly similar? Consider the correspondences between the traditional weekly sojourn to church or temple and the experience of attending the Sunday Game of the Week. In both cases there is an assembling with others and of bearing witness to the extraordinary deeds of 'transcendent' figures. Isn't there a quasi-religious devotion many people exercise when they link their destinies with the fortunes of their team? When they win, the fan feels his prayers have been answered; he has been blessed, and he basks in his team's triumph. When the Dodgers defeated the hated Yankees in four straight games to win the 1963 World Series, I remember feeling enlarged, elevated, empowered. Somehow, my fervent rooting had contributed to my team's success. The converse is also true, of course. When those same Dodgers lost to the Giants on the final day of the previous season, I remember weeping more than at my grandmother's funeral that same year. It took weeks to get over feeling devastated and diminished.

This longing, then, to identify with something greater than one's own personal struggles carries within it certain elements of a religious experience. So does the adoration of these athletes to whom we ascribe superhuman or semi-divine attributes. In the towering achievement of such figures as Muhammed Ali, Chris Evert, Cal Ripken, Michael Jordan, Jackie Joyner-Kersee, we pay homage to a higher ideal of the human being. Their skill, grace, endurance, and strength remind us of our own transcendent possibilities. In the deepest sense, to cheer on such champions is to honor the higher being in each one of us.

What about the legions of people who, instead of simply spectating, choose to participate directly in sports themselves? Is it only for the obvious health benefits? Or is there a deeper aspect as well to such physical activity?

Athletes who engage in marathon running and other long-distance tests of human stamina speak reverently about the altered state of consciousness that often accompanies extreme exertion. They may experience a sensation of floating, of lightness that carries them effortlessly forward. And in the moments after the race, runners also describe an almost inexpressible feeling that fills them with peace and well-being. Other athletes, who unaccountably lift the level of their game to extraordinary heights, describe a common experience of being in what many simply call 'the zone,' an almost supernatural state in which they feel in complete control of the contest, as if they can will the outcome. Basketball players suddenly feel gravity-free and the ball swishes through the hoop as if by radar. Hitters on a hot streak in baseball see the ball coming in slow motion, looking as plump as a pillow. Tennis players can suddenly hit every stroke into the deep corners, grazing the lines time after time. It is a paradoxical condition, in which athletes feel most confidently, comfortably within themselves and simultaneously elevated, lifted out of themselves.

All these descriptions begin to sound remarkably akin to a meditative state, reached most commonly by people on a spiritual path. No wonder athletes at all levels hunger for this experience. Isn't it ironic that sports, the most seemingly external and materialistic of activities, has supplanted religion for some as a way of fulfilling, however faintly, an inner longing for a spiritual experience?

Child sports prodigies: budding stars or burnouts?

One of the unfortunate leaps of logic that adults often make is, 'Well, if this activity makes me feel so great, it must be terrific for my kids.' Moreover, many parents subscribe to the increasingly popular idea that the earlier their children are exposed to a particular sport, the more proficient and successful they will become later on. 'If my 10-year-old picks this game up so quickly, I bet my five-year-old will be an all-star if I get her started now.' And so children are drawn into the world of sports at younger and younger ages.

On a certain level, this approach seems to work. Just as we can teach a three-year-old to read well before he is interested or developmentally ready, we can also start throwing a ball in that same three-year-old's direction or put our daughter on a balance beam in a harness. And if we enroll him in a peewee league or her in a gymnastics clinic soon enough, we may indeed have a star in the making. On the other hand, we may come too late to the painful realization that for every premature push we give our children, there may be a stiff price to pay later on.

On the most obvious, physiological level, we could look at any number of 'child prodigies,' who catapulted to the top of their sport, only to have their careers come to a crashing halt because their bodies simply couldn't handle the strain. The most dramatic example of this phenomenon is the story of Tracy Austin's rise and fall. At the almost inconceivably precocious age of 14, Tracy burst on the professional tennis scene in 1976, wearing pigtails, braces and a cotton dress with a big bow on the back. At the time, she stood 4' 11' and weighed all of 90 pounds. She electrified the tennis world by storming into the quarterfinals of the U.S. Open. Two years later she defeated the already legendary Chris Evert to become the youngest U.S. Open champion ever. But her reign was an unexpectedly short one. After winning eleven tournaments in 1980 and seven more in 1981, including the U.S. Open again, her body began to break down. She injured her neck, contracted tendonitis in her shoulder and then, most debilitating of all, suffered a stress fracture in her back. By the time she was 21, the age most young people are reaching their physical maturity, Tracy Austin had virtually retired from tennis.

More recently, the meteoric rise and fall of another tennis player— Jennifer Capriati—illustrates the soul damage that can also befall today's young athletes. Jennifer excelled at an even earlier age than Tracy Austin. At age 13 she became the youngest player ever to win the U.S. Open Jr. title. At 14 she accomplished what no other tennis player had ever done at so tender an age; she reached the semifinals of two Grand Slam events. A year later she was ranked sixth in the world and had already defeated four of the five players ranked above her. Her crowning achievement was to win a gold medal at the 1992 Olympics in Barcelona. By age 16 Jennifer Capriati appeared to be living every young person's dream: she had become a world champion, acquired global fame, and had earned more money than some major corporations.

The problem was that Jennifer was not a corporation. This had somehow been overlooked by her parents, agents and financial advisors. She had been groomed to be a professional athlete; the plan had worked to an extraordinary degree. But somewhere along the way Jennifer Capriati became a commodity instead of a young girl. She was packaged and marketed by corporate sponsors; she was mythologized, courted, hounded and, finally, exposed by the media for what she really was—a troubled teenager who could no longer cope with her celebrity status. Is it any wonder that within a year of winning her gold medal Jennifer Capriati was cited for shoplifting and, soon after, arrested for possession of marijuana? Or that even after undergoing therapy of various types, she had, at the time of writing, yet to return to the game and the media circus that had glorified her achievements while ignoring her inner needs?

We would be wise to ask ourselves what is the effect of all this early emphasis on drill and discipline, coordination and alertness, fitness and strength? Ironically, the consequence may be just the opposite of that intended by all those well-meaning, enthusiastic parents. A recent study published in the New York Times revealed that 75% of children who participated in organized athletics at an early age simply burned out in adolescence. By age 15 they no longer actively engaged in that sport. More tellingly, the study also showed that 'the earlier the children began playing the sport, the sooner they dropped out.' Those who chose to stop playing cited several factors; most frequently heard was the lament that 'the fun had gone out of it all.' And even those who stayed with a sport into their teenage years did so 'because their parents wanted them to.'[2]

I have a friend who fits this profile perfectly. His father was an inventor who designed a kind of miniature sports training center that provided a basketball hoop, a bounce back wall and a tennis net, all within a 15 foot enclosed structure. To prove the effectiveness of his mini-sports complex, my friend's father had my friend hitting a tennis ball in this athletic 'Skinner Box' by age three. Learning the basic strokes gave way to a weekly regimen of long practice hours. By the time he was 16, my friend had risen through tournament play to become the top-ranked tennis player in New England in his age group. Then, with a promising athletic future before him, including the prospect of athletic scholarship offers to college and perhaps even the lucrative possibilities of turning professional, or at least becoming a teaching pro, my friend simply walked away from it all. When I first met him, six years later, he had still not touched a tennis racquet. His reasons? He said he finally realized that he had been robbed of his childhood and had grown weary of living someone else's dream.

Are we clear about our motives when we sign our children up for little league or midget football or junior hockey? Are we attempting to resurrect, through our children's seemingly boundless promise, our own unfulfilled athletic dreams?

Letting children play

We have never harbored any long-term fantasies about one of our children becoming an Olympic champion or professional athlete. Yes, my six year old son will tell you, if you ask him, that he wants to be a baseball player and a backhoe driver when he grows up, but those aspirations are of his own choosing at this point in his life and are likely to change by tomorrow. We have never favored the sacrifices necessary to raise a child sports star. The disruption to family life, the single-minded dedication required of parent and child, never appealed to us. In fact, it seemed to represent a grievous offense against the nature of childhood, which is to play until the activity becomes tiresome, or until another form of play captures the child's fancy. The whole notion of training is alien to children before the age of puberty. They can be trained, of course; at a very young age they can be subjected to the most rigorous conditioning. But before adolescence the motive for such training almost invariably comes from outside sources—a zealous parent or coach who doesn't want the boy or girl 'to waste all this potential.'

The danger here is that, in the name of developing 'potential,' we may well be wresting away an irretrievable part of their lives. While our children are spending dozens of hours each morning training, what *aren't* they doing? Do they have an opportunity to be children, to play freely, to run through fields without being timed? To kick pebbles instead of footballs? to catch autumn leaves instead of baseballs? Yes, children love to play— movement is their element. But to a large degree, it is the adults in their lives who teach them to turn play into competition.

This transition from imaginative play to organized, competitive sports represents a major rite of passage for most children. The question for many parents is, when should this take place? For those who espouse the 'earlier-the-better' philosophy, the answer is easy—as soon as the league allows. It is not uncommon to see five and six year olds playing midget football or soccer or basketball on any Saturday morning in parks and fields all over America. But my impression is that team sports, especially those involving a ball, may do more harm than good to children under the age of nine or so. Why? Most children younger than that simply have not developed the requisite hand/eye coordination to catch or kick or hit a ball with any degree of proficiency. In addition, their attention span is rarely long enough to focus on, much less to understand, the complexities of a full-length ball game. The result can lead to discouraged children with an unhealthy case of 'sportaphobia'.

The most subtle reason arguing against early involvement in sports has to do with the child's psyche and sense of self. Two of the most critical lessons awaiting every child who plays on a team are: 1) how to balance personal goals with those of the team, and 2) how to win and lose with grace. How many six or seven year olds have the maturity to learn these lessons? For that matter, how many adults have mastered them?

Playing on a team can be one of the most effective ways of teaching a child the meaning of community. After the family, what other social unit comes close to providing the sense of identity, the interdependence upon others for success? But does a small child really have a developed enough judgment to appreciate true teamwork? One can only give up a lesser cause for a greater if one has something to give in the first place. Most children under the age of nine or thereabouts lack the sense of self and the perspective to maintain a healthy balance between personal and team identity. To make matters murkier, how many young children fall victim to the inherent flaw in competition which equates winning with 'success' and losing with 'failure'?

The dangers of competition

My second son has struggled for years now to rise above this 'I win, you lose' mentality. A born athlete, Benjamin had such remarkable coordination that even as a three year old he would draw attention from total strangers at the beach for his uncanny ability to hit a ball with a bat which was bigger than he was. Perhaps because he was a second child, he began competing with his older brother at a very young age and to take the outcome of these contests very seriously. It didn't have to be a ball game—they would race to see who could brush their teeth the fastest, who could jump out of the swing the furthest, who could hold their breath the longest. For Benjamin, these silly games were not games at all but ultimate tests of worthiness; they offered him an opportunity to dislodge his older brother, if only temporarily, from his 'favored' son status. Our family certainly didn't invent this dynamic; that honor goes to the First Family: Cain and Abel had a rather competitive relationship too. But then my sons finally did discover sports as the natural proving ground for their aspirations. We became concerned about Benjamin's extreme reaction whenever it even looked as if he might lose one of these contests. He would cry, hurl a stream of invective at his smirking brother, at his mediating parents and even at his unsuspecting baby sister as he stomped off. When he won, he would gloat, rub it in and bask in those magical words, 'I beat you!' To this day Benjamin considers the term 'loser' the single worst insult in the English language.

As one might imagine, Benjamin wanted to get involved in organized sports as soon as he became aware such leagues existed. We felt that to capitulate to his wishes we would only be fueling his competitive fires, so we resisted his entreaties until this past year, when he turned 11. He joined a very good team in a league so strong that its all-star team advances to the state tournament.

For Benjamin, playing little league had a wonderfully humbling effect. He experienced a stretch during the season when he went through a 0 for 8 dry spell—8 games, not at-bats. It was heart-rending on the one hand to watch him withdraw and brood over his 'slump.' But with each game,

Benjamin also began to experience a dawning truth that his world did not collapse when his team lost or when he struck out. He was not branded with the mark of Cain or cast out of his community. On the contrary, he was consoled, encouraged, restored by sympathetic teammates and understanding coaches.

It was also reassuring to see him stick with it, to witness a budding resiliency and even humor emerge as the slump turned into prolonged 'drought.' Post-game sulks passed more quickly; a new philosophical outlook began to surface as Benjamin tried to find the positives in every loss. Finally the drought broke, the skies opened, and Benjamin hit a game-winning triple toward the end of the season. On the ride home after the game, he seemed more relieved than boastful; he was proud all right, but he spoke without the bravado of the cool, conquering hero he had assumed at the beginning of the season. His good fortune had come only after protracted travails, and my son at this moment seemed to be more himself than I had seen him in years.

So what is to be gained in going from impromptu backyard games of catch into leagues with uniforms, lined fields, real dugouts, and enthusiastic parent/coaches? For my second son, it was clearly the humbling experience of having to confront certain limitations. He went from thinking he had some natural claim on becoming the next Barry Bonds to realizing that he would have to work hard to achieve the all-star status he coveted. At the same time, Benjamin began to develop the quieter confidence born out of perseverance through hard times. This self-affirmation may be one of the greatest gifts sports can confer upon our children.

What about girls?

Sandwiched among three brothers, my 8-year-old daughter already exhibits a certain indifference to competitive sports. She has never been drawn to ball games, and is frankly mystified by the level of intensity which colors her brothers' interactions. The boys have not exactly welcomed her participation in their games when she has expressed an interest:

'Aw, dad, she can't throw, she can't hit, and in the outfield she blows on dandelion puffballs instead of paying attention to what's happening.'

'So teach her how to play. You weren't such a hotshot at her age. How is she going to improve if you don't help her?'

I confess that I already harbor some concern that my daughter will grow up victimized, not by premature exposure to athletics, but by the 'lowered expectations syndrome' foisted upon her by her brothers. It is hard to know whether Caitlin's current lack of interest in sports prefigured her brothers' disdain of her capacities, or if it was the natural reaction to such criticism. But there is a third possibility: perhaps Caitlin's disregard for the world of sports at this stage is the healthiest approach of any of the children. She has even said, in a most sensible way, that 'I'm not ready yet,' when prodded to learn some basketball move or batting stance. Perhaps she will actually grow into adolescence without relying on athletic achievement for her self-esteem. She need never swing a bat or jump a hurdle or hit an ace, if that is her choice. But if she has already internalized the message that still stunts the development of so many young people—'because you are girls we simply can't take you seriously as athletes'—then we must do whatever we can to combat that constricting falsehood.

For those girls who take themselves too seriously as athletes, who become obsessively involved in competitive sports, another fast-spreading danger must be mentioned. According to the American College of Sports Medicine, over 60% of 'females competing in "appearance" sports (like figure skating and gymnastics) and endurance sports, suffer from an eating disorder.'[3] Such insidious illnesses as anorexia and bulimia are not limited solely to female athletes. Indeed, any girl or woman who believes in one of our most influential cultural imperatives, that 'you can never be too rich or too thin,' is a potential casualty. But the pressure on female athletes is especially intense. In an effort to shed the unwanted weight that they believe will prevent them from swimming faster, diving more gracefully or vaulting higher, these young girls starve themselves or go on binge-purge eating sprees while exercising four to six hours a day. For a while, such severe regimes may seem to work. But prolonged over time, these extreme eating habits often lead from temporary biological disruptions—loss of their menstrual cycle—to more permanent damage —osteoporosis, organ malfunction and, all too frequently, death. Weighed against the remote odds of achieving lasting glory on the athletic field or in the arena, doesn't the cost seem inordinately high?

Finding the balance

Balance is one of the most essential and valued of attributes in any sport. Is it not ironic that in our fanatical pursuit of fitness or of the perfect athletic program for our children, we often create the most unbalanced of situations for our families? With practices after school until dark, night games and weekend clinics, how much time is left for family to be together? How much time do our children spend engaged in non-athletic activities (watching sports on television doesn't count)?

We don't do enough in our family to counteract this frenetic centripetal movement which whirls all of us constantly away from the center. But there are obviously ways to combine both the need for physical activity and the need for family time. A whole dimension of non-competitive sports can open up to families willing to go 'only as fast as the slowest member.' On Sundays we periodically pile all the bikes in or on the car and go out to the country for a leisurely ride around a lake. We have done the same with camping trips when we have hiked and canoed for hours. Such outings provide more than exercise—they can be memorable adventures, which add to the family 'lore' to be recounted and relished years from now.

One of my colleagues, Eugene Schwartz, wrote an illuminating article about sports for the school newsletter several years ago. He identified two opposing approaches to the whole subject by associating the word 'sports' with the Greek city/state Sparta, and the word 'athlete' with Athens. In a period of history when athletic contests were really born, these two city/states had very different methods of preparing their young people for the Games. In Sparta, boys were taken away from their families when they were seven and subjected to the harshest physical training conceivable. They drilled, marched, exercised, for most of every day. The goal of the trainers was to so toughen and harden the physical bodies of these soldiers-to-be that they would be impervious to the elements, so well-conditioned that they could outlast any foe. The boys were taught that cowardice was the greatest shame, and the body-length iron shields were made so heavy that soldiers could not run away from battle and still carry them. (A soldier came home with his shield or upon it.) Indeed, the Spartan army became renowned as the most effective fighting force in the world. However, the Spartans' single-minded pursuit of soldierly perfection created a one-dimensional society. Culture was non-existent, art was an irrelevance, and leisure time was a waste of time.

Consider the striking contrast of this with the Athenians. Their formal education also began at seven, but boys had lessons in letters and music as well as gymnastics. In the mornings they recited Homer, played the lyre, learned mathematics; then, in the afternoon at the gymnasia, they engaged in a host of physical activities. The Athenians did not exercise simply because they wanted to keep fit, nor did they compete solely to win glory for themselves and their city/state. Their aim was nothing less than to develop the body as the purest expression of the spirit. To educate anything less than the whole human being would have been incomprehensible to the Athenians.

They also recognized an innate connection between artistic and physical activities. For instance, they believed that the best training for oratory was throwing the javelin; both require a 'taking hold' of a subject, an aiming at a 'target,' and a 'delivery.' Those who were drawn to philosophy trained in wrestling—what better preparation for 'grappling' with life's questions? In the Athenian polis, then, physical training was less intended to produce soldiers than harmonious, balanced human beings.

Our culture's approach to physical activity has clearly tilted in the direction of the Spartan model, of highly specialized training for the purpose of producing 'sports warriors.' Perhaps we need to re-evaluate where such a one-sided approach is leading our children. Are we interested in turning them into 'Spartan sports stars' or 'Athenian athletes'? Should sports occupy the pre-eminent position in their young lives, to the exclusion of other equally worthy pursuits? Or would our children be better served were they to follow the Athenian ideal of cultivating all aspects of the unfolding child?

In the end, we need to remember that at every level of athletic endeavor, we speak of 'playing' the game. Whether the activity is hopscotch or the World Series, the true wellspring of all games is the exhilaration we experience when we play, when we move our limbs through space with grace or speed or power. As long as our children relish the opportunity to do their best without wishing their opponent the worst, as long as their anxiety over the outcome of a contest does not obscure their sheer delight in playing, then athletics can be the enlivening and even elevating activity it was intended to be.

Notes

[1.] Rudolf Steiner. 1986. *Soul Economy and Waldorf Education*, Chapter 3, p. 40. Anthroposophic Press.

[2.] 'A Parents' Guide to Kids' Sports.' *New York Times Magazine*. April 26, 1992.

[3.] 'Special Report: Eating Disorders.' *Sports Illustrated*. October 24, 1994.

[4.] Herman Poppelbaum. 'Sport and Spiritual Development.' *Anthroposophical Newsletter*, Spring, 1981

Jean W. Yeager

In the first incarnation of this lifetime, I won international awards for radio/ television advertising copywriting. I wrote hundreds of commercials, corporate film/videos, television program treatments and scripts, speeches (including one for Ronald Reagan which was delivered to the National Association of Broadcasters) and Industrial Theatre including the Coca-Cola Centennial Bottlers' meeting which had a $2-million production budget. In my present incarnation, I am developing realistic approaches to marketing and communications for anthroposophical initiatives including the Bio-Dynamic Farming and Gardening Association. I live with my wife Marietta, an artistic therapist, and children Jake, Hallie and Gideon near Kimberton, PA. My favorite poem is 'The Song Of The Man Who Has Come Through' by D.H. Lawrence.

15
What does television do?

Scene I: Up from blacktime-1984

I was a freelance television/film writer. Like many of our friends, my wife and I used *Sesame Street* and *Mr. Rogers* as a way to keep our child 'entertained' while we were busy around the house. One day my oldest son, Jake, who was five years old at that time, had a neighbor boy come over to play. The child tapped on our front door and called out happily, 'C'mon out Jake! Let's ride tricycles!' And Jake replied in a very bored sounding voice, 'Naw—*Sesame Street*'s on!' In this instant, I knew something was wrong. A five year old should be active <u>doing</u> things. I got Jake up and out of the house and busy with his friend.

Dissolve to Scene II: Time 1986

We were visiting relatives who kept a television set on constantly in their living room. The audio volume was turned extremely low. I watched as my in-laws and relatives came into the room to 'visit' one another. Although these people hadn't been together for many months, they found it difficult to carry on a conversation as their eyes were slowly drawn to the television. Conversation was disjointed. Some drifted to the chairs my in-laws had positioned in a semi-circle near the set. My kids, of course, sat on the floor in front of the set and enjoyed the flicker and glow. They rebelled at the suggestion of going 50 feet to a nearby creek to play in the sand or hunt crayfish or frogs. I suggested that we turn off the television and met the question, 'don't you want to hear the news?'

Dissolve to Scene III: Time 1994

My 85 year-old mother, whom I have called an hour before to alert her to my coming to pick her up for an activity, opens her apartment door to let me in. I discover that she's not dressed, but has once again been captivated by the television and 'lost track of time.' In many instances when I come to my mother's apartment these days, I find that the television is on, but turned to a cable channel which is simply endlessly repeating a chain of video-text advertisements. She seems to find some comfort in the movement and colors.

Fade to black

I don't believe these scenes are unusual—television is a motive force in our daily lives. We all have 'television' stories. The electronic media, in one form or another, has been my livelihood since I was 20 years old. Over these past two decades, I have experienced the power of commercial interests and heard about the 'potential' that television has for educating, opening our understanding of the world, and other such benefits.

In the small scenes from real life sketched above, my concern is television as a process. It is vital for all parents to ask the question: What does television do TO us, to our children, to our social lives?

Consider, for example, what television does on the physical level. The little vignettes above show that television has the ability to capture people physically and hold them: either through the desire to watch what is 'on', or through the 'potential' for what might be on. The effect is to mesmerize us so that we lose our sense of reality.

Doctor Leonardo Fulgosi, noted Swiss pediatric specialist, points to the fact that television scans some 625 lines of 800 dots per line at a rate of 25 times per second—illuminating or exciting some 12,500,000 dots each second. This sensory bombardment stimulates the brain at a speed which is so rapid that the eye cannot detect any movement. And so, you sit passively and 'give yourself up to the image.' [1]

I explored this 'captivating' physical aspect of video with a class of 12th Graders at Wynstones School in England. At the beginning of a day-long workshop on media, I simply set up a television set to one side of the room and turned it on with no audio. The screen flickered and those within line-of-sight could not keep their eyes from glancing over at the screen. We observed that the physical flicker of a set seems to be irresistible. Try as they might, the students could not ignore the physical presence of an illuminated video screen. Only by physically turning away from the set, could they free themselves from being 'distracted' by it.

Consider how television affects our natural rhythms.

I worked for over 15 years in broadcast advertising. We made use of sophisticated systems for monitoring the popularity of television shows and commercials. The network television shows are very specifically formatted for commercials and the segments of 'program' time are usually no more than 10 minutes. We found that the 'industrial videos' we produced for corporations could not be any longer than 10 minutes before a break of some sort, because executives would become bored, restless and lose interest.

The clearest example of the power of television to control our 'time body' was the 'rating' system conducted by Chicago City Water Department employees. They simply measured the drop in water pressure at specific times of day or night. When these notes were compared with television logs, they showed which programs were the most 'popular', because viewers would not go to the toilet until a commercial break. The more toilet flushes, the greater the demand for water (and corresponding water-pressure drop.) This measurable drop in water pressure system-wide was logged and could be used to create an 'unofficial' rating of shows.

Television creates rhythms and patterns in our lives in other ways, too. From the broader television 'season' and 'premiers', we can also see social planning which reinforces viewing habits. How is it on Saturday morning for parents who try to get their kids away from cartoons?

Consider how the process of television—not the content—affects us psychologically.

Television has its own thought processes. As a writer, I can tell you that whoever watched what I had written was drawn into my thought processes. When television tries to present unadorned reality, it is boring. Have you ever watched the Senate or House debates? Did you long for someone to give you the edited 'highlights'? Logic and continuity—coherence—are not good television. Neil Postman's book, *Amusing Ourselves To Death*, goes into great detail on this point, and as a film and video writer, I recommend this book highly.[2]

Newscasts are discontinuous collections of stories with insufficient facts for forming judgments. In every-day life, this used to be called 'insanity.' And worse, the 'police/action' docu-dramas popular these days, are dressing fiction in fact's clothing, such fiction is 'based on fact' or 'appears to be fact'.

In order to communicate in a discontinuous, condensed atmosphere where logic is impossible, commercial advertisers seek to gain 'impact' for their 30-second commercials by focusing on the psychological or emotional needs of the viewer. They puff up our egos and tell us that if we buy their brands, we will be like this star or that. Or they present one-sided solutions to 'problems' that make use of stereotypes or clichés in order to communicate quickly. Or, even more outrageously, they have recently presented 'anti-commercial' commercials that say that the users of this or that product, are beyond being influenced by what they see on TV (including, of course, this commercial!) In the advertising which I helped create, we used humor, which proved to be one of the more powerful means of engaging a consumer.

The process of television imposes a reality on us that we are powerless to change or even discuss. We cannot argue with television. We cannot react or be active. That's not what television is for.

Consider what television does to the highest member of our being, our ego. Television does not ask us to be creative. It is a 'hot' medium which means that it does the 'action' for us. It asks us to be viewers only. Our job is to consume the story, program or commercial. Television gives us no time to assess, decide or act. It continues non-stop and we have no choice about what is coming at us unless we turn off the set. We take in someone else's decisions, creativity and work and are not asked or expected to do anything but watch.

And the more this happens, the more we want it to continue.

Television and addiction

Dr. Leonardo Fulgosi wrote a medical study in 1961 which enumerated dependency-causing 'drugs.' His ground-breaking research was the first to include television as a cause of addictive behavior. 'This study,' Dr. Fulgosi said, 'caused a storm.' Since then other researchers have accepted his thesis. A 1985 study in Berlin reordered Dr. Fulgosi's original listing of addiction-causing agents and listed the top three in Germany as: alcohol, nicotine and television. Fulgosi says that there is a growing body of evidence which shows that addictive behavior is now being seen as early as first grade.

Addictive agents affect the individual on different levels, causing physical or psychological dependency. The effect of these agents is the dimming of consciousness. Usually they cause pleasure for the addict who will also continually search for some new agent that can produce even greater pleasure.

'When a certain limit of television watching is reached, the phenomenon of addiction becomes stronger,' Fulgosi said. At a certain point, an addict will become 'void of consciousness' or confused and lose the ability for critical judgment. Fulgosi emphasized that addicts live in continual expectation: 'Television addicts believe that there is something "important" being broadcast which they should see and experience, and they very much regret it if they are not able to watch.'

Expectation is a powerfully motive force for us, but the key question is, who generates that expectation, where does it come from? Enthusiasm for life and action, an inner expectation or personal deeds, is one kind of process which should be encouraged in children. Television, in contrast, offers children no possibility of thinking for themselves, of doing anything about what is presented to them; it cleverly weaves in the writer's and/or producer's judgment and emotions.

Yet we do not really question what television does. In the motion picture Shane, Alan Ladd portrays a 'reformed' gun-fighter who, in the movie's turning-point, straps on his six-shooter and heads to town with a line that says something to the effect: 'A gun is a tool and neither good nor bad.' This is an argument applied to many technologies. But handguns can cause injury or death. One may disagree about the way technologies should be used, but this doesn't alter the fact that specific processes are built into each one—be that handgun or television.

Young children are particularly at risk from television due to the physical bombardment by images, which I have described. They have no physical defense against unconscious visual bombardment, which increases brain stimulation and causes stress and strain. Young children have also not experienced life fully enough to have a capacity for distinguishing between reality and television. They are therefore at risk of being unable to distinguish what is true.

Unplugging
Up from black—Scene III: Time 1984

When my son Jake went out to ride tricycles with his young friend, I unplugged our television set and moved it from the living room where it had always been part of the scene, and put it in an upstairs closet.

When Jake came home, he asked, 'What happened to the tee-vee?'

I told him that I had moved it to the upstairs closet and that we wouldn't watch so much any more. He threw a fit, whined and carried on for a while, complaining loudly about missing Mr. Rogers. In a while, he gathered up some toys and went out to play.

When the neighbors heard the news—which Jake probably communicated something to the effect: 'My dad won't let me watch tee-vee any more! He put our tee-vee in the upstairs closet!'—an amazing social process began.

'If Jake comes over to play, do you expect us to turn off our television?' We were interdependent with these families. Our neighbors, friends and families were in community together. We watched each other's children. We shared meals. We cared for each other. When we made a value shift in our family, there was a response.

My attitude was and has remained: my decision was my decision. We did not expect our friends or family to change their habits because of our change. We didn't ban television. We changed the process in our household. We de-emphasized television. I took it out of the living room and made it inconvenient for us to watch.

This meant that we had to be willing for our kids to learn to make choices. Sure, they were 'sucked into' the neighborhood television habits at times. On Saturday mornings, when we could be sure that Jake and brother or sister were at someone else's house 'playing' (read: watching television), we would call after an hour or so and ask the parents to send them home for chores. And, once home, the onus was on us to get them active and busy.

We rediscovered reading, story telling, conversation, games and many things to do. We actually began to look at the calendar and make crafts in advance. We prepared the house for festivals or holidays.

Scene IV: 1990—England

Teenage Mutant Ninja Turtles was the world-wide phenomenon of the moment. We were living in a small village south of London. We had no television, but my son Jake (then 12) and his sister and brother never really suffered. Everybody else around us had a television or two.

This was some five years after I unplugged our set. The kids were so busy with school work, soccer, scouting and their own projects, we didn't seem to have time for television if we had wanted it.

Media was changing. Video cassettes were getting widespread, and these (including some very violent subjects) were on offer at neighbors' homes, causing us concern. Many of our neighbors thought it was all right for young kids to watch anything they wanted.

We approached the situation by setting down special rules: Saturday was household chores day and the children cleaned their rooms and the common areas before they went out to play. This effectively cut Saturday morning in half.

Another rule we evolved: videos were not automatically 'okay.' After one or two incidents where our kids trusted a neighbor child's judgment and watched a video which caused some pretty bad dreams, they actually became leery of watching just anything at the neighbor's house. But they also didn't want to be impolite. So we gave them the option of calling home to check before watching a video. If we thought they might have bad dreams if they watched it, they could say we asked them to come home. It gave them options. Sometimes we disagreed with them and insisted that they find something else to do or come home.

Scene V: 1995

We have worked very hard to keep television from being a dominant force in our lives, especially when our kids were very small. It was actually no big deal.

Today, my kids are 16, 13 and 11. Watching a video is a weekend-only activity. My idea has been to approach watching of film/video historically, as the media itself has evolved. So, for some time now, but not in a regimented fashion, our one video per weekend has let us take a slow journey of exploration through different film genres—the silent movies, The Marx Brothers, Laurel & Hardy, Musical Comedies (a very big favorite!), and so forth.

But, just when you think you have things fairly well under control, along come pre-teen influences and Walkman, GameBoy, and CD Rock'n'roll.

Well, such are the ways of life!

Notes

[1] Dr. Leonardo Fulgosi. Notes from a lecture at Kimberton Waldorf School, 1993 and 1995. Written up by the author in the KWS Newsletter, 1993

[2] Neil Postman. *Amusing ourselves to death.*

[3] Jerry Mander. *Four arguments for the elimination of television.*

[4] Betty Staley. Article on television and the young child from Renewal.

Robert Hickman

Since writing the final draft of this article many wondrous changes have occurred. The campaign began on a small scale that laid a foundation for future growth. It has received tremendous support from educators and public officials. People and opportunities have appeared making progress possible. Most importantly, my confidence has grown owing to the awareness that there are spiritual forces supporting this initiative.

I have found inspiration from something Goethe wrote. His words aptly describe my experience once I made a commitment to follow through.

Until one is committed, there is hesitancy, the chance to draw back, always ineffectiveness. Concerning all acts of initiative (or creation), there is one elementary truth the ignorance of which kills countless ideas and splendid plans; that the moment one definitely commits oneself, then providence moves too.

All sorts of things occur to help one that would never otherwise have occurred. A whole stream of events issues from the decision, raising in one's favor all manner of unforeseen incidents and meetings and material assistance, which no man could have dreamed would have come his way.

From a small, one man operation, Home Together has grown into a statewide campaign in California that will begin during the season of Michaelmas 1996. I believe that other states will follow suit soon after.

A final thought sends a chilling warning and call to action. I believe the last hope for thwarting the growing menace of video lies in the hands of adults like myself who were born prior to 1960. We are the last generation to have early childhood experiences not wholly shaped by television. Many of us have memories of safe, nurturing neighborhoods, home and community-based recreational activities and involved parents that have instilled in our minds a video, media-free image that can be applied to the future. Collectively, we have the clout needed to promote public policies that support all families and children. By recognizing the problem, taking a stand, and acting on what we know to be true, the 'love and peace' generation will have the opportunity to change the world for the better. Home Together hopes to tap into that regenerative impulse.

16
Home Together: an initiative promoting alternatives to video media

When our home became TV-free over two years ago, it marked the beginning of a remarkable journey for me of personal growth, enlightenment and transformation. During my travels on this new path, I discovered the power television had on me, my family and other families. I also gained insights that guided the development of an innovative initiative aimed at alerting parents to the deleterious influences of the TV on their children and families.

My daughter Rose watched a lot of TV from an early age. As a preschooler, she watched hours of children's programming before school and when she got home. We didn't think that anything was wrong with it. My wife and I took pride in the belief that we were making decisions that took her needs into careful consideration. Although we both worked, we were almost always able to adjust our schedules so Rose would not have to spend a full day in childcare. However upon returning home, she would watch TV while last minute work was completed.

I now see that much of Rose's viewing was promoted for my convenience. It was easier to get my work done or even have time for myself if she was occupied. I now realize that I had become dependent on the TV as a baby-sitter, but I didn't want to believe it was hurting her.

Rose seemed to enjoy her programs and looked forward to them each day. On occasion I would join her. She could easily incorporate cartoon characters or songs into her play, which appeared imaginative and fun for her. Although she imitated what she saw on the TV, I wasn't aware of her being adversely affected. I chose to ignore the signs that she was watching too much. I noticed that it was difficult to pull her away; she would often whine or complain if I tried to set limits on the activity. She dictated the viewing schedule, but also became easily frightened by shows with violent or emotionally intense content which sometimes caused nightmares. I did not yet imagine how insidious the effects of television viewing had become.

When Rose entered kindergarten at the Waldorf School in San Diego, California, I began to hear about Waldorf Education's strong position on television. However, I couldn't see how it applied to my wonderful daughter since the kindergarten teacher spoke very highly of Rose's experience in the classroom. Her play seemed very creative, and she easily interacted with her peers.

First grade, on the other hand, proved to be a more difficult experience for Rose. I remember reacting with surprise when the teacher told us she watched too much TV. After the second warning, I began to feel annoyed. I couldn't believe, no I wouldn't believe, what she was saying—'short attention span for her age, imagination filled with images and songs from cartoons, restlessness'. She's not talking about my daughter! My denial was so entrenched that the teacher's warnings did not get my full attention for over a year.

I finally got the message after reading a Waldorf article on reading-readiness. I could not ignore the threat the TV was to Rose developing a love of reading. I became aware that her preference for watching TV was inhibiting her interest in reading. When that connection was made, disconnecting the cable was relatively easy. I found I could even live without it. What's more, I became aware of the effects of the TV on other children and families.

In my work as a marriage and family therapist, I began to see the TV's ruinous influences not only on children but also family relationships. One three year old 'hyperactive' child calmed down considerably when the mother began to strictly limit the amount of TV he watched. It was also common to see children acting up in the home while their parents watched TV to escape the pressures of work and family. Each scenario highlights the dysfunction commonly seen in many families and ignorance of a problem that is so pervasive in American society.

In many homes today, TV viewing has become the most commonly pursued activity. A *Time* survey revealed that 30% of American homes have three or more sets. Families spend less and less quality time together engaged in conversation and other activities that can be truly interactive, like mealtimes, game-playing, story-telling and outings. Consequently, children are not getting enough of the positive attention they need.

Life without TV has promoted remarkable changes within my family.

Rose has become an avid reader and good student. Both the quality and quantity of time Susan and I spend with each other and with Rose have increased dramatically. We have created a haven in a hectic media-filled world. There is ample time for reading alone and together, story telling, game playing and performing. My biggest fear—that Rose would not know how to entertain herself—turned out to be unfounded. Instead, we have experienced unbelievable enrichment and fulfillment. Moreover, I felt relieved that no lasting damage had been done.

About a year and a half after the cable was disconnected, another door of awareness was opened. I attended a lecture given by two outspoken critics of video media in Waldorf Education, Nancy Poer and her son, Colin. They gave a presentation on Virtual Reality that introduced me to the idea that excessive viewing of the various forms of video media influences how a child's brain develops and sets him or her up for learning and behavior problems. As I began to read literature on the TV and its effects, I came to understand the causes of Rose's classroom problems.

The presenters strongly recommended that I read the book *Endangered Minds: Why Children Don't Think and What We Can Do About It*. The author, Jane Healy, Ph.D., introduces the theory, taken from neurophysiological research, that brain development is shaped by a child's active, hands-on exploration of an enriched three-dimensional environment composed of interesting objects and familiar people. She argues that children who watch excessive amounts of TV are not having these enriched activities and are consequently not fully developing their cognitive and language capacities. Applying this to my family, I could see how fortunate we were to catch the problem early.

I also entered a period of great clarity. I began to understand how our culture has succumbed to the lure of the TV over the past 30 years and is now experiencing the consequences at unprecedented levels. I regularly see children entering school lacking the readiness skills for classroom learning. Moreover, parents and children are increasingly resorting to aggressive styles of communication and problem solving. They view violence and bullying in a passive and disengaged manner, tolerating and even condoning its destructive consequences. In my opinion, America's fixation with the TV has contributed to the rising tide of intellectual mediocrity, the rupturing of the social fabric of our communities and the weakening of family ties.

The estimated average daily viewing time by American children, three—seven hours, is shocking, but not a surprise. When I realized the pervasive denial of TV's influence in our society, I wanted to do something about it.

Rose's teacher had helped me to see what I was doing to her. Maybe there was something I could do to alert other parents.

For most of my adult life, I have had the belief that I can promote positive change. I have developed several innovative programs that produced benefit on a limited scale. I have introduced stimulating play experiences at an orphanage and a center for abused children. I also organized a mutual-support network at my church for members experiencing crisis in their lives. In addition, I developed an intervention-procedure that effectively promotes change and problem resolution in abusive families. Moreover, my work as a therapist has helped numerous families. So I never hesitated when I began thinking about solutions to the TV problem.

Many of my ideas on program development have come from flashes of insight. Intuition and inspiration are the dynamic result of the mind's struggle to find answers to compelling questions. In my mind, I can envision effective responses to problems I am concerned about. As I strained to find a solution, I discovered several related ideas within two *Time* articles that prompted the beginning of this process.

Research evidence indicates that excessive TV viewing causes attention-span problems. My clinical experience suggested that the TV is often part of a pattern of overstimulation in the home. So it bothered me when an article on 'Attention Deficit Disorder' did not mention the TV or other sources of environmental stimulation like diet and lifestyle-pace.

The second article was a commentary on the 25th anniversary of the first moon walk. The writer, an official in John Kennedy's administration, was reflecting on how the space-race captured the country's imagination and support. He then reflected on how there hasn't been a unifying movement since then and wondered if there ever would be another. Soon after reading this, I had the idea that has inspired me to help other parents, for a media awareness campaign, Home Together. This was modeled on the American Cancer Society's 'Great American Smokeout'. I have identified groups such as educators, preschool teachers, school nurses, pediatricians and parents who shared my concern about the TV's negative influences. We have formed a coalition that has identified ways to bring the following message to parents—your children may be watching too much TV and this activity may be preventing them from reaching their full social and intellectual potential.

Waldorf Education has the clearest and most accurate view of the problems TV causes children. Its unequivocal position has guided me as I develop and implement the campaign. Each school expresses its concerns to parents in a straight-forward manner. Teachers are aware of the signs of excessive viewing and are quick to talk to parents about the effects they see in the classroom. This approach helped my family and can be used by other educators and health care professionals who work with children and families.

For too long there has been little parents could do to avoid the effects of the media. Much attention has been given to content-related problems: if only there was less violence and sex and more quality programming for children, then the problem would disappear. Several organizations are calling for improved fare. On the other hand, little attention is paid to the process-related effects that cause the behavioral and cognitive changes commonly seen in heavy viewers: how are children being physically affected by the process of watching excessive TV? What causes parents to become dependent on the TV as a childrearing tool? It is the energy from this examination that is being harnessed and channelled by the initiative.

From the birth of Home Together, I have envisioned Waldorf schools playing an important role in raising these issues in their communities. I have developed a process that will serve as a model for other communities. With the assistance of the Association of Waldorf School of North America (AWSNA) an information packet has been sent to representatives of each school. They have also been offered assistance with organizing a campaign in their community.

Home Together is an on-going campaign. Parents and children are invited to participate in the campaign through their elementary schools and child-care centers. An array of classroom, school-wide and community events and activities create awareness about why we watch so much TV, what it does to us and what people did with their time before it was available. They also identify and plan activities to engage in during the annual TV-turn-off week. Thereafter, families are encouraged to continue to do without TV.

Experience from other TV-turn-off campaigns shows that some families will not choose to participate. If the effects of heavy TV use is apparent in any of these children, teachers are encouraged to begin a dialogue with the parents about the TV-related problems they are seeing in the classroom. Home Together offers written materials for parents that reinforce the teachers' concerns. When parents have accurate information they are able to make informed decisions on how to improve the quality of family life without TV.

Parental empowerment is the phrase that best describes the objectives of Home Together. My life changed when I realized that I could do something concrete to diminish TV's effects. My family's decision to remove it from our life is affirmed as I talk to more and more professionals and parents. I am convinced that other families will benefit as they move away from a TV-centered household to one in which parents and children regularly participate together in conversation and activities.

Deep down, I believe that most parents want what's best for their children. They want them to realize their fullest potential. I am convinced that when parents learn what the TV and other video media are doing to their children, many will do as I did. Once they are awakened from their TV-induced slumber, they will feel empowered to take the steps I did. And they will experience the rewards and benefits of their families sharing time at home, and becoming more creative together.

Carole Cole

Throughout my childhood I moved with my family from city to city, country to country and language to language. Among many other things, this gave me a golden opportunity to discover not only the diversity within humanity but also what is universal.

This quite naturally led to university studies in psychology and sociology and later graduate studies in education. After a brief experience teaching in special education, I spent four years in Saudi Arabia teaching multinational elementary school classes. I was also fortunate to be involved in establishing the first public girl schools in Saudi Arabia.

Upon returning to the United States I spent a year taking further courses in education and working with the Hmong and Mien refugee population in Oregon. I learned many things from these quiet, gentle people as they shared with me the riches of their oral traditions and thereby rekindled my interest in the story, their story.

In 1982 I moved to the San Francisco Bay Area. Over the next 10 years I co-founded a socio-economically diverse nursery class. Through participating in the struggles of these children who were often in difficult and painful circumstances, I began to have a more and more clear idea of what would be necessary in their education and environment to support their growth and make possible the full unfolding of their destiny. It was at this point that I, at long, last found Waldorf education. After taking the teacher training, I spent three years at the San Francisco Waldorf School. There I was able to give depth and breadth to the stories I had cherished for so many years through so many places. It was a joy to work with the fairy tales in combination with the many other healing aspects of the Waldorf Early Childhood work.

1994 brought the end of apartheid to South Africa. Camphill Hermanus, outside of Capetown, wrote that they would like to found a multiracial kindergarten for normal and handicapped children. Who could turn down such a request? The next two years were the most shattering, enlivening, exhausting and revealing years of my life. The massive amount of resistance to opening a multiracial kindergarten in the new South Africa was overcome by the miraculous appearance of children of all races who simply arrived— often on their own at the age of four. It was amazing, it was as if they were waiting for their school. Some walked down from the mountain, others came in on the farm transport and others were already a part of Camphill life. Some children were very hungry each day when they arrived. Many more wore the only clothes they owned—cleaned and pressed anew each evening.

Their play was fed by the rhythms of cooking, painting, modelling and the beauty of the surroundings. And we told stories, our own stories, fairy tales and country legends in four languages. The children acted out the rituals of life in their various communities.

Through their play they showed one another how life and death is experienced and so a deep multiracial exchange took place. We found our differences, we found what is universal. The grannies of the township declared the little Waldorf nursery a healing place for the many deep wounds. I believe this way of working with young children can heal the wounds in all places where there are wounded little ones—that is, everywhere.

The nursery is now taught by Xoliswa Mabel Saul, a Xhosa woman from the township. Xoliswa and I worked, trained and lived together for a year and a half. She now lives in Camphill with her two children.

I now coordinate the children's program at Raphael House, a family homeless shelter in San Francisco. I am confident that the stories and fairy tales will once again guide us through the challenges of finding who we are, honoring the differences and binding ourselves to one another through love, through the universal.

Before beginning that task I was fortunate enough to be asked to join in the celebration of the 8th grade graduation of the San Francisco Waldorf School.

What follows is the commencement address for the class of '96.

17
An eighth grade commencement

It is wonderful to be a part of this very special event. Over the past few weeks I have had the opportunity to spend a little time with the 8th grade. We have spoken about the importance and significance of fairy tales. These stories are found around the world; one hears very similar stories in Africa and in Asia. This is so because they are universal. The fairy tales deepen our experience of turning points in our lives. These young people are at a turning point. As Waldorf students they have had the possibility of living into these great inspirational, imaginative pictures that the fairy tales give. As young children they experience them through their will, acting them out, dancing and singing their way through them—and later through their feelings. Now at this time in their lives they will be asked more and more to sharpen their thinking. To be analytical but to do so with a thinking that has been warmed through the heart. It is this thinking, this heart-warmed thinking that will enable them to direct their will in a healthy way. Please accompany us as we look anew at the story of Briar Rose together with the question that was asked—what does the world need?

So this day is here quite suddenly and at last. I want to use the story you know of Briar Rose as a vessel for our exchange. This story is about the very journey you are now undertaking. Even in the oldest translations it is about events that take place in the 15th year of life. The year all of you are living now.

In the beginning of the story there is a king and a queen. You know in the fairy tales each character represents a part of ourselves. The king and the queen do not have a child but one day the frog tells them they will. Do you remember when frogs could speak? This is at the beginning when you were very young. The princess is born and there is a great celebration, a feast; just as the day when each of you were born. There was a great celebration and the wise women of the kingdom are invited and they bring gifts. There are thirteen wise women but only twelve are invited. Perhaps they are the wise women of the Zodiac. The wise women of the starry world, each one giving a particular gift—beauty, strength, modesty, humor. Each of you brought with you your gifts. Then the 13th wise woman arrives. She seeks a reckoning for not having been invited. It can be said she is life on earth; awakening us all with a start. She proclaims: In her 15th year the princess will prick her finger on a spindle and die. But the twelfth wise woman has not yet given her gift. She cannot take away the sentence but only soften it. She is our education, the love of our family and friends. Love can soften, alter our destiny because love can change and transform life. An eye for an eye is no longer the way, for that is how the whole world becomes blind. Instead we now go forward with a love filled with understanding. The world needs this.

So the princess, who represents the soul, will not die but go into a deep sleep. But the king does not accept this and he orders that every spinning wheel in the kingdom be burned. Still one cannot keep a destined meeting from happening. On her 15th birthday the princess is left alone in the castle. She finds her way to a tower, walks up the winding staircase, finds an old woman spinning, pricks her finger and falls into a deep sleep.

The time of childhood is over. The soul is now asleep and must be awakened. The prince comes. The prince is our actions, our deeds, our living in the world. Now the story gives a beautiful picture of the journey at this stage. The princess is asleep in the tower. The prince is on a quest to find the soul. It is a picture of the task at hand—the task is to answer the question: who am I?

The world needs people who are asking the question: who am I?

And now comes a difficult part. How will I find who I am, what is needed? Many princes, many attempts have been made to get through the thorny hedge into the castle but they have failed. Still the prince says: I am not afraid. I will see Briar Rose. I will find myself. There may be fear but the fear does not become me. Courage, courage for the truth is needed to go forward despite obstacles, and there are many obstacles to the truth in our time. We live in a culture that values packaging over substance and publicity over vision and service. It takes tremendous inner courage to stand by what one knows is true and right. The possibility of practicing courage is given in small ways every day; for example when, as so often happens, a good laugh is had at the expense of someone else. To stand up to this sometimes means being left out of the group or activity oneself. In fact there is often very little reward for doing the right thing. Do it anyway. The world needs people who will do it anyway. Out of this grows the courage that Martin Luther King spoke of—the courage for active non-violent resistance to evil.

Evil has many faces as do beauty, goodness and truth. To see the inner reality, the truth of people and things, what really is, this is your task.

How to go about finding the inner realities—the truth—is the great spiritual question. These inner realities exist but we have largely lost the way to them. You must find the way. I think the form of the tower where the princess is sleeping gives us a key to the way. The gesture of the tower is round. The prince must wind his way up the spiral (circular) steps within the round tower.

The story tells us we need to look at things from all sides, in all ways to find the inner reality. In our time, quick snappy answers are valued and the complexities are often ignored. But you know from your work at this school that to arrive at a full understanding you must look at it from all sides, paint it, sculpt it, see it in light, in shadow, through the heart, through thinking, through observation, through what others say, in quiet and in motion. The tower's roundness is a reminder of this necessity.

As you meet experiences: sex, drugs, what used to be rock and roll but now is perhaps performance art, you will be challenged by the many faces each will bear and you will have to look fully and deeply so that the inner reality, what is really true can speak to you, and it will speak to you. The sunrise and the moonrise will also wish to speak and they too require a depth of looking to be understood.

So the prince climbs the stairs and comes into the room and meets the princess. There is great joy. The most important meeting is the one with my true self. It will color all other meetings—and there will be many meetings. The whole world is waiting to meet you. To meet though is not simply to name something and go on, or only to see how it affects me and go on. A real meeting is only possible if we can be quiet enough, free enough to hear what the other brings. The other can be a poem or a tree or most important, another human being. What does the small child from the South African township have to say? If we truly meet we can understand her story and how her story lives in us—we can begin to know what has made her life the way it is and we can know what her life gives to us—not only what we give to her. A real meeting is an exchange, each party is enriched. You all have great capacities for real meeting. The world desperately needs real meetings.

Now we come near the end of the story, this part concerns later years, perhaps after high school. The prince and the princess go out into the kingdom. This is about relationships to the world and to others. Relationships require ongoing artistic work, but that's another story and not really yet the transition we are celebrating today. The great work is the true meeting. This time of your graduation and turning toward high school is an exciting, invigorating time of great highs and lows. You are ready.

What the world needs is each of you, with all that you bring, who you are, and who you are becoming. Congratulations. Go Well!

Kay Hoffman

I have never forgotten the agony and the ecstasy of being an adolescent. At fifteen I felt shaken by the certainty that although I must have a life task, I had no idea what it was. I remember the pain of searching for myself while being caught up in emotional upheavals. A teacher of mine pointed out to me that sensitivity can become a barrier to the world if it focuses one inward, that sensitivity becomes constructive when it is focused toward others. That thought has helped me as a parent, spouse and teacher.

I am grateful for the events and people leading me to work with adolescents and their parents. As is usually the case, I have learned more than I have taught. My own struggles have been those of a mother of four, married, then left to cope alone, single, then remarried with the task of recreating a new family. It has also been my particular destiny to stand first on one side of an experience and then on the other—to be a faculty spouse and then a teacher, first a parent of young ones and then suddenly a teacher of teenagers, a faculty member and then an administrator. The role I have valued most has been that of a mother because it is there I have been stretched the most. My children, and my students as well, require that I be sensitive to them rather than to the way they react upon me. That is a constant lesson in self-development.

18
Adolescence:
the agony and the ecstasy

When we adults think back to our own adolescence, that tumultuous time between childhood and adulthood, we must try to recall vividly what it was like for us—not necessarily so that we can remind the adolescents we know, of what we did and how tough things were back in our day—but so that we can be sensitive to what young people are experiencing. That is what working with adolescents is all about—developing the tact needed to be in touch with their lives and struggles.

At the onset of puberty, young people are cast out of paradise. The gates of childhood close behind them, leaving them bewildered and even afraid of what lies ahead. They are looking back with longing toward a simpler, more protected time. It is quite wrenching to see how hard it is for some of them to accept that they are suddenly changing in such a dramatic way and that they have to learn to live with it. Many times they admit, 'I don't want to grow up'. In addition, they have all kinds of sexual questions to face; the hormonal roller-coaster ride has begun. In the coming seven-year period they will make independent life steps toward their own future, no longer so closely connected with school or family. They will have to separate inwardly from home and family in order to become fully individual.

Yes, they do look backward to their childhood. At the same time, they are peering forward into the future, toward their true 'becoming'. They do so with anxiety. But we hope they also look forward with the assurance that the adults around them will offer the necessary guidance. Such supports help them to be strong enough to continue on the journey, and not to withdraw from the challenges into self destruction through eating disorders, violence, substance abuse, or suicide. Even those who take on the challenge must undergo/experience pain. No adult can honestly remember adolescence as a time of pure joy, unless there has been a major memory lapse. In the time of transition between childhood and adulthood, one's natural, God-given gifts suddenly change or even disappear, and must be relearned through conscious activity. A child who was harmonious, who moved with great grace, becomes awkward and uncertain, overwhelmed with apparent limitations. The words of an eighth grader express eloquently her feelings of homelessness:

> Young woman, you are a poem without meaning,
> A loom without warp, a shoe without a sole,
> A bird that flies, yet a bird that has fallen from heaven;
> An impossibility.[1]

According to Rudolf Steiner, at the onset of puberty the child's feeling life separates from the organs of the physical body so that the feeling life becomes individualized. What does this mean and what significance does that separation have for the parent and the teacher? It means that the teacher can no longer present lessons through pictures and expect to affect the feeling life of all children in the same way. Suddenly, the adolescent has a feeling life which is held separate from others, a secret to be protected. There is also a difference in the feeling life of boys and girls. Boys tend to protect their inner life in such a careful way that we cannot tell what they are feeling. They may be outwardly playing all kinds of pranks and apparently without a care yet inside they are very delicate. Girls, on the other hand—and bear in mind these are generalizations—exhibit their feelings as if they were on stage and in a daytime drama. This should not suggest that they are without their secrets, too, but they give more clues.

Both girls and boys feel pain and an extraordinary vulnerability. Their longing for the security of the spiritual home from which they have come is accompanied by a growing awareness of death. One adolescent expressed it thus:

> You see me stand before you,
>   shrouded in my cloak of sin.
> You cannot light those shadows,
>   nor see my face within.
> I am the King of Darkness, and
>   Death my other name.[2]

Another adolescent writes graphically about the awareness of her own isolation, separation from the world:

> Wake up from your tormented dreams, and stare frightened into the sneering shadows of your room. Grab for a stuffed bunny—a faded, raggedy, one-eyed remnant of a time when you were still ignorant to the meaning of loneliness. A poor substitute for a friend, it is cold...it lacks the warmth of human life. It does not hold onto you even when you've let go—it doesn't look into your soul with worried eyes, feeling helpless to your sorrow.[3]

They experience alienation. They exhibit negativity in a way reminiscent of the 'terrible twos,' when in order to learn something new about themselves they must push others away and examine at a distance what is happening around them. So what can we adults do when an adolescent is criticizing us and everything else? We can work with those feelings of antipathy, because they form the basis of our thinking, our separation of the one from the other. In the curriculum of the Waldorf High School students are asked to exercise the forces of antipathy. They are asked to make judgments in the world of ideas. That activity of judgment is a kind of 'feeling-thinking'. Adolescents are first asked to look at the world and make judgments about it. When the history teacher is talking about the legal system, he presents a particular case from the perspective of the prosecution. At the end of that presentation the ninth graders are already saying, 'He's guilty! He's guilty!' Then the teacher reveals the case for the defence and they are startled. They say, 'Aha!' Their capacity for judgment is being exercised in the realm of thinking, where it is appropriate.

But if the capacity for judging and antipathy falls into the realm of feeling, a hard-heartedness leading to anti-social behavior may result. If that antipathy holds sway in the adolescent's will life there is a desire for power. He or she may become aggressive and even destructive. Antipathy in the sphere of feeling and willing manifests as divisiveness and violence among adolescents (as well as adults). Adolescents must therefore be prepared and carefully guided if monumental pitfalls are to be avoided. They must be taught in the first years of the high school by means of imaginative presentations, which are also the basis of the Waldorf elementary school curriculum. This artistic approach can lead them through pictures, examples, and stories, into the realm of ideas, but only gradually. That is how young people meet the challenge of thinking, by being nourished through an interest and an investment in the world.

It is interesting to observe a class of ninth graders pushing and shoving their way, as ninth graders do, into a math class where their thinking is challenged, where they are being asked to really think. And as they begin to do so, they become more calm, more confident; in fact, it is clear that participation in the objectivity of thinking is very strengthening, or as one might say 'incarnating'. Rudolf Steiner tells us that the soul of an adolescent enters the gateway of the world through the mind. Through exercising judgments, an adolescent's thinking becomes more and more objective, more mature. By the age of 18, a young person has achieved the capacity for independent thinking. Up to that age, parents and teachers provide the models of clear thinking-processes which are imitated by adolescents. This does not mean that we tell them what to think, but that we must make our thinking-process clear so it can be followed. While avoiding sentimentality, we need to infuse everything we teach or 'model' with enthusiasm. Otherwise adolescents will have neither interest nor confidence in the world of ideas. Proof that the world we present to them is worth the effort needed to work in it and to understand it, is what we must give them. No matter how hard it may be, we must not be lazy or jaded or cynical. We must work as hard as we can to show them what challenges there are and how to find the tools needed to meet those challenges.

One of the benefits of working with adolescents is that they challenge us all the time, often in an unforgiving way. They remind us swiftly when we forget to give them what they need. It is indeed a humbling experience to be reminded of our failures and to be called upon to live up to our ideals, both for ourselves and for them.

So what is the best way to present ideas to adolescents? What is meant by imaginative teaching? Recently I attended a conference in which such questions were discussed. A veteran Waldorf teacher described a lesson in the ninth grade block on Art History. The purpose of the course is to give students a panorama of the evolution of consciousness from early times onward and to give their hungry souls an appreciation of beauty. This particular teacher spoke about working with Da Vinci's Last Supper. He spoke about the painting and its use of perspective for dramatic emphasis and continuity. He gave its historical background as well. But because of that painting's importance for our civilization, he also orchestrated an experience of the Last Supper for his students. After telling them about the disciples, he asked them to imagine they were present at the moment depicted in the painting; he invited them to take the positions of the various disciples in the tableau and to imitate their gestures. And then he asked the students to adopt a gesture which might have preceded the words 'And one of you will betray me,' and then change to gestures appropriate as a response to those words. The students not in the tableau at that time would watch how the various groups reacted to one another and make suggestions. The class worked on this exercise for part of each lesson, over a period of several lessons. What did such an exercise do? It gave the students the chance to imagine what was happening inwardly as well as outwardly. It gave them an imaginative picture with which to work. They could even identify temperaments with the disciples. Although it might seem excessive to spend so much time with one topic, yet paradoxically there is economy in it because the students gain so much; they live into an experience which they can translate into many other life situations. That, for me, is a fine example of awakening thinking through imaginative teaching.

If we as adults and teachers live up to this challenge, we can help distract the adolescents from preoccupation with their own inner pain. There exists a mighty danger of self-involvement and self-preoccupation. The more they dwell upon their inner pain—for indeed their 'soul separation' is painful, the less awake they are to the world. We must help them direct their thoughts and feelings elsewhere. Otherwise there is a danger that they will escape into the sexual preoccupations which take place when one's feelings descend into the sexual organs; such a descent leads to extreme sexual consciousness. Healthy social interaction is an antidote, which the adult can help provide.

All this guiding and advising and teaching cannot be done without humor. Adults must use humor appropriate for high school students. Why is this so vital? We all know how something funny releases the tension, the contraction in any situation. We laugh and there's a real release, and then something new can happen that would not have been possible before. We need that; they need that. Of course we have all been exposed to the humor of an eighth and ninth grader, which is almost exclusively sexual in nature. As you are driving them to and from their social engagements, you might encounter a very dangerous situation: the temptation to cover your ears, which unfortunately means taking your hands off the wheel!

Much that happens around adolescents can be read as symptom of inner chaos, the silent hurricane. We have to take care not to judge that what we see as words and acts is all that is happening; there is a more delicate inner life, protected carefully from all eyes but the most loving and accepting.

Darkness surrounds me like a thick blanket
    -but it does not comfort me.
It keeps me from the pain and fear of life
    -but it does not protect me.
I hide behind it, only looking out
    -but it does not shield me.
I am wearing one of many masks
    -but it does not fit me.

I met someone
    -she flipped the switch.
She has given me a lighter blanket
    -one that comforts rather than surrounds.
She has brought me fear and pain
    -but not from the outside, from within.
She sees inside of me
    -my shield has been penetrated.
My mask has fallen
    -it never did fit right.[4]

Beware of intruding into such a delicate space; only through our understanding can we penetrate the mask enough to let them know we know they carry an inner life, abundant in feeling.

The genius of Waldorf education presents the students with what they need to meet their own struggles. Another example of a ninth grade block of lessons is that of the history of drama, in which they study comedy and tragedy: the antithesis between fear and courage, love and hate—all exercises in contrasts, in dichotomy. Through such a study they can arrive at a new balance:

Where is the center?
I am pulled to one side and then the next
Constantly off balance
With fear each side regards me,
One with love, the other blindness.
I defend my ripped soul
And tie it firmly to my body.
There is not enough to give away evenly,
Therefore I exist, balanced, until I fall again.[5]

Often we meet adolescents struggling between sympathy and antipathy, overwhelmed with feelings of alienation from others. A typical example is that of a ninth grade girl who came as a new student to our Waldorf High School. Her mother described her as bright, having been in accelerated classes all through school. Until 7th grade she had been an excellent student. Then she lost interest in school and didn't want to do anything anymore. Her mother was baffled because all the tutoring, computer work, accelerated reading courses, summer seminars had not come to fruition. This is a common outcome when a preadolescent is asked to call upon powers of judgment and abstract thinking before her soul capacities are ripe enough to nourish her in those activities. At puberty there needs to be an inner fullness, not exhaustion, a wellspring from which the adolescent can begin to draw, but in the case of this student the well was prematurely depleted. That brings about an alienation: everything feels inaccessible because one does not have the forces to approach it. One is cut off. Strangely enough, a premature assertion of pseudo-individuality appears at the same time. 'I don't do French. I don't do math.' Underneath these assertions lies a longing to belong. It is therefore very important how such a situation is handled, how ways are found to satisfy such a longing—which may, of course, include cults, gangs, E-mail etc.

When a young person withdraws socially, adults must often take on the responsibility of establishing contact and teaching social skills otherwise learned through peer interaction, in an attempt to put a young person in touch with his own age-group. A young person whose early education has been overly intellectual will have made his way into the adult world prematurely. That is why such young people relate to adults better than to peers. It does not work to put him or her into a room with other students from a different background and expect them to work it out on their own. We have to offer special attention and nourishment in order to move from alienation to involvement.

Once an inner separation has occurred at puberty, a degree of healthy alienation we hope, the adolescent moves toward a synthesis in the feeling life. Young girls develop a mad crush on some lad. With a young boy it may be hero worship or a strong friendship with an older person. These are gestures of longing for a reunion, a spiritual reuniting. Many such relationships are not so much sexual as motivated by the need for a 'soul' mate or a person who can listen and answer questions about life. Of course other consequences can arise out of this intensity of feeling, but we applaud it as a prerequisite for making a commitment to future ideals, tasks, and people. Through an experience of sympathy, girls may be led toward the aesthetic, the beauty of the world and therefore toward the world of ideas. Boys may be led inwardly toward a resolution to take courage for doing the good in life. One eleventh grader writes sensitively about searching for ideals:

> It is a quiet, clean morning and
> The smoke rises off a quiet fire.
> It rolls, it folds, it spins, it twirls
> A dance whose movement grips you,
> Rolls you, folds you, spins you, twists you.
> A ballerina whose dance is pure and seductive,
> Whose body and whose movement are perfection
> Yet you grasp for her and she eludes you,
> The more you reach, the further you scatter
> Until she is gone and you are lost.[6]

Another eleventh grade student expresses the kind of courage a knight needed to face the battle:

> His lance splintered with a force that almost sent him
>   from his horse.
> Drawing his blade he saw his grievous predicament.
> He stood alone now with only sword and shield.
> His foes were far too numerous to count,
> Each with a blood lust in wild eyes.
> Time stood still as his thoughts wandered far from this
>   bloodstained field
> To a woman for whose love he now fought.[7]

It is so fortunate if friendship can ripen without early sexual activity, if one can at first experience love from afar. Later that is not the case and many high school relationships are sexual as well. Students can maintain only minimal interest in an English lesson, a science lab or a language class if sexual activity has become the overwhelming experience. People often express regret later at the toll such an intense experience can take socially and educationally during adolescence. 'I wish I had waited until later on.' Yet it is tricky for adults to work through such knots with young people without being old fashioned, judgmental or just plain insensitive. When must we merely watch what is unfolding and when must we interfere? We may perhaps be guided by bearing in mind how important this new stage of sympathy is in adolescent development.

Imitating a person one admires, and adopting a certain stance—even just to be noticed—is an important act of affirmation of the world. If adolescents have had a rich education worthy of imitation they will have a better sense for what is worthy of imitation, who is worthy of adulation; such imitation helps them to avoid trivialities and make their way playfully into the adult world.

> Ha ha! says he, and maliciously grins
> Those who work hard are more likely to win.
>
> Don't you want to succeed
> And get what's best?
> Don't you want to be better
> Than all the rest?
>
> Oh woe, says me
> And helplessly sigh
> Must I toil until I die?
>
> Buy the right shoes
> Get the right date
> Finish your homework
> Have you lost any weight?
>
> My ears catch his words
> Like paper to flame
> My innocence and joy
> Burn just the same.
>
> No no: no complaining
> Not a peep or a cry.
> If you don't smile,
> You'll never get by.
>
> But look, says I, at the glorious day
> My feet can't stay still
> They want to go play!

His laugh is like thunder
It rolls in my head
Like a child I wish
I was tucked safe in bed.

Now is not the time for fun
There are clothes to be bought
Work to be done.[8]

Our culture recognizes the need for children to be teenagers before becoming adults. During this transition we must also encourage the young people to look behind the facade they present, to find out who they really are and will become. That is a task worthy of our attention at any age.

When will you realize that a mirror simply reflects,
distorting, giving you an image of self
before your self exists?
I know you're seeing beauty,
but don't let it fool you into thinking it's truth.
Look inside to find your life
before you start living in a reflection.[9]

In order to help adolescents understand who they are and will become, adults must understand the underlying questions which the young people are unable to articulate. If we do not fathom their unspoken concerns, and then bring the questions to light, we will have failed and they will become bitter toward us because of it. This frightening responsibility: to hear the riddles posed and then work on them. Otherwise it is reminiscent of the joke about the child of five who asks his parent, 'Where did I come from?' The parent thinks, 'Oh, I've been waiting for this,' and explains (with diagrams) the whole cycle of reproduction. After the lengthy explanation the child answers, 'Oh, I just wanted to know whether I came from New York or Cincinnati.' The trick is understanding the question and knowing the context behind it. Otherwise a door shuts, communication stops.

Of course we should not expect that they will communicate with us about everything. They need to protect their space, to spend time preparing themselves for dawning adulthood. We must make sure there remains a lifeline, a crack in the door reflecting their ultimate confidence in adulthood, the world.

A big door stands between us
    it has for many years
I can't remember the last time it was opened
    or how it got shut.

The gray paint has begun to fade
    and is peeling along the sides.
There is a cobweb a spider just made
    around the insides.

The door is heavy
    I feel the weight on me suspended across my back
Just a small movement
    could cause it to crack.

So all these days peering through the keyhole
I wait for you to come
Turn the knob
    and set me free.[10]

The way in which we guide cannot be the same as it was when they were younger. For the younger child it was very important that teachers and parents knew what was needed and made the decisions; otherwise the child's force would be sapped by too early decision-making. 'Would you like to wear your brown coat or your red jacket, your yellow gloves or your blue mittens. Maple syrup or strawberry on your pancakes? The museum or the zoo?' How often have we heard such a grilling?

The child flourishes in the security provided by the authority of the adult. However, the adolescent will not tolerate the adult's authority to the same extent. It is a measure of growing independence. Strangely enough, though, a child who has had no restrictions and has made all his own decisions, becomes as an adolescent indecisive, afraid of making any decisions, a kind of recoiling from independence; or she becomes rebellious, having never developed confidence or respect for adult direction.

If an adolescent lacked the guidance of authority from both parents and teachers, he or she will need more authority than is usual in the transitional time from grade eight to ten. Equally harmful to an adolescent is authority from teachers and parents continuing rigidly throughout the high school years. That causes anger, restlessness, in some a kind of indifference, apathy, lack of confidence in others. Unfortunately, childrearing practices do not recognize when authority is required and why, as well as when authority must be relinquished and why. Independence is vital for maturity and it must be offered and won, hopefully not wrenched away from the adults.

> I will leave. I am a girl no longer
> And the candy you lured me with is no longer sweet,
> But has grown stale and hard.
> I am leaving
> And though you grapple with the line,
> The fish is tearing his bloody insides from the bait and hook
> I have left.
> And you will restrain me no longer.[11]

At the time of separation, when the gates of Paradise slam shut, the young person must find his identity, recognizing his selfhood, his own destiny. Once that occurs, he will gain power for his work, strength to develop his capacities and discernment to guide his work. That is the power of self-esteem. Self esteem comes through being challenged, being tested. She becomes stronger by trying something she is not even sure she can accomplish. If she fails, she tries again until she does succeed. Think of how false it is to face situations which are not truly challenging, where there is little possibility of failure; a kind of pre-digested trial.

> Our father, who has created all things; the sky, the earth and all...
> Why must I suffer so? All was well until the suffering came.
> Thou, whom I have served; whom I have served with heart
>   and soul,
> Must surely see I love thee; for all your creations I love thee.
> But will you let me love thee for thy mercy? for this I will pray
>   with heart and soul.
> Is it to punish; that you make my bones brittle?
> Is it to punish; that all I have left is the water beside my shack?
> No, oh no, that cannot be;
> You understand that even better than I.
> After long thought my thoughts have arrived at one reason only.
> To become close to you, even so close as I am to my bed at all time
> This suffering is to purify. A time when great knowledge comes
>   to life.
> For one must suffer to become truly wise.
> I thank thee.[12]

So we do stand back, hold our breath, watch, pray and try to understand the threads of their destiny as they weave their own tapestries. We rejoice in the failures which will teach more than the successes; and by doing so we let them know that we have confidence in them, in their potentials. We must allow them their interests (within reason) which may be unlike ours. We must not fall prey to the notions that exam results reveal the value or lack of value of the young person. We must develop realistic expectations and then allow for surprises (miracles?).

I have a personal abhorrence for parents or teachers brandishing their own childhood accomplishments or hardships in the face of the young person, either as an example or an unsolicited admonition. That denies their own separate identity. This is saying: 'You have to be like I was'. It also denies the different life and social circumstances which exist in each generation. A young person feels fervently attached to his own moment in time. Education will help him expand beyond those limits. This poem gives us a humorous picture of ourselves as adults. Perhaps it will encourage more sensitivity in all of us.

> 'When I was a boy I earned my money honestly.
> I fed the cows every night.
> At dinner I spoke only when I was spoken to
> if I misbehaved, Father thrashed me
> out back in the woodshed.'
> 'Sure. I bet you also walked uphill
> to and from school,' said the kid.[13]

For every step they take forward, we take a step backward. They have to 'go it alone'. They must go by the way of suffering and loneliness. Facing up to pain, they will survive it and know they will be able to do so again and again.

> I am the only one here.
> I am lost in this vastness,
> I am...alone.
>
> Too many times this feeling has devoured me,
> But I have survived.
> And I will survive.
> I will know that these feelings pass;
> Being alone does not last.[14]

They come to their time of crisis. Everything that was outward becomes inward. Then comes the question, 'What is my task, why am I here?' They come to a synthesis in their will. No longer merely feeling strongly about this or that, no longer merely thinking about it, but instead resolving upon carrying out their ideas. This occurs around the age of 18—the point when they are usually ready to go out into the world. It always makes me smile to think that by 18 they have become quite civilized and articulate and then—they leave. 'Life is like licking honey off a briar.'

What stance must we take as parents and teachers of young people? We must strive for objectivity and tolerance, avoiding sentimentality. If we are weeping with them and denouncing their lamentable fate, they cannot be certain there is an order and reason for their experiences. However, viewing their experiences with the calm objective eye of a scientist, and the flexible creative eye of an artist, we can help them come to an understanding too. Most difficult and most crucial of all is our example. We must try very hard to be objective about our own life experiences. Oh, there's the rub! A friend once warned me that parenthood is a path of initiation. I think she was right. It can and should be a change/challenge to one's self development. If we have achieved objectivity in the realm of thinking and tolerance in the realm of feeling, we will have accomplished a great deal, for their sakes as well as our own. As we all know, the 'finished' part of the adult does not affect the children as much as our perpetual striving; that is what will educate the younger generation, lending them the strength to persevere.

If I can stand on my own soap box, I would emphasize the importance of choosing our battles very carefully. Obviously, as adults we must guide and educate the next generation. But we have to choose what is really worth the fight. Do I say, 'O.K. Four earrings in one ear and a nose ring. That's enough!' Or do I bite my tongue? If I corrected everything I didn't agree with, I would spend all my time doing that and they would eventually tune me out anyway. We have to avoid expending all our energy on the small stuff and save our voice for the greater issues. That will demonstrate, better than words could express, that we have gained our own objectivity in thinking about them, their friends and their actions. What better examples than that for them to imitate as they mature!

Today's youth is faced with the dissolution of family life, often as a result of abandonment or divorce. This is a battlefield on which we all show our true colors. Do we rise to a mature level of communication with ex-spouses? Do we treat one another as fairly as we can possibly manage? There is no more tragic picture than the possibility, like King Solomon with the two mothers, of having a child rent in two between two adults whose will to have the child is stronger than their love of the child himself. It is tragic to see situations in which the children are forced to be mediators, to play adult roles. It is possible to watch the news about the horrors of war and famine in other parts of the world and imagine we have been spared; we must face the challenges of our own family and social circumstances with grace and determination to be truly human. Sometimes, if we remember we are doing this for their sake, we will succeed.

So we must realize what an important role we play as adults in the lives of adolescents; helping them do what Bernard Lievegood calls the main business of an adolescent: to stop being one. When a young person is well along in his or her teen years, we may notice a nascent individuality coming from the future. We cannot take credit for, or be held accountable for what he or she becomes. But we can recognize when he or she has arrived at clear and independent thinking, a balanced feeling life, and a purposeful direction toward the future. We can then say that he or she has survived adolescence, which Rudolf Steiner describes as a protracted illness, and has arrived at maturity immune to the disease.

Notes

The author and publishers would like to acknowledge and thank the following poets from the Green Meadow Waldorf School for the use of their poems in this chapter:

1.	Jennifer Mankoff '91	8.	Tara Stone '88
2.	Jocelyn Head '93	9.	Johanna Stoberock '88
3.	Crika Babar '91	10.	Laurie Newmark '91
4.	Kristine Trepte '92	11.	Deborah Blossom '89
5.	Alissa Tallman '90	12.	Bruce Muirhead '91
6.	Jeb Metric '89	13.	Peter Burger '89
7.	Shane McTarvey '91	14.	Deborah Friedman '85

J. Eva Nagel

Scene I:

9AM National Cathedral, Washington Waldorf Kindergarten, Feb. 1975

What is this realm of rosy, draped fabric, golden wood, and joyful children? I knew nothing about the philosophy but I knew I had come home. Returning to school at the University of Maryland, I had managed to design an independent study on Waldorf Education. I was determined to discover what this Rudolf Steiner guy said about teaching children. Well, I found out, and continued on to do my teacher training at Garden City.

Scene II

6pm, Congress Park in Saratoga Springs, NY; November 1984.

Three dozen small children are holding aloft the paper lanterns they have scrupulously created out of their colorful paintings. The shimmering light spills into the frigid night in the shape of stars and moons cut into the lantern sides. We wind along the paths singing, 'Laterne, Laterne, Sonne, Mond und Sterne, brenne auf mein Licht, brenne auf mein Licht, aber meine liebe Laterne nicht.'

Though the light outside is fading, the glow within can grow until the light returns to us once again. This is the Spring Hill Waldorf School. I began the school in 1980 with 12 nursery age students (one of them my own daughter) on the upper floor of Temple Sinai in Saratoga Springs.

Scene III

1:30 in the afternoon, a cafe in Boscastle-on-Sea, England; August 1989

A deep valley in Cornwall where our bikes are leaning against a wall. Time for a tea break. Sitting at an outdoor table with Avi who is three and Shanti nine, my husband Lee and I confer. We have become separated on this rather eccentric bike venture from 12 year old Kiara, 16 year old Moses, and his friend Adam. What to do?

Our objective is to trace King Arthur's path on bikes. We have fought plastic sword battles in every old castle and standing-stone site on our path. We rented these old clackers amid polite stares but conspicuous silence from a family-run bike repair shop. Nobody here seems to have heard of journeying by bike in this rather hilly region. We stop every afternoon in a sheep pasture, eat our bread and cheese, read and doze while Avi naps. Idyllic, indeed. But what happened to our other children? After an onslaught of uneasiness we continue on into Tintagel, our destination— King Arthur's birthplace. There in the central square are the three teenagers calmly eating a vegetable pastie, 'What took you so long?' they ask.

Thus began our passionate tradition of roughing it, which led us to family travel—Morocco, Turkey, India, and Mexico. What an education, what a bond, and what fun!

Scene IV

7:30pm, old building- 2nd floor, Downtown Saratoga: September 1993

A small room filled with curved back chairs and round tables, a stage with microphones up front, the smell of coffee and the musty air of years gone by. A room with 14 people hunched in close and earnest conversation. This is Caffe Lena, at 36 years old the oldest coffee house in the US and perhaps the most widely recognized. An important start for many in the acoustic music business: Bob Dylan, Arlo Guthrie, Nancy Griffith, Tom Paxton, Oddetta, Don McCleen, the litany marches on. Although started and solely run by Lena Spencer for almost 30 years, since her death in 1989 it has struggled to survive as a nonprofit establishment. I serve as the President of the board.

The music keeps singing.

Scene V
5pm Union Center Office, Schenectady, N.Y. December 1995

Eight teenage girls sit on pillows in a circle. One girl stands to name the voices that she hears speaking in her head. As she identifies them she selects different volunteers to represent each of the voices: the parents, her critical peers, her grades and school pressures, and such larger issues of concern as pollution and global warming with their devastating consequences. Now these voices are circling around her and calling out. 'You're stupid, you dress funny, you are not good enough, I don't trust you, you are going to die anyway.' The other girls can relate to this: no wonder they feel anxious and stressed. Where is the core voice, her own, the one which answers and quiets these others? That is the one we want to encourage.

These are clients from my psychotherapy practice.

Scene VI
8:30am our farmhouse in rural Saratoga Springs, 199_

I squat between the chard and the broccoli, weeding the herb circle. The sun, the bird calls, the rampant green surrounds me. On the two outer back walls of my house is the mural I finally completed. Here time stops; I am renewed. My home, my family; my guides, my compass. Three of our four children were born here.

Scene VII
6:15am, a small hotel in Siem Reap, Cambodia, October 1995

The phone rings, 'Jon here, you wanted to see a school. How soon can you be ready?' 'Give me 10 minutes' is my unhesitating response. Less than ten minutes later I am clinging tightly to Jon on the back of his motorbike as we bounce over the ruts and through the mud puddles to an outlying village.

I am in Cambodia on the invitation of a friend. We are here to assist an American Health Maintenance Organization in creating a medical partnership and service opportunity. Expecting simply to help with organization and communication I am surprised by a continuing request that I start a school in this radiant, but devastated country. Education is their best hope and they know it.

The wheels begin to turn; I can't help it. The good-hearted people, their overwhelming need and the lure of a challenge begin to wind their web around me. Soon there is funding, some assistance, Unesco backing, a growing array of contacts and connections, and an evolving plan.

These are simply scenes from a life; my life. My life is woven of many such vignettes. I offer them to you. Be gentle with them. God bless you.

19
A sacred ceremony

Choking sobs assault me from all directions. The air feels dense, shapes are only dimly perceivable. I am standing in the center of a dark basement surrounded on all sides by weeping teenagers. They are sitting two and three deep against pillows, huddled on laps, perched on tables, leaning against walls and knees. And still more arrive, walking down the stairs in twos and threes. They have rings in their noses and lips, shaved heads, jewelry made of screws, nuts and bolts. Their clothes are ripped, ragged, and layered. Hair runs the gamut from purple to orange to green and combinations thereof. Today they are hurting.

It is 5pm on a Monday evening in March. My husband, Lee, and I are in the center of this crowded basement that is filled with expectant silences and charged emotions. There is a sense of danger, of desperation. Why are we here? What could possibly connect this group?

Most of these young people are friends of a blond, cheerful, skateboarding 16-year-old boy. Three days ago, at dawn, he stood at the school flagpole and shot himself in the head.

Today is his funeral. These people, his friends and schoolmates cannot attend that funeral. The family will not allow them in. The school will not acknowledge the death for fear of copy-cat suicides. The message they are being given is 'Forget about the whole thing.' 'No way,' they scream, 'that is not possible.' They must find some way to acknowledge what happened.

Everyone in this room has been touched in some way by this boy and by his (and our) senseless tragedy. They have been churning all weekend with disbelief, horror, anger and loss. Where do they put it? How do they make sense of tragedy? How do they choose to go on? What about the many who have themselves considered suicide during long nights past and are afraid? Where are the available adults willing to talk about life and death ? Where are the wise elders ready to offer advice?

It seems to be up to us, a couple in our middle years with teenagers of our own and more questions than answers. Everyone in this room is looking to us. What do we hope to offer? How can we ease the pain, comfort the mourning, and reassure these many pairs of eyes now turned beseechingly in our direction?

This basement is the home of Rob, a middle-aged, unemployed artist. He saw the rebellious youths of the town struggling on a local street corner and invited them to gather and organize at his house. One day our 15 year old daughter informed me about a meeting at the home of this older man. 'Hmm, this sounds a little strange.' I reacted with suspicion. So I gave him a call. 'What's this I hear about meetings at your house (and who are you anyway)?' Before we finish the conversation I have offered my help. Pretty soon he has a regular group of 15 or 20 kids meeting twice a week. I bring food, guests, and a listening ear.

This continued in a quiet way for a couple of months. Then came the suicide. With nowhere else to go, knowing instinctively that they could not be alone, the students left school and headed to the dark but familiar place. They brought friends. Word spread; more showed up. This began early Friday morning after word of the death spread throughout the school. School officials allowed the students to go to the guidance office, but they could offer little comfort and no discussion or symbolic words. The adults were paralyzed by their own fears and rules. Unable to tolerate the gaping silence in the face of this soul-shaking event, the students began to leave the school in small, silent streams. On Monday, incensed by the school's refusal to even mark the boy's passing with a moment of silence, and their exclusion from the funeral, they cut class and headed to The Basement. By noon the numbers were growing. I received the call, 'What should we do?' After a quick consultation Lee and I announced that we could be there at 5 to conduct a ceremony. There was no formal way to announce this: word simply spread.

So here we are, with little time to prepare, no time to consult each other and no professional support, ready for...what?

The school administrator calls and asks if we would please have these kids back to normal so they do not play hooky tomorrow. The reporters from the local newspapers are elbowing their way in, and a few parents, looking bewildered and concerned, stand around the doorways.

We begin by taking a deep breath. Then we set some ground rules. Safety is a priority. We are here to support each other. When one person is speaking everyone else is listening. Then we explain what we are about to do, step by step. Lee says a few words of opening and prayer, and speaks about what happened. I sing a Native American song:

Ancient Mother, I hear you calling
Ancient Mother, I hear your song.
Ancient Mother, I hear your laughter.
Ancient Mother, I taste your tears.

It is a mournful, haunting melody. As the echo of the notes dies away the room is left in absolute, unbroken silence. Not a cough or a shuffle mars the empty, almost holy silence.

We set the main candle on a small table and say, 'This candle is Tommy. We ask you to come up, one at a time, light your candle from the main one and say a few words about Tommy, or how you are feeling, or simply stand in silence.' Rob, as their spokesman and trusted adult, lights Tommy's candle and speaks first.

I am wondering, 'Will they come up? Will they participate? What if no one responds? What if they hate the whole idea?' All these doubts are rumbling around in me even as the procession begins. In respectful order and stillness they step forward.

T. was so much fun
You left us too soon. Why'd you do it ?
I love you, man.
You were so beautiful. I miss you.
I didn't really know you but I wish I did.
Man, I know what you were thinking.
I'm so scared.
You could have asked us for help. Or run away...or something.
I won't forget you, buddy, you were my friend.

The room grows brighter...and brighter.

Tommy's girlfriend (who first heard the news over the loudspeaker at school) comes up to speak and collapses in paroxysms of hysterical sobbing. She is held and rocked and stroked by others as she returns to her place. There is an amoeba-like quality to this group, as if they are a single organism that gently thrusts out one unit from time to time and then gratefully receives it back into the whole. A few people come up and simply light a candle and stand in silence for a moment before being swallowed back by the group life force.

I look around the room: everyone is holding a candle. The dark room is glowing brightly but the despair is pulsating, pounding. What is this force we have unleashed? Do we know what we are doing? Can we keep these young, wounded souls from drowning in it? Can we turn the pain into healing?

Lee steps forward and asks everyone to look at the light all around them. 'This is your light. You have created it, together. It is Tommy's gift to you. Please blow out the candle but allow that light to penetrate through to your hearts. When you are feeling overwhelmed and hopeless think of that light and remember that you're not alone. Tommy's death will not be in vain because it has brought us together; it has given us a family where we can belong. It has given us a voice. I want everyone to stand up. Now reach out and be sure you are in contact with at least one other person. We have each other. We are not alone. We have formed a community.'

And then we began to sing. The words, the notes swelled as our voices were joined by almost 100 more:

> Amazing Grace, how sweet the sound
> That saved a soul like me.
> I once was lost, but now am found
> Was blind but now I see.

At last we blow out Tommy's candle. It has been snuffed out in the world and now in the basement. We are in darkness. There is silence broken only by a few sobs, an occasional sniffle. Silence.

There has been a shift here in this airless basement space. A group of random teenagers have changed. Yes, they are scarred and will never be as innocent again. But they have grown. There is a dignity, a pride in their mourning. Some will grow stronger, kinder, more compassionate. They will be heard. They will choose life, with its bumps and hard edges, and injustices. But LIFE all the same. That, in the end, is Tommy's true gift to us.

Sometimes it seems that we have all had it up to here with our adolescents. They are causing just *too much* trouble: too much violence, too much crime, too much sex, too much laziness, too much criticism, too much drugs, and too much suicide. They are responsible for conflict on our streets, in the classrooms, and in our living rooms. They have so many things, why are they complaining so loudly? I have heard parents refer to this time as the long, dark tunnel...and these were the optimists! Witness the jokes and rolled eyes at the mention of teenagers. Some of us cross the street to avoid them. Many would prefer to lock all twelve year olds in a distant warehouse and let them out at twenty. What a wonderful world it would be.

But would it really? What would a world without teenagers look like? It would be a passive, status quo, dying existence. It might at first seem peaceful, but would soon become boring and lifeless. Our world would lack the yeast, the juice. How would our creative bread rise and our pot of soup on the cauldron of life bubble up? Teens are the barometers of the world. They reflect the worst of us, the dark recesses, the narcissism, the decadence; yet hint at the best. If we learn how to read the barometer, and perhaps even how to adjust it, we will be doing the whole country a favor—not to mention calling a tentative truce in our own homes. We who are parents, teachers, counselors, friends, and relatives of teenagers (that includes just about all of us) must try to gain some perspective.

The body's sudden growth and eruption at adolescence is an outer metaphor of the powerful changes manifesting inwardly. The body is growing, erupting and changing, the mind is stretching and the morals, values and individually molded truths are trying to keep up. Adolescents are shaping their individual identities and values. No wonder this sometimes involves rejecting the family. They are searching for Truth. No wonder they are sometimes angry. They want the world to be just. No wonder they are sometimes discouraged. They think about death because they are evaluating life. 'Why was I born? What is the purpose of my life? Do I want to live?' They now see that life is filled with struggle. This is where we must be ready to step in and say 'Yes. It is hard. Here, take my hand and we will go forward into life.'

The struggle is good. It is the striving that creates strength and integrity, but it does not have to be alone, and we can sometimes offer a safety net.

In order to progress through this difficult phase the young person needs to feel a connection (through a person, a God, a sport, an animal, a cause) to the world. She must believe that there is a point, a meaning to the struggle, that she personally can make a difference—she matters. And that she belongs to something, a family, a community, a country. This is where we, as adults, enter the picture: we can be the contact. In *The Child's Changing Consciousness*, Rudolf Steiner says, 'Will the young people, as they enter life, find the right human contact in society?...Puberty is the right time to make the transition, leading the adolescent into the realities of outer life. And that those elements will have to play more and more into...life that, in a higher sense, will make the human individual, as a being of body, soul, and spirit, a helpful and useful member of society.'

How can we help these teenagers receive the crucial elements? What are these elements Steiner speaks of? Adolescents are the prophets, the ones who force us to re-examine our ideals. They make us uncomfortable.

Gratitude and Love of the early years give rise to Duty, which I also define as Purpose. As a good mother I would never let my child go without a meal. God forbid she should be hungry or wanting. Yet here are teenagers all around me who are starving for spiritual nourishment, for Direction. Duty is taken up out of a commitment to Purpose. 'I know where I am going and what I must do to get there or at least to find out.' The teenager who can say this (even occasionally) is going to be all right.

Imagine my excitement when I read Steiner's words in *The Younger Generation* spoken about the needs of youth 73 years ago: 'The fundamental question is: how can original, firsthand experience, spiritual experience, be generated in the soul?'

In old cultures, the youth were given a vision quest, a rite of passage. Today just living the years into young adulthood is the rite of passage. The tests and suffering and terrors are there. The guiding vessel of the wise uncle/aunt, grandparent, midwife, Shaman is missing. They need that spiritual experience now more than ever.

You and I can be the elders. It doesn't require a major leap. It is rather the guiding force of the lighthouse which stands tall and bright amidst the swirling water. By honoring the past, working in the present, while looking with them to the future we will bring the work of the angelic world into consciousness. Pay attention. It is happening.

Again from *The Younger Generation*, 'Modern youth...is demanding to be awakened in its consciousness. And this can only happen through the Spirit, can only happen if the Spirit actually sends its sparks into the communities people are seeking for today.'

Let us take our place in the community for these young people. If we reach back to the strength and wisdom of our Elders in the past and shape it to the needs of today we will find the way to do the right thing. We are talking about mighty transformation. We're on our way to the future. And what a fantastic journey it is! Stay open, laugh a lot, pray when possible, hold hands. Here we go!

20
A test of love
J. Eva Nagel

Let me start right off by confessing: my son lives on the streets.

I don't tell this to just anyone. I feel her out first. In response to a casual inquiry about him, I usually say, ' He's doing great.' If pressed further I say, 'He's travelling.' No-one can fault that, after all; many restless young men spend a year roaming before they settle down and go to college. Get it out of their system, sow their wild oats, find themselves...you know. But questioners may remember this is his second year out of school. How many wild oats has he got?

And the interrogators drop away. They may be too busy with their own life dramas. The facts may not be that interesting. Or perhaps they feel some great darkness lurking behind the answers, a darkness they're afraid to step into. It'd be like asking a depressed person 'How are you?'. Do you have an hour to listen? Do you really want to know?

But some people are tenacious. 'Where is he?' they want to know. Fast paced scenes from *Around the World in Eighty Days* have popped into their minds; exotic locales, wild beasts, babbling foreign languages...a tale of intrigue is on the tip of my tongue, but for some reason I am compelled to tell the truth, so I answer, 'New York City.' I hear the wheels turning. How long can you be travelling in New York City? There's a lot of sights, a few good day-trips, some excellent restaurants, but, hey, two weeks ought to do it. Once I admit my son is living in New York City, a huge writhing can of worms gapes open: 'What's he doing? Where's he living? How is he supporting himself?' And then the oozing, 'Why?'

My son is a street person.

I am a failure as a parent.

That's the shocked response I glimpse before it's stuffed away. That's what they're really thinking when they avoid the subject. It's as if my son were dead. That's what I think sometimes, and the thought gnaws inside me despite my efforts to believe, *It ain't so.*

Let's take a look at the sociological data. The studies all concur: street kids come from: 1. divorced, 2. alcoholic, 3. abusive, 4. unloving, 5. uneducated, families. That's the classic profile, but it's no portrait of my son. For a moment let's examine these one at a time.

1. My husband Lee and I, have, amazingly enough, been married (and frequently in love!) for 21 years.

2. We've never enjoyed alcohol, and despite my genteel attempts to cultivate the pleasure of a glass of wine now and then, I must admit, the stuff puts me to sleep.

3. I scolded my son and sent him to his room on occasion, even grounded him once or twice. But he was an easy child and in our family yelling is something you do on the sidelines of a hockey game (we even have a short tune any family member can whistle in order to get someone's attention and avoid yelling in public places). I'm not defending it; a good scream would at times be a relief, but we tend to talk things out.

4. Unloved? This child has been adored, admired, enjoyed, and cherished since he was conceived. To this day he lights up a room when he walks in. There is an energy, a zest for life that can't be missed. At three, he dressed as Curly and sang the entire score of *Oklahoma*. At 16 he conducted elaborate plastic sword duels with his little brother amidst the ruins of King Arthur's castle. Passing tourists would give them a cheering ovation after the death scene. So please don't say it's lack of love. I did not do everything right each day of those 19 years, but love him? That I did.

5. Which leaves only education on our sociological checklist. Education runs on both sides of the family. My masters degree will soon be replaced by a doctorate. His dad has a PhD. Our family tree is practically sprouting with doctors, lawyers, and MBA's. This kid's so smart his high school teachers still talk about him.

Having eliminated all the usual paradigms of homelessness, 'mentally unbalanced' is the only label left. He must be crazy, right? Well, I wish you could talk to him. He's the most rational, common sense, understanding person you could hope to meet.

We've got to revise our definition. What would inspire my beloved son to choose a life on the streets? He is not roaming the streets homeless or living out of a cardboard box. He is a squatter. He has joined together with others to occupy an abandoned building that is city owned. In large cities there are plenty of these eye-sores. They take up residency, begin repairs and avoid authorities. Others link in and soon there is a community of sorts with rules, guidelines for joining, and extended support from older, neighboring squats. I wish I could tell you his is a rare case. But since I've been forced to become an expert on the subject, take my word for it: he is *not* alone. There are teenagers from all over this country choosing a similar life. Your child might very well be next.

I have talked to many of them. After overcoming my initial reaction to body piercings, ripped clothes and dyed or shaved hair, I find them to be kind, intelligent, thoughtful people. They are searching for something.

You see, my son has *chosen* this life. He is not there because he's failed, he's there because he's succeeded, as Don Juan says, ' in finding a path with heart.' It is not a last resort, a desperate attempt to survive, a dead end. He wants to be exactly where he is and he's happy about it. Nor did he do this out of a romanticized notion of what it would be like. He's tried it out in NYC, San Francisco, St. Thomas, and Seattle. He knows the hunger, the fear, the loneliness, the violence, the disease. His is not a romantic ideal; it's an informed choice.

When my understanding has evolved to this point, I face the next hurdle. It goes something like this: It would be all right for him to live like that (with those people, in that neighborhood) if he were planning to write a book or article, make a film, or organize assistance for the homeless. In the beginning I actually imagined that this was the plan. I had it all worked out. My son the social activist, the do-gooder.

It turns out this brilliant plan of action existed only in my imagination. My son did not go to NYC to *help* those 'poor people'. NO. He just wants to be, to live. In fact, he claims, any other way would be a form of manipulation, taking advantage of street people, standing apart and observing. He is living his life. Though he comes home for occasional visits he does not ask us for any money or help.

Day after day I ask myself 'Why?'. Why did he end up in this place, this predicament? I will never be able to fully understand or accept it. Of me it requires only surrender. I can not change it or approve it, or even explain it. Yet it doesn't go away. That is my child out there.

After my initial horror, I begin to comprehend some of the appeal of the life he has chosen. It is a day-to-day existence. The people choosing this way of life do not worry about career goals, or what the neighbors will think, or making their mark in the world, or paying bills, or even about entertainment. They focus on the basics of existence: How are you going to eat today? Where will you sleep? How will you keep warm? Where will you relieve yourself? These are questions which inspire considerable passion.

They take up a major portion of each day. After these are settled you are free to pursue your own thoughts and daydreams. No-one can claim a piece of them. There is, indeed, a freedom in the squats. The price is danger, discomfort, bugs, and ill health; the street beats you up and ages you quickly. But the freedom is there. It is not pretty or pastel or romantic, but beneath the dirt and the desperation I can sometimes see it through the eyes of my son.

A strong sense of community exists with these people. There are a few categories: the down-and-out families that are there as a last option. The drug dealers and users. The desperate runaways. And then there are the ones like my son who are there by choice. Some of these are old timers, others are new to the life. They have organized their places of shelter into a network of communication that could be a model for any revolutionary group. Within ten minutes a hundred people can be gathered in support. There is an excitement and purpose in their rejection of a world order they consider to be decadent and off target. No-one here is abusing the earth, or taking advantage of people, or accumulating wealth. They may be more sure of what they do not want than what they do, but at least they do no harm. They live in the buildings abandoned by society, eat the food our civilization throws out in vast quantities, and scrounge the clothing and comforts of life from the discarded piles on the curbstone. Books on revolution and philosophy are passed around and discussed late into the night. After all, no alarm clock rules these lives. They offer each other protection and help, often giving their only dollar away to one whose need is greater. A pride grows in their ability to survive. Perhaps if we dare to listen to them they are telling us something about the disfunction in this nation of unhappy, out-of-control, futile consumers.

Before I become so convincing that you move to the nearest city with only the clothes on your back, let me assure you, I have considered the drawbacks. On those long nights when fear grabs hold of me and will not let go, I see them clearly. I imagine all those guns in NYC. I see berserk crackheads or aggressive dealers pursuing my innocent child. I picture him caught in crossfire or poking his head in the wrong dumpster or simply ticking off some hothead. I see him cold and shivering with no respite. I see him dirty and lice-covered (and this one I'm not just imagining). I see him sick, his immune system weakened and all those monsters—AIDS, Hepatitis, Tuberculosis—ready to ambush him. I see him falling in love and wanting to settle down but afraid and unprepared for a ' normal' life. There are times I long to brag about him to acquaintances...but briefly, what can I say? I see these things, and for all my attempts at understanding, I am simply a frightened mother.

What is the price he will pay for this lifestyle? I don't know, though I try to guess. I do know that he is young and his goals will change (though the college graduate we once imagined is a dream long deferred). I am much more clear about my cost: the nightmares of imagined dread and the endless days of worry, the incessant wondering about what we could have done differently. The hesitant greeting I give him while I examine the sores on his face with a growing dread. Yet is this so different from any parent? I may think my case is more dramatic and extreme, but in the end we mothers all worry and pray for our children whatever their age or whereabouts. Our inability to insure their safety and happiness never changes the longing.

Yes, there is a disquieting mix of embarrassed chagrin when I am questioned. I know I am about to advertise myself as a failed parent. And sometimes I believe that is true. Yet there is also my pride. This handsome, vibrant young man to whom I gave birth nineteen years ago has found the courage to take control of his life. He is on a quest. It is no less a search than the one for the Holy Grail even if its goal is not a golden chalice. And like Perceval, or Thomas Merton, living in Christ-like simplicity could mature into true insight and wisdom. He is searching, learning, seeking. He is questioning everything. What will be his future? What will be the future of his world? In some ways he has travelled to the last remaining frontier. In the old days he might have gone west or searched for a river's source; today the cities have become our wilderness. Perhaps he, more than I in my frenetic, practical life, has found what it is all about. Who can say for sure? Perhaps it is, after all, a chalice of gold he seeks.

I do know that when he comes home to visit I welcome him with open arms. The prodigal son. That is all a mother can do. That and feed him!

Perhaps I am a failure. But for now I hope you will withhold judgement; the evidence is not all in. So listen, now that I have confessed, you will better understand my request. If you pass a strange, scrungy kid on the street wherever you might be, don't look away or grimace in disgust. Look him in the eyes, talk to him, at least give him a greeting—he might be my son.

Olivia Stokes Dreier

I live on a small farm outside of Amherst, Massachusetts with my husband
and two teenage boys and work as a psychotherapist at a local medical
clinic. I did my graduate training in clinical social work when my boys were
small and worked first at a university mental health center. My husband
and I also helped start the Hartsbrook Waldorf School in nearby Hadley.
Our eldest was in the first class, and we have remained very involved as
trustees. In my practice I work with adults, teenagers, couples, and families
on a wide range of issues, and, as Amherst is a university town, I have the
opportunity to work with people from all over the world. I find my work

deeply engaging. While humbling and at times difficult, it is also a real privilege to accompany people as they grapple with life's challenges.

When the call came for chapters, I felt strongly about doing something on body image and eating disorders. As a therapist, I have come to feel something is seriously harmful in the current pressure on women to be thin. It deeply affects self esteem and confidence, undermining our capacity to act powerfully in the world. Teenagers, of course, are the most vulnerable.

Throughout my life, finding my identity as a woman in the world has been an important theme. As a member of the first class of undergraduate women at Yale University, I was, at 18, acutely aware of receiving mixed messages; everything was now to be possible for women, but the old stereotypes still held sway. In these last years, finding a balance between actively nurturing home life and developing my professional work has been a challenge, and trying to integrate these into a coherent sense of self, a conundrum!

I am delighted to be part of a book encouraging women to articulate and reflect upon their experience, and I know how difficult it can be to find the confidence to do so.

21
Why are they starving themselves?

Girls' adolescent development, body image, and eating disorders

Bean lean, slender as the night, narrow as an arrow, pencil thin, get the point?

(Advertisement from Bloomingdale's Department Store)

When you are so unhappy and you don't know how to accomplish anything, then to have control over your body becomes a supreme accomplishment. You make out of your body your very own kingdom where you are the tyrant, the absolute dictator.

(Words of a young anorexic)[1]

Clad in baggy jeans and T shirt, lank limbs draped over my office chair, Heather describes a shrinking world. Six months ago she was happily engaged in her teenage life, confident, a star athlete, a good student, busy with friends and quite content with her strong muscular body. When a fellow athlete returned from summer vacation 30 pounds lighter, Heather began to compare herself unfavorably and to panic about her size. For a while, she enjoyed the feeling of mastery and control as she ate only a bowl of yogurt for breakfast and an apple for lunch. Now 40 pounds lighter, mastery has long since been displaced by a host of obsessional fears. Whenever she eats, she is convinced that her stomach protrudes, and if she crosses her now meager thighs, she is disgusted by what she regards as folds of fat. Food at meals is carefully weighed, but subsequent bouts of hunger lead to nibbling which fills her with a sense of failure and self-loathing. She still forces herself to take her daily run, but feels weak with exhaustion. At school, she can no longer concentrate, and is, instead, preoccupied with comparing herself to other girls who appear thinner. Heather has developed anorexia, and as her body has shrunk, so has her internal world: from a lively brew of adolescent query to a narrow focus on body size and food.

While Heather's problems have become quite severe, most teenage girls have at least some of the same concerns. In a recent discussion group with high school students, many reported to me that they no longer know what is normal eating or normal body size. Most feel embarrassed to be observed eating. To eat heartily is as uncool as wearing the wrong outfit. For adolescent girls of the 1990's, body size has become perhaps the most important measure of their self-worth as they struggle to conform to an impossibly thin ideal of female beauty. This struggle has lead to a host of problems, including the loss of a natural relationship to eating, the tendency to develop a negative self-image, and an alarming rise in the number of adolescent eating disorders. Anorexia, self-starvation to the point of dangerous weight loss, and bulimia, a compulsion to binge eat and then purge, were rare psychiatric disorders before 1960; now they are commonplace. Once established, they are difficult to treat and very harmful both to the physical organism and the psyche.

As a psychotherapist, I have long been troubled by the fact that most of the women I see, no matter what issues bring them to my door, no matter how successful they are in their careers, are, at heart, deeply disturbed by what they regard as imperfections in their appearance. Though opportunities have grown enormously, women continue to feel they will be judged by their looks rather than their actions. At the same time, the modern Western image of feminine beauty, tall, long-limbed, and rail thin is unattainable for most body types. While I am concerned for all women, I am especially concerned for our daughters, as they traverse the perils of adolescence, trying on identities for size and seeking models and images as beacons. Why our image of feminine beauty has become hollow-cheeked, gaunt, and emaciated and how this image affects girls' development are questions in need of our attention.

Girls' adolescent development and body image

Adolescence has always been characterized by tremendous inner upheaval. Looking at emotional development during this phase may shed light on why girls are so deeply affected by today's strange standards of beauty. Developmental psychologists have long observed that with sexual maturity comes a new experience of one's separateness and with it a new consciousness of one's own internal world. Rudolf Steiner describes the process as a severing of the child's natural unconscious link to the world of spirit, leading to the birth of true subjectivity.[2] No longer feeling simply a part of things, the adolescent awakens to his or her own inner life. This experience of increased independence allows for a new objectivity in thinking and the capacity for abstraction, but also leads to the intensification and extremes of feeling so apparent in these stormy years.

Though the adolescent is acutely aware of feelings, he or she has not yet developed a coherent sense of the self who feels or the capacity to guide and form feelings with the force of his or her own personality. It is as though one is suddenly aware of being at sea in one's own boat, but not yet aware that one has the capacity to steer. There is also a fragility and delicacy to these first nascent stirrings of self which lead to extreme self-consciousness and, at times, a defensive glaze of insecurity and confusion, especially if not met with adequate encouragement and affirmation. Unable to stand fully alone, the adolescent looks for some external means of self-definition; peer groups, clothing styles, and appearance all become important props. For an adolescent, the experience of self is 'I am as others see me,' making her extremely vulnerable to the opinions and norms of peers, whom she assumes are always observing and judging her.

When we observe adolescent girls, it is clear they revel in their newly enriched life of feeling. They are astute, sensitive observers of the nuances of human relationships, and can spend hours discussing intricate shades of feeling. Steiner describes the adolescent girl as more at home in her subjective life than boys, as her ego or sense of self does not penetrate as fully into her physical body.[3] The adolescent boy is more apt to experience himself through what he does rather than how he feels, and his emotional life often remains a confusing mystery to him. While he may be more concerned with his power to affect the physical world, adolescent girls are especially attuned to their affect on other people. Naturally drawn to aesthetics and self-expression, a teenage girl's 'look' or presentation becomes an especially important medium for experimenting with different identities.

Unfortunately, today's teenage girls and boys embark on their rudderless exploration of identities with little guidance and in a minefield of dangerous influences. As psychologist David Elkind has eloquently described in his book, *All Grown Up and No Place to Go*, today's world offers few protected spaces for measured, controlled development into adult life. Stress, over stimulation, early exposure to sex, alcohol, and drugs, parental and cultural confusion over values, the absence of any kinds of rites of passage, and exhortations to be anything you want can all lead to what he calls, a 'patchwork sense of self', rather than a coherently integrated one. This lack of defined values or meaningful rituals surrounding the process of coming of age is particularly damaging to adolescents as they are natural idealists. Steiner has described the development of ideals in adolescence as the building of the scaffolding of inner life, as essential as bones to the structure of the physical body.[4] If not adequately fed, this idealism can flip into the kind of nihilism and despair one senses in so many teenagers today, dressed in black, as though in mourning, bodies heavily pierced, listening to dark lyrics.

With their thirst for aesthetic images and their heightened sensitivity to social expectations, teenage girls may be especially vulnerable to the confusion of the culture and especially at risk in finding their way. Recently, increasing attention is being paid to their plight. Psychologist, Carol Gilligan, in her studies of school age and teenage girls, observes that as girls reach adolescence today, their budding individuality seems to go underground, masked by excruciating self-consciousness and loss of confidence.[5] IQ scores and competence in math and science plummet, while preadolescent tomboyishness, spunk, avid interests and hobbies, and grand dreams for the future all but disappear. Gilligan's interviews with preadolescent girls sparkle with imagination and lucidity, but with young adolescents are characterized by vagueness and a refrain of 'I don't know.' Rather than delighting in self-expression as they explore their budding sense of self, these girls seem to have lost their voice. Mary Pipher, author of *Reviving Ophelia: Saving the Selves of Adolescent Girls,* and Gilligan both note that teenage girls turn their acute powers of observation to reading social and cultural cues to determine what is expected of them; these cues are, at best, extremely confusing. On the one hand, girls hear that for women today there are no barriers, that they have equal opportunities, that they should compete academically and train for significant careers. On the other hand, the traditional social prescriptions for women to be nice, cheerful, not too competitive or aggressive, and above all attractive are still just as strong. Girls are surrounded by media that emphasize a women's sexual role above all else, advertisements that use women's bodies to sell everything from toothpaste to cars, and teen magazines that affirm the old stereotypes. Pipher and Gilligan suggest that girls develop a kind of false self to meet perceived social expectations at the expense of hiding their competence and disowning more authentic thoughts and feelings.[6] This results in confusion, a crisis of confidence and a greatly impoverished sense of possibility.

Modern Western culture presents both teenage boys and girls with numerous challenges, but they are affected differently. Teenage boys inwardly long to test their power in the physical world, but finding few venues, may instead be diverted into a kind of obsessive engagement with spectator sports, violent video and computer games, and action movies. Teenage girls, inwardly seeking an aesthetic ideal of beauty in all its manifestations, are caught by a culture obsessed with women's looks, with beauty that is skin deep, and with the insistence that what is beautiful is flesh which hugs the bone.

At puberty, it is natural and biologically necessary for girls to greatly increase their body fat. Fat gives the female body its contours and is the location for the production of estrogen which governs the reproductive cycle. If these layers of fat are depleted, ovulation and menstruation cease. And yet, just as the adolescent is beginning to inhabit the fully developed female form, she is taught to regard it as fat and ugly, and the endless diet, a rather sorry substitute for a rite of passage, begins. My teenage sons eat with extraordinary appetite and are constantly trying to gain weight. They take pleasure in the growth of their bodies. Increased bulk and muscle mass clearly increase their sense of power in the world, giving a slight swagger to their stride. But the teenage girls in my practice are afraid to eat and afraid to develop curves. Feeling adrift and confused by the numerous, but ill defined options that lay before them, they focus on their bodies as a kind of anchor. Desperate to meet expectations and to find something within their control, they seek solace in the exactitude of the calibrations of the scale and much of their energy is spent trying to achieve 'the look.'

Evolving images of beauty

The adolescent girl encounters few living models of the impossibly thin 'look' she is to achieve, but is virtually swamped with images of it from the media. This starved, bone thin, practically prepubescent body is plastered across billboards and displayed in the sharp, angular mannequins of store windows. It fills the pages of every fashion magazine and crops up in virtually all television and magazine advertising no matter what product is being sold. The average teenager is probably absorbing dozens of such images daily, and always they are associated with glamour, success, and popularity. Unfortunately, our teenagers do not realize this starved look has not always connoted beauty, but is, in fact, a rather odd, modern aberration. The story of its evolution is very revealing of our current confusion over the place of femininity in our world and the impossible pressures driving so many adolescents towards eating disorders.

In most cultures throughout most of time, feminine beauty has been associated with a plump, full-figured form. The history of art until the turn of the 20th century indicates changing styles in the depiction of the female form, but it is nearly always portrayed as robust and often resplendent in curves and fleshiness. In early Neolithic figurines of Venus with exaggerated breasts and bellies, the association of fat with fertility is evident. Until recently throughout Eastern and Central Africa, 'fattening sheds' for adolescent girls were commonplace. Teenage girls were deliberately overfed and kept from exercise and then ceremoniously displayed. In cultures where food is scarce, plumpness in women indicates social rank and prosperity.

The cultures of Ancient Egypt and Greece offer an interesting exception. A lithe, slender form was highly valued in women, and it is said that the Greeks envied the Cretans for possessing a drug which kept them slim no matter how much they ate. In Roman times, women began starving themselves to stay thin, and, of course, it was Roman culture that developed the vomitorium. In the Middle Ages and Renaissance, a full, rounded figure was again preferred as is evident in the art of that period. Raphael's depictions of the Virgin Mary are statuesque, Titian's Greek goddesses powerfully built, and Botticelli's Venus curvaceous. In Oriental art, one also finds a full figured form with breasts and hips emphasized by their roundness.

In the Romantic Period of the first half of the nineteenth century the fashion for corsets and the hour glass figure led to clinched waists, at times damaging the rib cage and internal organs. Still, while waists were to be tiny, the rest of the body was to be ample, and overall thinness was considered ugly. The French epicure of the period, J.A. Brillat Savain, describes thinness in women as 'a terrible misfortune...the condition of the individual whose muscular flesh, not being filled with fat, reveals the forms and angles of the bony structure...The most painstaking toilette, the sublimest costume can not hide certain absences, or disguise certain angles.'[7] In the Victorian era, fat was regarded as a woman's 'silken layer', as 'stored-up force' and was associated with good health and emotional well-being. At the turn of the century, as Impressionist art turned its gaze on domestic life, women are portrayed with grand proportions. Renoir's women are never angular, but always full fleshed with dewy soft skin, and even Degas' dancers are hardly svelte.

Already in the Victorian era a fashion for slimness was emerging in the upper classes. A thinner, more frail body symbolized a spiritual, feminine nature, a rejection of carnal appetites in favour of finer sensibilities, and demonstrated distance from the sturdier working-class woman. It was only in the 1920's, however, that the hourglass figure was fully rejected and the thin tubular look took hold. The constrictive corsets were discarded, but replaced by equally constrictive dictums about diet, as women's magazines began to rail against the evils of fat. Interestingly, this shift occurred just at the time in America when women achieved the right to vote, and one cannot help wondering whether changing styles reflected social confusion over how much space a woman should take up, and whether she could be powerful in the world and maintain her feminine form at the same time. This was also the time when ready-to-wear clothing began to be marketed, giving rise to standardized sizing and the notion of a normative range. The desired look was, however, still plump by today's standards. One of the great beauties of the day, swimmer, film star, and fashion commentator, Anette Kellerman, was 5ft. 3 3/4 in. and weighed a solid 137 pounds. In the 1920's, the divorce rate was also on the rise, and wives were warned by commentators of the time to attend more seriously to their physical attractiveness. Cultural historian Joan Brumberg notes that by the 1920's outward appearance had become more important than inner character, because 'sexual allure had replaced spirituality as woman's 'shining adornment.'[8]

In this country, there was less emphasis on slenderness during the Depression and War years, and with the post-war emphasis on domesticity, there was a return to a more voluptuous, full-figured look as epitomized by Marilyn Monroe. It was in the 1960's glorification of the model Twiggy— boyish and almost gawkishly bony—that the tubular look was reestablished. Women's clothing became skimpy and revealing, drawing more attention to the body itself than to the clothes adorning it. Again, the change of fashion coincided with women breaking out of the limited roles dictated by the culture. Twiggy accompanied the advent of birth control pills and the dawn of the Women's Liberation Movement.

The late 20th century diet craze

Since the time of Twiggy, fashion models have become progressively thinner at a frightening rate. Thirty years ago, the average model weighed 8 percent less than the average American woman. Today, she weighs 23 percent less, and many suffer from eating disorders. Today's standard of beauty is, at best, only attainable by the naturally thinnest percent of the population, leaving the vast majority to feel that something is very wrong. The decline in ideal body size has led to a huge increase in girls' and women's dissatisfaction with their bodies. A study in *Glamour Magazine* in 1984 of 33,000 women aged 18-35 found that 75 percent thought they were too fat, while only 25 percent were medically overweight, and nearly half of those who were underweight thought they were too fat. Sadly, nearly half also indicated losing weight as a priority over developing a new friendship or success at work.

While all women are affected by the pressure to be thin, studies show adolescents to be particularly vulnerable. A study of 3,000 adolescents found 2/3 of girls 13-18 trying to lose weight, while most of the boys were trying to gain weight. When girls 11-17 were asked to list three wishes, the number one wish of most was to lose weight and keep it off. An even more alarming study found that 81 percent of *fourth graders* in a San Francisco school district were trying to diet. Not surprisingly, women's increasing dissatisfaction with their body size has been a boon to the diet business, which in the US has tripled in the last 10 years, to a $30 billion a year industry. And diet books have an ever present place on best-seller lists. In addition to causing physiological and emotional damage, most diets do not work. Research indicates that 95 percent of dieters who lose 25 pounds or more regain the weight within 5 years.

How ironic that this craze for dieting should occur in an era of such material plenitude. Indeed, the contradiction is strikingly played out on the pages of women's magazines, where lavish recipes are placed side by side with articles about dieting and fashion displays with waif-like models. Women are still expected to take an interest in their roles as nurturers, and food is still associated with festivity and happiness. But the message is clear: it is dangerous for women to indulge themselves in the pleasures of eating.

Losing weight and getting in shape has, in fact, become the new moral imperative and, for women, virtually synonymous with self-improvement. It is assumed to be what is meant when New Year's resolutions are referred to, and when teenage girls speak of being 'bad', they are more likely to be referring to eating than to sexual exploration. A recent magazine ad has the word 'sin' emblazoned across an ice cream sundae and the word 'salvation' across a diet drink adjacent to it. An ad for a butter/margarine blend is entitled '40% sin' and '60% forgiveness.' Diet plans speak of 'the thin person within' waiting to emerge. How sad that urges toward self-discipline, self-development, and spiritual growth should be largely channeled into curbing our natural hunger and starving our bodies. Diet and fitness have taken on all the attributes of a religion and a sadly dogmatic one. This has led to the worship and hatred of the physical body at the same time. Ironically, it has left women as enslaved to biology as ever.

Most perplexing is the aesthetic appeal of this gaunt, angular, hard-edged look now considered beautiful. Cultural historian, Roberta Seid, wonders what meaning future generations will find in this strange ideal, 'this unique fashion for bare-boned skinniness':

> Future historians might conjecture that Americans had fallen in love with death, or at least the mortification of the flesh...They might argue that we had been so influenced by modern art, Bauhaus aesthetics, and contemporary steel architecture that our ideal human body also had come to consist only of the scaffolding that held it up and of the machinery that made it move. ..Even more, they might contend that we had dehumanized, not just masculinized, the human form. ..They might argue that we had come to idealize technology, and also (befitting our secular age) to distinguish humans from other animals and the civilized from the uncivilized not by the presence of consciousness, a soul and a conscience, but by the suppression of animal fat.[9]

There is, indeed, something strikingly cold, steely, and soulless in this image of beauty, a beauty without any softness, grace, or subtlety. It also suggests a profound confusion and ambivalence about the place of the feminine in the world. With the recent popularization of the 'waif' look, we saw models so thin they looked as if they would topple in a breeze or simply fade away. Rarely do we see models who smile or strike a pose which is confident. Usually the gaze is downcast, the posture slumped or constricted, and the face pale. A recent fashion supplement to the *New York Times* depicts women dressed in little girl's frippery and menswear. The text touts the remarkable range of choices a woman has today for self-expression, but each image is either infantilized, sexualized, made masculine, or needy and vulnerable. Rarely is there an image of mature and confident beauty or of a woman proudly taking her place in the world. Now, magazines are starting to use computer imaging techniques where the 'model' is not even a real person, but a composite of different women. This image can then be air brushed to further shrink the contours, creating a truly impossible ideal, but one which looks all too real to the observer.

Interestingly, full-figured women are depicted in pornography, but in those images the figure is usually in some way bound. The culture seems frightened to grant the feminine an unfettered place in the world, or to endow it with any strength or power.

These then are the pictures of beauty, the images of womanhood and the cultural ideals that teenage girls drink in as they search for models by which to forge their emerging identities. At the same time, other voices are telling them their options are limitless. But how can the anorexic-looking model appear strong enough to accomplish anything? And what encouragement do teenage girls receive that the culture will value more than their looks? No wonder they are confused, and no wonder eating disorders have become so rampant.

Understanding eating disorders

Though the notion of 'eating disorders' is new, such illnesses have no doubt existed in some form for centuries. Their meteoric rise among young women in the last 30 years, however, suggests their current manifestation is largely in response to cultural pressures. Anthropologists have described such syndromes, unique to a particular culture in a particular period, as 'culture bound illnesses,' known to come and go throughout history. In Indonesia, in a culture which demanded a high degree of control over aggression and deference to authority, men occasionally developed the illness, Amok. After an accumulation of insults or stresses, a man would initially withdraw and brood, then embark on a murderous rampage, finally lapsing into amnesia and exhaustion. The 19th Century in Europe and America was a time of sexual repression and sentimental emphasis on female frailty and domesticity. This was coupled with the expectation that women were to be the beacon of moral strength with full responsibility for home and children. Some women responded by developing hysteria. With paralyzed limbs and countless other perplexing symptoms, these women became the focus of wealthy households, wielding great power in their passivity. Similarly, eating disorders have become a disease of the times among young women in modern Western culture. They are a response to extreme pressures and contradictory demands, and, in the case of anorexia, offer a grotesque caricature of the current ideal of female beauty. Eating disorders are overwhelmingly a female disease (only 5% occur among men) and until recently were found only in developed countries, usually among the educated or prosperous (although now with the universalizing influence of media they are beginning to cross all class and national boundaries).

Though there have been other periods in the history of Western civilization when abstinence from eating has been popularized, historical investigation reveals that its symbolic meaning differed in important ways. In the 13th-15th centuries' world of medieval Catholicism, adolescent girls fasted for spiritual perfection, claiming to need no other food than the Eucharist. St. Catherine of Seine is said to have lived on a spoonful of herbs a day. If forced to eat, she put twigs down her throat to bring up the food. During the Reformation, such abstinence was seen as the work of the devil, and some young fasters were burned as witches. The tradition of fasting continued, however, and these 'miraculous maids' became the object of much fascination in the popular culture of the time. Insisting they required no earthly sustenance, they posed a challenge to the growing scientific rationalism, provoking 24 hour watches by physicians, magistrates, and clergy. In most cases, they either died or were discovered to be sneaking tiny amounts of food. In Victorian times, 'fasting girls' were again the subject of much debate and touted by the Spiritualists as living proof that life could be sustained by spirit alone. Medical explanations held sway, however, and in the 1870's, the English physician, Sir William Gull, coined the term 'anorexia nervosa' (a nervous absence of appetite). Increasingly, food refusal was seen as a nervous disorder and not as an act of piety.

In the early 1900's, the case of Ellen West received considerable attention in psychiatric circles. Ellen was a young Jewish woman whose family moved to Switzerland when she was a child, and who from age 20 until her suicide at 33, suffered severe symptoms of anorexia and bulimia. Her symptoms are strikingly similar to those of modern sufferers, and her diaries offer extraordinary insight into how her obsession with food and weight became a battleground for internal conflicts. She longed to express her impassioned nature, to break out of the limited possibilities for women, and to live out of her full humanity, but she was caught in a restrictive bourgeois society. Her words ring forth as a harbinger for the struggles of the masses of young women suffering from eating disorders today. By all accounts Ellen was a lively, athletic, headstrong girl, a brilliant student, keenly concerned about the social problems of the day, and very ambitious. Frustrated by lack of opportunity and forced by her father to reject a suitor she loved, Ellen began at age 20 to eat compulsively. Teased and mortified by her weight gain, she then began fasting and hiking up to 25 miles a day. The rest of her life was characterized by extreme cycles of fasting and then gorging, vomiting and laxative abuse.

At 21 before she was entirely consumed by her obsessions, Ellen writes of her frustrated longings.

> I must again take my notebook in hand...It is really sad that I must translate all this force and urge to action into unheard words instead of powerful deeds...For what purpose did nature give me health and ambition? Surely not to stifle it and hold it down and let it languish in the chains of humdrum living, but to serve wretched humanity...I am 21 years old and am supposed to be silent and grin like a puppet. I am no puppet. I am a human being with red blood and a woman with quivering heart...Oh, what shall I do?[10]

Earnestly she longs for a venue for serious work and the opportunity to make a difference, but instead all of her energy becomes enslaved by her terror of growing fat and focused on desperate attempts to control her insatiable hunger. She describes her panic over eating as a single idea that fills her entire soul with the result that 'all inner development was ceasing, that all becoming and growing were being choked.' And, much as her reason at times rebels against it, she tries 'by will power to drive this idea out'.[11] Her effort is in vain and the obsession in the end destroys her.

Until the 1960's, both anorexia and bulimia were still considered rare, somewhat exotic psychiatric disorders. But in the 1970's with thinner and thinner standards of beauty, the rise of dieting, and increasingly complex, conflicting pressures, many young women began echoing the struggles and suffering of Ellen West; anorexia and bulimia began to take on epidemic proportions. Studies of incidence have had varied findings. Conservative estimates suggest that 0.5-1% of high school and college age girls suffer from anorexia and 3-20% from bulimia. Among middle and upper middle class families, the numbers are higher, with many more exhibiting at least some symptoms. Most teenage girls are enormously affected by the pressure to be thin, and while they may not develop eating disorders, they find it difficult to sustain a natural relationship to eating. It is estimated that 10% of those who develop full blown anorexia die from medical complications or suicide, making it the most lethal psychiatric disorder. Something is seriously wrong.

Anorexia, as we know it today, usually develops between the ages of 11-19 and invariably comes as a shock to the family. It seems to occur most frequently among 'model daughters', who have always desired to please, and been good, conscientious, high-achieving students. It often starts with dieting, in response to a comment about weight or when a still fragile sense of independence is challenged after the loss of a friendship, rejection by a boyfriend, a perceived failure, a move or a death. Among these strong-willed, perfectionistic girls, the dieting becomes more and more extreme, and soon it becomes a challenge to eat as little as possible. There is a fascination and preoccupation with asceticism, to go one more hour without food, to run one more mile, to swim one more lap, or to withstand the cold without warm clothing. Perhaps the body becomes something seemingly tameable, a stand-in for the external life that seems so difficult to control and so full of complicated choices. Decreasing numbers on a scale at least offer tangible evidence of effectiveness in a world which offers too few opportunities for girls to feel truly effective. At any rate, the young anorexic masters her appetite with a vengeance, and in the early stages, this new found discipline and display of mind over matter can lead to a feeling of moral superiority and even euphoria. Girls at this stage have described to me feeling quite triumphant discovering their will to resist the food that others find so irresistible. Some spend hours cooking for their families and then proudly deny themselves the results of their creations, even though ravenously hungry. Others describe how prolonged hunger creates heightened sensations, more vivid colors, or a sense that life is more ethereal. As the body shrinks, there seems to be a desire to pull back from the complications of earthly life altogether and a longing for something transcendent. Hilde Bruch, an American psychiatrist who did ground breaking work in the study of eating disorders, offers the following remarkable quote from one of her young patients.

> The more weight I lost the more I became convinced that I was on the right way. I wanted to learn to know what was beyond the ordinary living, what happens in after life. Abstinence was in preparation for special revelations; it was like the things the saints and mystics had done. I also wanted to be praised for being special, and I wanted to be held in awe for doing what I was.[12]

As though brainwashed through some form of self-hypnosis, the anorexic girl becomes more and more enslaved to her ascetic goals. The most puzzling aspects of the disease are the extreme distortions in perceptions of body size, leading her to see herself as still too large when she is dangerously thin. Unfortunately, many tell me they are complimented for their weight loss and envied by their peers right up to this point. The young anorexic's view is thus supported by what is becoming a culture-wide delusion about appropriate body size.

Gradually, the initial feeling of euphoric control is usually replaced by an extreme fear of gaining weight and a host of obsessional anxieties which become quite debilitating. Prolonged hunger may lead to small binges which easily create a sense of panic. Malnutrition induces its own psychic changes, including irritability, confusion, apathy, and depression. The physiological effects of chronic starvation are numerous and many are dangerous. Many of these girls grow so thin they look like concentration camp victims. They are weak with exhaustion and cannot stay warm. Lanugo, a downy baby-like hair, grows all over the body. The heart muscle can shrink, causing a low or irregular heart rate and low blood pressure. Growth is stunted, menstrual cycles cease, and insufficient estrogen production can lead to severe osteoporosis at an early age.

Hilde Bruch observed that girls who develop anorexia often grow up in families where there are very high expectations for achievement, but little room for individual expression and very controlling norms for behavior. She suggests these families give the paradoxical message: accomplish great things and be a strong independent individual, but only do so in a manner we approve of. The girls then become paralyzed by a sense of ineffectiveness and inadequacy and work furiously to control their bodies. Among psychologists this view has largely held sway. But as anorexia has become so widespread, it no longer makes sense to blame the family, especially as these very same conflicting pressures exist in the culture at large. Our culture seems to say, 'Achieve like a man, but stay feminine, compliant, and beautiful, and above all minimize the amount of space you take up in the world by staying thin.' With perfectionistic drive, the anorexic girl outdoes the cultural expectation, becoming stubbornly independent and defiant in her pursuit of emaciating herself.

I also sometimes view the illness as a kind of hunger strike, as if the girl is saying, 'I won't grow up and develop a womanly body in a culture where that appears to be a losing proposition, where I will be judged by my body or met with too many expectations.' And other times the disease seems fueled by a desire to shrink back from life, to literally fade away.

Bulimia is the most common eating disorder and quite rampant among college age women. Apart from the institutionalized binges and purges of Roman feasts, it seems to have few historical antecedents. As with anorexia, it usually starts with the continuous pressure to lose weight just at the age when one's body is naturally putting on weight. At first, it appears to be a magical solution; one can eat as much as one wants and then simply regurgitate the unwanted calories. The problem is that the behavior becomes highly addictive and compulsive. Binges tend to get bigger and bigger, at times leading to the voracious consumption of entire cakes and quarts of ice cream. And the frequency of binges and purges easily grows from once a week to several times a day.

While those with anorexia will often deny that anything is wrong and are usually brought to see me by concerned parents, those with bulimia tend to be by nature more impulsive, readily admitting that their life has become desperately out of control. Often considerable shame and secrecy surround their behavior. Planning how to manage the next binge and purge becomes a total preoccupation, resulting in a complete withdrawal from family and social life and causing feelings of irritability and depression. Many have described to me how they experience the force that leads them to binge as something quite external, outside their control, generating tremendous anxiety if they don't give in to it. Following the binge, they feel enormous guilt and self-disgust. The purge becomes a purification rite, and for a while there is a feeling of freshness, of a new beginning, with a temporary restoration of self-worth. But soon after, anxiety over the next binge sets in. Medical complications of bulimia are serious and include dehydration, an upset in the electrolyte balance, which can cause potentially fatal cardiac arrhythmias, tears in the esophagus, and an eroding of tooth enamel. If laxatives are abused there is irritation of the colon and interference with absorption of nutrients.

Those who suffer from bulimia quite literally enact a cultural paradox. On the one hand, we meet over-consumption, a bombardment of material plenitude, and a dizzying array of foods. On the other hand, as women we hear incessant exhortations to deny ourselves food and to maintain discipline over our bodies. The young woman with bulimia is caught swinging from one extreme to the other. The teenager with anorexia responds to overwhelming pressure by latching on to a cognitive delusion about her body size and with steely will seeks to discipline her body, often succeeding too well. The teenager with bulimia usually has a more conscious understanding of the pressures in her life, but becomes panicked over her inability to direct her will or control her behavior. Bulimics feel they are at the mercy of their impulses and are also susceptible to substance abuse and promiscuity. Some girls recover from anorexia only to develop bulimia.

Others binge without purging and become compulsive overeaters. These girls feel no need to purge as the sensation of being overfull is experienced as calming. Food becomes a narcotic, a salve to soothe emotional pain or feelings of emptiness. After a while, all emotions, be they excitement, sadness, anger, fear, or insecurity, become experienced as hunger. These girls lose touch with physical sensations of hunger and satiation and eat to fill an insatiable emotional hunger. Growing fat may also provide an escape from the pressures of dating and sexuality. Unfortunately, developing this kind of relationship to food in adolescence can lay down a life long habit which may be quite difficult to undo.

Eating disorders often go undetected until they are well established, but there are warning signs that parents should be aware of. Rapid or large weight loss, restrictive dieting, avoidance of fats, weighing food or other ritualistic behavior around eating are all early signs of anorexia. Secretive eating and regular use of the bathroom after meals, combined with irritability, depression or withdrawal from family members may indicate bulimia. If these disorders are detected early, they are much easier to treat. A few months of bulimic behavior is fairly easy to turn around, but after a year or more, it becomes a very entrenched habit. Anorexia is also not as difficult to treat if the psychological effects of starvation have not yet set in.

Girls who develop eating disorders tend to be among the brightest and most talented. Their joyful engagement with the world becomes sadly disrupted as their ambition to grow and achieve is redirected toward maintaining an impossibly thin body. Their youthful idealism gets lost, replaced by a rigid, dogmatic adherence to a narrowly defined physical ideal. How can we help to free them of this obsession and to enable them to broaden their horizons? In working with these girls, I try to help them articulate their feelings and ideas, to encourage their initiative and sense of autonomy, and to instill confidence in their voice so they no longer resort to using their body as the only means of self-expression. I gently help them to see that their preoccupation with food and weight has become a cover up or a distraction from what truly concerns them, be it the vicissitudes of their relationships or larger fears over finding their way in such an uncertain world. The process is a delicate one. With anorexia, denial of the problem, distortions of body image, and real panic over the prospect of giving up hard won control can be quite powerful, and I must be careful not to challenge these beliefs head on. The teenager with anorexia must be gently coaxed back into experiencing that her hunger is safe and healthy and that she can tolerate her feelings of insecurity. With bulimia, as with any addiction or compulsive behavior, it is more a question of helping a young woman to experience that she does have control, that her capacity for self-determination is a stronger force than her addiction. As these girls begin to heal, it is also very helpful to enlist them in the process of observing the tyrannical effect of the culture and the mania for thinness. As they become freed of symptoms, many will eagerly participate, clipping offensive magazine ads and challenging their peers. Once reawakened, their natural idealism is easily fired to work toward creating a freer world where their individuality can find fuller expression and where, as human beings, they will count for more than their physical appearance.

All teenage girls need help finding broader concepts of beauty than those dished up by the media. Girls have a natural pull toward aesthetics, but need help enlarging their experience of beauty to include all its forms, physical and non-physical. They can then learn that they are beautiful inwardly and outwardly and fully capable of beautiful deeds. To develop a healthy relationship to their bodies, girls need for their mothers to also abandon their diets and free themselves of their preoccupation with weight. How many of us realize that it is a natural biological process for women to gain 10-15 lbs. with the birth of each child and to keep that weight on?

Teenagers also need to experience meals as relaxed social occasions where the sharing of food can play its age-old function of building community. Teenagers are surrounded by fast foods and an approach to eating that is becoming more and more like grazing. Food seems to accompany virtually every activity, but is often eaten on the run. Busy lives and hectic schedules make the family meal often impractical, but probably more important than ever.

My generation grew up rebelling against an image of female destiny too narrowly defined. Our daughters face an image that is still, in many respects, quite limited, but in others, overwhelmingly vast and filled with contradictory expectations. For many, the cult of thinness has become a way to flatten and simplify the whole process of identity search. In my practice, I try to offer these girls a safe harbor, a place to express turbulent feelings, to temper expectations, and to regain a sense of play around possible identities. They need to feel that there is time enough to explore and that they can enjoy trying on different identities for size to see how they fit with their still nascent sense of self. Clearly, this is a need not just for those with eating disorders, but for all teenage girls, and should not only be addressed in a therapist's office, but also at home and at school. Girls need help finding other measures of self-worth than physical appearance. They need active encouragement to explore a range of options and to develop their many different talents, but less pressure to succeed everywhere at once. Most importantly, we need to realize that by cultivating a fear of appetite in girls, we are as a culture cultivating a fear of living. Our daughters need all the encouragement they can find to pursue their natural hunger for life and all the reassurance we can offer that they will find safe passage into an adult world where they are invited to express their full humanity.

Notes

1. Hilde Bruch, *Conversations With Anorexics*, New York: Basic Books, 1988, p.134.

2. Rudolf Steiner, *Waldorf Education for Adolescence*, Forest Row, Sussex, U.K.: Kolisko Archive Publications, 1980.

3. Ibid.

4. Ibid.

5. Carol Gilligan and Lynn Mikel Brown, *Meeting at the Crossroads*, New York: Ballantine Books, 1993.

6. Mary Pipher, *Reviving Ophelia: Saving the Selves of Adolescent Girls*, New York: Ballantine Books, 1995.

7. Quoted in Roberta Seid, *Too 'Close to the Bone': The Historical Context for Women's Obsession with Slenderness*, in Fallon, Katzman, and Wooley (eds.) *Feminist Perspectives on Eating Disorders*, New York: Guilford Press, 1994.

8. Joan Jacobs Brumberg, *Fasting Girls*, Cambridge: Harvard University Press, 1989.

9. Seid, p. 12.

10. Quoted in Ludwig Binswanger, *The Case of Ellen West*, in Rollo May (ed.), *Existence—A New Dimension in Psychiatry and Psychology*, New York: 1958, p. 243.

11. Ibid, p. 246.

12. Bruch, p. 143.

Tamara Slayton

My biographical initiation into the question of gender began at my first pregnancy at 15 and the subsequent giving away of this child after his birth. (Yes, I have found him, he is well and there is love between us.) This decision was made within the then prevailing silence regarding a young girl's emerging fertility and the difficulties of parental alcoholism within my family. As many women in the 20th century have begun to share, I lived in the wilderness of post-industrial family life. I have since come to see this striking experience as linked with the imagination of the woman in the wilderness giving birth to the child as the dragon stalks (Apocalypse of St John, Chapter 12).

As an individual concerned with the fruits of spiritual endeavors, I believe I lived through themes, pains, losses in this first encounter with fertility and pregnancy that prepared me to take up the tasks I am currently involved in. Now I travel throughout the United States and work with groups of girls and their communities encouraging the growth of their self-knowledge, self-care and self-esteem in relationship to the fertility of the heart *and* of the womb. I suggest that life will be challenging enough without the unnecessary baggage of mentstrual shame and fear of fertility.

I have also come to understand that the experiences I encountered in the 60s have prepared me for the 90s. I now see these girls-becoming-women, and watch the softening of boys witnessing this new picture of girls' outer changes. I observe the parents' joy at finding a creative relationship to emerging sexuality.

I have come to understand myself as an *American* anthroposophist, understanding the consequences of materialism in my own body. My early childhood and teen experiences, my participation in the revolution of the 60s and now my coming awareness of anthroposophy give me a fuller picture of the tasks at hand.

I am deeply concerned about the difficulties youth have in finding their way in current social complexities of gender, economics and power. Again Steiner has helped guide my thinking about how to remedy these difficulties, and has led me to a growing understanding that the spiritual forms within his thinking are now arising everywhere in America. His 'premature seeds' of the threefold social organism are alive in the hearts of people seeking to revitalize their lives, the strivings of corporate America to revision itself and honor the worker as partner not slave, the hunger of education for an artistic and social approach to learning and the dramatic changes in scientific thinking regarding the nature of reality.

I currently raise the two of five chidren who are still in my home. I experience them as teachers. I am active in developing new business forms based on new social forms,such as a cloth menstrual pad worker-owned cooperative, a natural death care worker-owner cooperative, and a combination high school and adult education worker-owner cooperative based in the facilitation of leadership through cooperation.

The writing of this contribution for *More Lifeways* arose out of my dialogues with parents and teachers in 18 different Waldorf schools. This article allowed me to further articulate the necessity of an entirely different approach to the needs of today's youth.

22
Creating communities of the heart—meeting the adolescent in freedom

Contemplate, for a moment, the dramatic and yet subtle changes that envelop a child emerging into the stream of adolescence? A daughter, a gangly girl goes to bed, the next day a shimmering maiden emerges clothed by the stars, her skin scintillating. A son, an awkward boy withdraws to sleep and returns the next morning, a royal personage with lance held high. As adults we may have all experienced the sudden leaping of our hearts at beholding this change from child to teen, at seeing the future standing there in pyjamas with tousled hair, at witnessing the fruit of the spiritual world— *hope.*

This capacity to see what is invisible is the task of any adult striving to parent a teen to adulthood. The challenge is to learn to sense subtle perceptions that are quickly washed away by the images of modern culture—pre-packaged and marketed images of adolescence that include irresponsibility, lying, promiscuity, deceit, laziness, and sullenness. Just before materialism creeps into our perceptions of the teenagers who share our lives, there lives another perception—*a perception of the heart.*

Hans Mueller-Wiedemann, referring to Rudolf Steiner's insights on adolescence, says: 'Something quite different is expressed by the concept of earth-maturity than by the concept of sexual-maturity. The concept of earth-maturity points to something which is invisible and seemingly hidden, like in a chrysalis...'[1]

From this perspective of 'earth-maturity', we are witnessing the *birth of the soul* that is now mature enough to begin to take up the tasks of earthly responsibilities. This is a most profound distinction compared to how modern science, psychology and sociology often minimize the teen experience as *originating* in sexual development. For Rudolf Steiner, what we are witnessing in the outer manifestations of hormonal influences is actually the result of the soul's maturation and not the defining element. Continuing with this image of the soul birthing—which happens as we pack our lunches and prepare for car-pool daily—Steiner describes 'how around the time of earth-maturation, the heart, the sun-organ, becomes the central organ of the body. What a human being does from the moment of earth maturation on, what he aims at with the ideals and ideas by which he acts, is inscribed into the wonderful soul-etheric formation of the heart. The human being is also presented at this time with the gift of an organ of perception with which, now and in the future, he can perceive his own individual destiny; this is the perceptive organ of the heart, forming itself within.' [2]

As parents seeking an expanded understanding of human nature, we can contemplate the significance of what Dr. Steiner is imparting. An invisible birth is occurring and a gift is being given—*a birth requiring tender midwifing and a gift that can become a guiding light for all future discernment.* This is sharply contrasted to the current, on-going interpretation of life-cycles dependent upon raging, imbalanced hormones. Women, in particular, have labored under definitions of pre-menstrual syndrome and menopause as diseases treatable by plant or animal-derived hormonal intervention. Repeatedly, young girls are put on the birth control pill to address their 'hormonal fluctuations.' The prescription is intended to standardize the individual, to assure she fits into a rhythm acceptable to mass consumerism and the ticking of the mechanical clock. Our loss of cyclical consciousness is in part the result of the evolution of the factory model for efficient production implemented during the Industrial Revolution.

Imagine that each time a girl began her menstrual flow we celebrated this proclamation of her heart shining like the sun, of her soul flowing to meet her destiny. And when a boy experienced his first erection, we smiled inwardly and knew that destiny was calling. Imagine that we understood in our depths that these physical changes revealed the soul's emerging intentions. Blessedly, the imagination *can* stretch to meet such a necessary correspondence between the inner life and adolescent physicality. The teenager brings the adult the opportunity to become disciplined in witnessing the activity of the spiritual world while penetrating through the restrictions of modern stereotypical interpretations of adolescence. *The imagination breathes from the heart and this breathing can be practiced by any adult seeking the true human being.*

My intent in developing these larger thoughts regarding the soul-being of the adolescent is to inspire the reader to look at the more difficult issues of living with teenagers, particularly the issue of their emerging *fertile sexuality—to view the physical from the perspective of the spiritual.* As an educator, my primary inquiry for this life time has been into the development of human fertility and Western culture's manipulation and categorizing of this basic human condition. I have repeatedly witnessed the most illuminated parents flinch when it comes to representing and articulating their understanding and ideals regarding menstruation, ovulation, spermatogenesis, intimacy, and procreation. We have all, to varying degrees, been trained in knee-jerk responses of self-righteous dogma or embarrassed silence in the sexual dialogue. Or we have been converted and tormented by the possibility of having 'the Big Talk' in hopes that *one* conversation can handle the demands of human evolution.

I have been blessed with an ongoing dialogue with teenagers seeking to share their process of attraction for others, the beginnings of intimacy and the consideration of first intercourse. I attribute my ability to breathe deeply, relax my shoulders, and cultivate a sincere interest in their sharing to my ongoing study of Rudolf Steiner and other contemporary thinkers as a primary antidote to my automatic response of wanting to lock them in a room and make sure they never have contact with the opposite sex until they are mature enough to do so! I have had to re-educate myself to the developmental process of the inner and outer life and include both in my assessments as parent and teacher.

In a rare moment when the world slows down long enough for us to be there for one another, I have sat at my kitchen table and dialogued with a sixteen-year-old girl, who has been educated through a combination of Waldorf pedagogy, the echo of the ideals of the 60's and the best of modern feminism. She shares with me that she has discovered she can attract boys and 'Oh, by the way, I have my first hickey'. This moment demands all the compassion, empathy and love I can muster as the rich purple blues of passion are revealed on her soft peach neckline. As I dialogue with this girl-exploring-temptress, I strive to stay genuinely interested in *her* process, *her* discoveries, *her* insights, as she leans a little closer into the mystery of our shared bond and she listens to what I have learned about the responsibility of attraction. Like a wild animal, discovering civilization, I can't look her directly in the eye but must keep my gaze soft and words tender as she steps out of her childhood garden and into the rights and responsibilities of being woman. If I cannot breathe with the contractions of her inner labor and the birthing of her heart, she pulls herself away and I have lost an opportunity to contribute the life experience I have to share. If my insights and worldly wisdom become more important than witnessing her journey, the difficulties in the conversation multiply and the delicate bridge between us wavers. I must strive to see the emerging of her heart.

What is the heart of the teen seeking and what are the difficulties we might find in our attempts to nurture this emerging inner life? The human soul is seeking images, archetypes, ideals that meet the spiritual images, archetypes, and ideals it carries from its sojourn in the spiritual realms. And what does it find here regarding menstruation, ovulation, spermatogenesis, intimacy and procreation? Most often, teenagers are exposed to hardened, automatic pictures grounded in fear and lack of knowledge and rarely ensouled with beauty, truth and reverence. Or they are silenced in their questions and held in contempt if they violate an undeclared policy within the family's values regarding bodily processes, intimacy and involvement with others.

A second difficulty arises from the fact that many of these souls have incarnated during a time when uninformed, unconscious sexual encounters are risky. Parents often seek out 'experts' to inform their children of the *dangers* of sexuality in the 20th century, but many of these experts have a one-sided world view that leaves the children cold in their questions. Frequently, the modern sex-education curriculum illustrates the many pathologies the young person must be aware of before embarking on an intimate encounter. The tone of such information is threatening and illustrated with images of disease and death. The tactic is management through fear.

Of course these concerns are real and must be met; adults need to act responsibly by informing their children of the condition of human sexuality at the turn of the century. But repeatedly, educators emphasise modern conditions at the expense of the evolving human being. If, as Rudolf Steiner is asserting, the *heart* is the central organ (not the genitalia) emerging during adolescence, we would do well to develop a fuller picture of the relationship of the heart to the adolescent's intimate encounters. During puberty and adolescence the heart is developing its *discerning* capacities, which are what we most need to cultivate in the 20th century—knowing who the other is to you and intuiting what is the appropriate form of relationship for each encounter. We need a sex education that includes emotional literacy and communication skills, not just disease considerations.

Thirdly, our unexamined responses to children's sexual maturation hinder the creation of a new imagination, new artistic ways of representing the mystery of male and female physiology, and leave us prey to medicine's relentless manipulation of human fertility. The intimate relationship to the awakening heart and the development of human sexuality will require a new science that merges the invisible and visible. 'Physical pleasure changes into spiritual enjoyment...Similarly, sexual love gradually leads to the highest spiritual love...Without the school of sensuality, we could never reach spirituality.'[3]

This awakening heart, and its attendant outer signs of fertile sexuality, leads a young person towards the future. The arising of attraction for another in the rhythms of hormonal ebb and flow facilitates the fulfillment of an individual's destiny. Teenagers, through the ripening of seed and egg, are drawn to each other to begin their entrance into the community of the world. The heart, as the central organ of perception evolving during the teen years, is responding to inner-pictures, imaginations carried from the spiritual world to guide individuals in making their way towards the fulfillment of their life's purpose.

Rudolf Steiner tells us that 'Pre-natal pictures are living in you, and you must bring them alive during life'.[4] As Maria Röschl-Lehrs illustrates in *The Second Man in Us*, these pre-natal pictures offer us solutions for the current cultural crises that the soul will encounter in modern civilization. Creative solutions to homelessness, starvation, environmental degradation live in the hearts of the youth incarnating at the turn of the century. These solutions are facilitated through the activity of attraction to the other individuals in a teenager's life. If a culture primarily focuses on managing and medicating the attraction, the 'pre-natal' pictures grow dimmer and dimmer and the heart grows weary with its unfulfilled intentions.

Maria Röschl-Lehrs goes on to state, 'Anyone seeking to bring up children in true line with the needs of our time, however, must go quite the other way and make every effort not to kill these pre-natal pictures. If the teacher (parent) seeks out of the picture-creating power of his own soul...then the pre-natal powers of pictorial presentations are reinvigorated and enlivened.'[5] This is the key to our concerns regarding first menstruation, ovulation, spermatogenesis. What are the picture-creating powers of the teacher/parent in the picturing of human fertile sexuality to a modern adolescent? And if the parent or teacher primarily utilizes the picture-creating powers of the media in all forms and the unexamined experiences of their own adolescence, their options for 'picturing' are limited. The heart's understanding of human fertile maturation must become an essential element in our picture building to nurture these gifts from the spiritual world arising in the hearts of young people.

Fertile sexuality, as embodied in menstruation, ovulation, sperm maturation, and the longing for the other, can be re-envisioned by parents who can appreciate the 'pre-natal' pictures arising in their children's inner life. By embracing the outer manifestations of the fruits of this heart-maturation—menstruation, ovulation, spermatogenesis—we can educate for the awakening to destiny, rather than to protect the children from the world they came to meet.

So where do we begin to listen with our hearts, to speak the challenges of sexuality in the 20th and 21st centuries and to fashion new images of this holy mystery? As adults, as parents we begin with ourselves. We feel back to our own first passions, interests, encounters and strive to remember the multiplicity of experiences that drew us to another. We ask ourselves what are the thoughts, the feelings, the deeds which are the true inner aspects of human secretions, human seeds, and how do we carry these chosen ideals within us in relationship to our children? We educate ourselves in the scientific understanding of human fertile sexuality and we can become *spiritual*-scientists in our pursuit of knowledge. We merge the memories of our own teen experiences with the wisdom of self-reflection to offer the stories of our youth to meet the questions of our children.

In my work with adults 'preparing for puberty' we always make our way to our own adolescence and retrospect to the life experiences that embodied our maturation. This is often delicate work, even for those who have understood the deeper meaning of their own difficult childhood experiences. Women often find that the difficulty they now have in speaking to their daughters about first flow and human fertility derives from their own first menstruation. The combination of shame and lack of celebration has often hardened a woman's heart to her own biological beauty and restricts the potential for dialogue with her children. For men, the sadness of having been left in the dark about female adolescence brings tears for years of wanting to understand the rhythms of a woman's body and having to keep a tough silence. This silence could now cost them their loving playfulness with their daughters who are becoming the women they never could understand, as well as a creative and informative dialogue with their sons.

But adults can begin their own healing of the heart and evolve a new imagination of the unfolding life mystery of the human being. Adults who were not allowed to vivify their own 'pre-natal' pictures are often struggling with a sense of aimlessness and longing for purpose. Many of these adults, standing before teenagers representing the potential for the renewal of modern civilization, have compromised their own inner life to accommodate the demands of materialistic thinking and a consumer-based culture. The demands of the times and the needs of youth can become an opportunity for adults to reclaim their own 'pre-natal' pictures and reconnect with their sense of mission and destiny as they facilitate a future intended by their children.

Notes

1. Hans Mueller-Wiedemann, *Earth Maturity as a Stage in the Maturation of the Soul*, Goetheanum, 8 October 1980.

2. Rudolf Steiner, Dornach, 26 May 1922.

3. Rudolf Steiner, Third Lecture, June 28—July 11, 1906.

4. Rudolf Steiner, 'Geisteswissenschaft als Erkenntnis der Grundimpulse sozialer Gestaltung', lecture of 11 September 1920 (Complete Edition No. 199, Dornach, 1967).

5. Maria Röschl-Lehrs, *The Second Man in Us*, East Grinstead: Henry Goulden Ltd., 1977

Ann Elizabeth Barnes

When I received this chapter back from the editor with the comment 'More personal experience would be appropriate here', I was startled. And when I wrote my mini-biography and showed it to my husband and he said 'This isn't about you, this is about your children', I was forced to go deep inside and contemplate these two comments. This is what I came up with: I am afraid to speak in my own voice. I am afraid that if I relate personal experiences I will be regarded as romantic, blurred, hazy, vain. And yet I am invariably unaware of this underlying infection. I think I am writing personally, sharing experiences. But I have come to the conclusion, again, that I have spent more than half my life disguising who I really am. I do understand the universality of the human experience. Aren't we all struggling with similar issues? Aren't we interested in other people's experiences? I know I am! Then, be brave enough to write about my own!

I am a human being, a woman, a wife, a mother, a step-mother, a person in the world. I am 42 years old, I have a degree in Natural Science (my passion). In 1989 I helped establish and run a non-profit organization for five years. Currently I am in the process of establishing another non-profit organization focusing on outdoor education. I am fascinated by the natural world. I have a goal of learning the name and habit of every bird, tree and stone in the Berkshire area of Massachusetts, where I live. I have a life-long desire to understand how everything fits together.

I am made up of the thick, multi-hued, patterned threads that have woven the tapestry of my life. There is lots of red and yellow in the tapestry with many large patches of blue and green. I look at it and know I am the sum of all my experiences, and yet I am more. I didn't arrive on this earth a clean slate, to be filled in as my life took shape. I came with my essential being and my destiny, the broad brush strokes of this tapestry. I am filling in the nuances, the subtle colors, the shapes that are me, that are the way I do things. But the primary me, the fundamental me, is there fashioning my life. Does this make sense? I have a burning desire to succeed at my life's work: working with adolescents, helping their transition into adulthood by providing the proper forum for their journey. I have begun work on this. I am putting considerable energy into it. And, I want to be a good wife and mother. These are compatible goals, there does not have to be a pulling in many directions. And this is who I am in this chapter of my life in the closing half of the last decade of the 20th century.

I have three children, Nadia, Shawn and Jonathan, who were all born in Switzerland. Their father and I lived in a small mountain village above Dornach for eight years. For all those years of motherhood I could think of nothing more satisfying than raising these three children. I revelled in every aspect of childcare and care of the household. Then, this dream fell apart and I found myself the sole provider for three children six and under. Their father no longer provided for us. I moved back to America, to Massachusetts, to start a new chapter in my life. I went back to school, studied biology, became an ardent environmentalist and naturalist, and forgot all about housework. But my children remained the center of my existence. Nothing that I did outside the home interfered with their needs. I was very fortunate to be able to arrange my schedule so that I could drop them off at school, go to my own classes and then pick them up at 3 pm and be home with them for the rest of the day. This went on for five years. I got my degree and began working full time. I found that the first thing I needed to do was rearrange my priorities again: household and housework became more of a team effort, but a lot was also left undone. It was a one-parent household: things that I couldn't fix didn't get fixed. It never occurred to me to hire anyone to fix things. We came to know the various broken items in the house as 'the screen door that doesn't close, the light that doesn't work, the burner that doesn't light.' When I look back on this it seems wacky but it truly didn't occur to me that the physical aspects could be remedied. I was much more at home on the emotional/psychological plane. I worried and planned and researched and felt guilty about so many things. I tried so very hard to give my children a balanced and nourishing life. They were not able to see much of their father and so there was lots more to feel guilty about. And then, suddenly, they were teenagers with new sets of challenges and the guilt had to be cast away. It did not serve at all. I had to accept that what I had done was the best I could do at that time and move on from there. And when I was successful at that then, lo and behold, I met my soul-mate and we got married and he fixes everything in the house and the children are happy and almost grown and I am just grateful to have been given so many gifts, especially all the trials and suffering, the special learning experiences that are mine.

23
Turning points: the role of ritual in the life of an adolescent

I received a letter...in which was asked: 'How does a human pass through youth to maturity without breaking down?' And (the letter) answered: 'With help from tradition, through ceremonies and rituals, rites of passage at the most difficult stages.'

Wendell Berry, *The Unsettling of America*

The cold November air is filled with the smell of burning sage. Slow, rhythmic chanting from the circle of dancers fills the air. The throb of the pot-drums increases in tempo. The tension becomes palpable. People watching stare into the bonfires, mesmerized by the rising fervor and energy of the dance. Young Brave Least Bear is standing in the center of the circle of men. His face is painted bright red with black slashed across the cheeks. He holds a rattle in one hand and an arrow in the other. He has just spent three days and nights fasting in the wilderness in preparation for tonight when he enters the company of adult men. He has been waiting for this moment with increasing trepidation and eagerness ever since he can remember. No longer will he have to play with babies, live with the women and children; now he will have rights and responsibilities, be respected by his peers and older men. Tonight he will spend with men in the kiva. He has come of age.

The hero severs the ties to the maternal world and steps alone across the threshold into the sacred world of Nature. In this world, the wind and the stars, the stones and weeds, the sun and waters are symbols of regeneration. In this world the terms of life and death are clearly

defined: The Great Mother gives and the Great Mother takes away.
Hers is the testing ground, the arena upon which the quest is staged.
Symbolically, the wilderness is a grave or a womb, wherein the hero
dies and is reborn.[1]

Ritual and rites of passage have been an integral part of the lives of early
cultures. They served to mark the transition periods experienced by each
individual, whether it was at birth, marriage, parenthood or death. The
changes of seasons were observed with ceremony and ritual, each harvest
was celebrated and praised; a young boy's first hunt and act of manhood
was extolled with a ceremony. The significance of the passage of time was
recognized; each transition was acknowledged and celebrated. Such
attention to the cycle of nature, the passage of time, and the development
of the individual, was the norm. It served to order, to give a sense of
security to the people. Children, especially, knew that at a certain age they,
too, would be welcomed into the community in a new way, and that their
new capacities would be recognized and called forth. This had a powerful
effect on their ability to mature and socialize within the group. They knew
what was expected of them, what the rules of the game were. They felt safe.
For a well run society, where there is appropriate give and take and respect
and recognition for the gifts offered by each generation, this is
fundamental. Our primitive cultures knew this instinctively. And our
modern, end of the millennium culture, must take this acknowledgment up
in a new and conscious way.

In some European countries, ritual is still firmly ingrained in the
culture. Birth, christening or baptism are marked with elaborate and
significant ceremonies. Choosing godparents is a careful and lengthy
process: one is honored to be chosen. Many of the Saints Days are observed
with specific customs such as St. Martin's Day or St. Nicholas Day, which
both involve the celebration of children and the coming inner light of the
winter season. But something creative is being called from us at the end of
the millennium, something that reflects a new consciousness for a
spiritually based understanding of the passages of development that each
one of us experiences as we walk our paths of life. I became interested in
ritual and rites of passage as I watched each of my children develop into
bigger and more capable individuals. They did it on their own without
much fanfare, but it all seemed to happen so quickly and without much
ceremony. I found myself trying to hold on to moments, so I could
remember how each child was at each stage. Family customs and
conventions soon became a way of freezing the moment in time, of making

passages memorable. And these evolved into various rituals that were unique to our family and served to order and pass on a feeling of confidence. Even so, I felt more consciousness was needed.

Due to the fact that I became a single mother when my three children were six, four and one, I became interested in all sorts of child-rearing practices. Besides being overwhelmed by the prospect of providing for my children on my own, of having to play both mother and father, I worried about the lack of male role models in their lives, especially for my youngest, my son. I was very much a woman of my times and knew that it was important to provide as balanced a milieu for my children as possible. Despite my own best intentions, though, I had absorbed from our culture, and a college education, a heavy dose of Freud. Throughout my adult life I had been constantly aware of Freud and his assertion that a mother is an overpowering and somehow indecent figure in her son's life. I felt trapped as I imagined myself and my son marching inexorably on, he towards adolescence and me towards my inevitable downfall as an effective parent. It felt predetermined, as though I was powerless against this fate.

Feeling a burden on my shoulders, I assumed that my relationship with my son was doomed. I felt that nothing I did was ever going to be able to save him from me. I worked very hard to find the appropriate balance to my innate shortcomings as a parent. But I felt uncomfortable with this picture, felt uncomfortable enough to try and find evidence to the contrary. In my research I did find room for a little comfort because, according to Freud and others, my two daughters, aged four and six, would be considered safe with me until adolescence! This allayed my fears about their well being for the present. I realized that eventually, of course, they'd have to go through their own process of detachment, and I'd have to find the proper forum for that to take place. But that was far enough in the future. In the meantime I leaned heavily on my father for male influence and on my son's godfather for advice and companionship for my children.

Things went well. We had a wonderful Waldorf school nearby which provided an imaginative and rich curriculum to balance out what I could not give them at home. But all along I felt this persistent, outraged presentiment. Why, just because I was a mother, was I condemned to be the wrong person to bring up my son to be a healthy integrated male? My parents live nearby, through the orchard below us, and so they played an important role in my children's upbringing. But my father is an intellectual, a Puritan with deep New England roots. Although he loves his grandchildren, and is loving when sought out, he is not directly involved in their daily activities. My mother, in contrast, comes from a warm and loving family. She is always involved in her children's and grandchildren's lives, communicating, supportive, cooperative and willing to take time to give of herself. In short, the females in the family appeared healthy and fulfilled, while the men appeared confused and, in the case of my children's father, absent. This was the way it was for my children. Not atypical! And this subject became the topic of numerous conversations among my friends, male and female alike. Yet all of us, influenced by Freud and the common perceptions of our culture somehow did not feel strong enough, or imaginative enough, to break out of tradition and do something completely new. We looked for direction, but finding none, went about the business of our already overburdened lives.

That is, until my children were starting adolescence and I read a book about ritual and rites of passage and the role older, unrelated men can play in the lives of adolescents. A friend handed me *Iron John* by Robert Bly. Upon reading it I experienced an absolution, a complete justification for the research I put in to disproving the undercurrents alive in our culture. Nothing changed outwardly in my life, but the inner release I experienced is indescribable. Much has been written about ritual and rites of passage since then, but this book will remain for me the jumping-off point into the new world of understanding about life's journey. Robert Bly takes the Grimm's Fairy Tale, *Iron John*, and uses it as a metaphor for the development of a boy into an adult. He describes the stages he must pass through, and the *wounds* he must receive before he can call himself a man. Part of a boy's task is to become independent from his mother. This does not mean that his mother was the one who inflicted the wounds or never had a healthy role to play in his life. This is merely a natural step he must take in order to become a man. And, very importantly, this process must be accomplished with the support and aid of older men. In an ideal world the mother hands her son, at puberty, over to the male world. And, ideally, there is a defined male world to hand him over to. Otherwise the deed will not be accomplished. This also means that a mother is not responsible for her son's initiation. It means she will hand him over to the older men in her family or circle of friends. *They*, hopefully armed with *Iron John* wisdom, will do what is necessary and, in the very doing, will *themselves experience a healing*. And the boy will begin the process of feeling his way into the world of men. He will find his own experiences and initiations appropriate to his age and consciousness. He will carry his own wounds, which won't only have been inflicted by his mother.

To me this vital new consciousness was very important. I experienced it as a great gift. What a relief to know that we all are allowed to have wounds!

Wounds are sacred. I don't need to over-protect my children! The wounds won't cripple us; they will contribute to growth! I hadn't really understood this, although I had heard it in other ways. 'For the truth is that everything in life that flowers and bears fruit is an outgrowth of pain and suffering...though it is also true that real human strength can only be developed by rising above suffering and making it a living force, the source of one's power to overcome'.[2] In actuality I felt as though these thoughts gave me back my son. Because of the men's movement, I am able to experience his adolescence without the guilt creating a pretended curtain between us, without me artificially withholding my love because I was afraid of being too overpowering. My son is 16 now and we naturally have arguments and disagreements as he experiences his rites of passage, but I won't have to withhold my love for fear of provoking an experience in him that both of us would regret.

After I'd read *Iron John*, I finally understood that it was in my power to do what was right not only by my son, but also by my two daughters. Robert Bly describes the role of the mother as being entirely appropriate and natural in raising young children. Only during adolescence is it necessary to turn them over to the male or female adult world of other people. In the case of sons, it is essential to have a male, or group of males, to whom to hand the responsibility of launching a male child onto the path of mature development. For daughters, a group of closely connected females is essential to help the female child understand and welcome her femininity as universal and not as only related to her mother. Most adolescents go through their entire youth without any one event marking the beginning of adulthood. They receive no indication that, from here on, they are a part of the adult world.

If a child is lucky s/he will experience a religious rite of passage such as confirmation or bat/bar-mitzvah. Although it is not overtly stated in most of the preparation classes for these events, this is the moment when an adolescent steps over the invisible line that divides childhood from adulthood. But for most teenagers the sign-post is not clearly marked. The guidelines for behavior, the answers to the uncertain questions that most youths carry, the forum in which to phrase and re-phrase one's questions, are not there. Anxiety, uneasiness, dread, as well as the fear caused by lack of clarity about the adult world's expectations of them, become just another trial for the adolescent. The uneasiness evaporates over time, as do most things. But this lack of clarity leaves a pall over the adolescent's ability to manage life's larger challenges. A sense of loss lingers, making the loneliness of life that much more poignant and baffling.

Struggling with this awareness of the need to celebrate transitions in my children's lives, I began planning my son's rite of passage two years before it actually happened. It would stand as a marker on his path towards adulthood and eventual maturity. He was sceptical and resistant to becoming involved. He felt self-conscious about this new-found focus on him and 'what would be good for him', as he put it. His childhood differed from children in native cultures who have the anticipation built into their lives. They grow up looking forward to their initiation into the world of adults. My son suddenly had this thrust upon him, with only a little preparation. And, none of his friends were having to do this. Nevertheless, because of my conviction that this was the right thing to do, I persevered. I knew it was important to have the right men involved in the ritual, men who knew my son and whom my son respected. His godfather was the obvious choice and we began discussing what would be stirring, significant and appropriate. Rather than seek out more literature on the subject, I relied on conversations with men I knew who were involved in various men's groups. I knew that their personal experiences would make the ceremony more vibrant. I asked them if they knew anything about rites of passage, or Native American culture, or the new men's movement. One person in particular had spent years working locally to establish a meaningful arena where men could meet, feel safe, and explore what it meant to be men today. With his help an evening was designed that each person felt would be substantial and momentous.

Nevertheless, I experienced an intense ambivalence. He was my youngest. We had a very warm and loving relationship. I was unconsciously holding back the time when I would have to relinquish him. I knew this was selfish and inappropriate, but that did not alleviate the soul pain. My higher self, the part of me that usually knows what is right, was able to realize that time waits for no person and that I must flow with the process or run the risk of being left behind. I realized the rite of passage was going to be as much for me as it was for my son!

A month before the ritual was to have happened, my son, who is very athletic and risk-taking, had an accident on his all-terrain vehicle. It left him flat on his back for 10 days and in a wheelchair for two weeks. During this time he was in intense pain and unable to move. I had to feed him, care for him and stay with him day and night. He was terrified. It was as if he had climbed back into the cradle. The 10 days that he was flat on his back went by like a dream. I stayed home to tend to his every need. We experienced a closeness that I knew was a gift, a closeness that could never be repeated. Remarkably, we both somehow understood this. Once the initial shock was over and we knew that he wasn't paralyzed, we approached each day with respect. I carefully lived into the moment and treasured each hour we spent together, each conversation we had, each encounter that allowed me to remain close to him just those few days longer. This included the inevitable need for entertainment. I had him captive, and read many of the books we had missed reading together because he was the third child and too young to remember. The twinges of guilt I had felt occasionally during his middle years as I stopped the nightly ritual of story telling was finally laid to rest. We didn't finish too many books but the fact of actually going back to an earlier time was potent! The potentially grave accident turned out to be a gift. I had been given a grace period, a brief return to the days when he was in the cradle, to cherish for one more quick moment.

We both knew it would not last. When the time came for his Confirmation (attended while he was still in the wheel chair) I was able, without much anguish, to send him on his way. I also realized that the time for the ceremony had passed, the people involved were unable to participate, so we decided to wait until the following summer and concentrated on getting him strong again. By the next June it was all arranged. He was very embarrassed, unwilling to admit it might be interesting, and very vocal about his complete indifference to the process. He wasn't going to have any part of it. Nevertheless, I went forward with the plan. His godfather came up from Washington DC. Three other significant men in the life of the family convened in the woods behind our house one Friday night and built a fire, arranged drums, and began burning bundles of sage. Before my son was to join them in the woods his godfather had given him the task of thinking about any questions he might want to ask the company of men, burning questions, or seemingly insignificant ones and to carry them to the fire with him that night. As the time to leave grew near, his godfather said, 'Come up alone to the fire in half an hour'. My son's friends were all at the house, being a part of the next day's component of the rite of passage and they were playing basketball. My son embarrassedly said he probably wouldn't come. His friends were silent and strangely supportive. They knew, deep in their bones, that something important was about to happen. When 25 minutes had gone by, my son appeared in the kitchen with a sense of purpose and dignity on his face. He said, 'Bye, Mom', and walked out the door. I experienced a sharp and sudden sense of loss and ran out the door to accompany him to the hedge to say a real good-bye. And that was that. He was gone for three hours. When they all came back it was late and no one talked much. Later, I heard vague references to four fires, four men, drums and questions asked. Since then, though, there is a marked difference in his demeanor and carriage. There is a certain sense of dignity in him that one doesn't often see in a 15 year old. And some of his friends have asked for something similar to happen in their lives.

After this experience I felt something must also be done for my daughters even though they were well past the age at which this is usually done. I'd only recently become aware that my first daughter, who is 21, had not really been given the tools to genuinely love herself as a woman. Two souls live within her breast! The one yearns only to be wife and mother, to find herself through relationship with a husband and children. The other strides assertively forward, claiming no one shall tell her what to do, demanding a life devoted to her chosen profession. And she can't reconcile the two. She struggles constantly with what her task should be and how to play her role as a woman. I feel that, had I been able to offer her a rite of passage at the relevant moment, had I been aware of the need to welcome her into a circle of women, helped her to rejoice in the feminine soul, feel the strengths and joys of being a woman, her confusion would be the less. She's had no real markers, no clear signs to follow. She hasn't been able to identify with the wide multiplicity of roles a woman might play. My second child seems less confused about her role as a woman. And yet, she, too, struggles constantly with potentially conflicting beliefs: that she has a right to make independent decisions, and that being in an intimate relationship with a man can be a path of inner development. She won't settle for any relationship, just to be *in relationship,* but this often means she is alone. Her first year at college, looked forward to for so long, has left her with a feeling of emptiness. She had a few boyfriends, but none of the relationships were what she was looking for. So she has chosen to focus on her career, her professional interests. This makes for very intense discussions with her sister. Both of them had gone through most of their adolescence without a significant marker, other than Confirmation and the Youth Conferences, to signal their passage into adulthood. I just had not been aware of what could be done for women, of how young girls needed to be welcomed into the company of women.

Feeling the necessity of planning, anyway, to celebrate their entry into womanhood, I asked around the community for help. I found that a number of women had been concerned with the same issues. They had organized a ritual designed for young girls when they begin to menstruate. They advised convening a group of women who knew my daughters well and would want to support them, separately, through a significant ceremony of welcome. When I approached my daughters I was surprised to learn that each of them and their friends already understood the value of ritual and had already incorporated aspects of ceremony and ritual into their own daily lives. For example, when my second daughter and my niece went to college last year their friends and cousins had designed a ritual to mark the significance of their leaving home for the first time. They wanted to mark the taking of that first real step out into the world. This was natural for them, and I had known nothing about it!

In the end they said they didn't want anything done by me. They tossed off the idea and said that they were fine with what they had done themselves and with their friends while they were teenagers. The ritual they had created for themselves involved water, in the form of a scented bath, and smoke, in the form of burning incense and cleansing herbs. They chose, for that evening, a ceremonial casting-away of a tendency or habit they did not want to take with them into their adult life. My niece threw away her tendency to defer always to others, while my daughter cast off her negative attitude towards, and fear of, change. Having had this elegant ritual described to me, I realized that ritual can be simple and short. It needn't involve intricate preparations or many people. It can be done on the spur of the moment. It's the inner attitude towards change, transition, the little deaths and rebirths we inescapably undergo that make ritual profound and meaningful. And so, despite the odds, and probably because of their Waldorf education, these teenagers have made ritual their own, something that reflects Generation X attitudes, needs and distinctive challenges.

Upon reflection I realized that the idea of ritual and ceremony had been made conscious in their minds through their exposure both to the Youth Conferences they had attended throughout their adolescence, and the conversations of adult women over the years. I was overcome with feeling when I heard that these young women were worlds ahead of me in taking care of the turning points in their lives. I thank the community of adults they were fortunate enough to grow up amongst for their ability to be so wise in their view of the world.

The Youth Conferences, which I am convinced also had a lot to do with this are offered by the Christian Community two or three times a year. They have become turning points for numerous young people in America for a number of years. The Christian Community was founded in Switzerland in 1922, in connection with the work of Rudolf Steiner, and it has grown into a world wide religious movement with 30 churches, some ten in the United States. Twice a year priests from the North East Christian

Community meet with a group of young adults, ages 14 through 18 to discuss what is on their minds and in their hearts. The burning questions that arise are formed into themes for the next conference. The priests find and narrate the biographies of significant people whose lives were influenced and shaped by the same questions. It is a very powerful and moving experience for the adolescents to hear adults articulate their own deepest questions and concerns and relate them to the lives of well known philosophers, musicians, pacifists, revolutionaries, explorers and inventors. It is a threshold experience for them as they try to articulate questions in a safe forum among learned and wise adults who have been struggling a long time with the very same universal issues. I have heard many teenagers exclaim in admiration and awe, 'How can they talk so effortlessly and articulately about such important issues? About questions that I have been asking myself for so long and found so few answers?' The organizers are deeply aware of the importance of the design and content of the conference. They want these youths to know that there are adults who are concerned with turning points, with questions about justice and war, the meaning of life, and whether death is the end or not. They want them to feel cared for on that inmost level, and know there is a place where these questions can be asked and taken seriously. The social aspect is intense and deep. Lasting friendships are forged among these teenagers from all over the area. They sanction the meetings that occur on a deeper level than most are used to because they know that such experiences can brighten the darkness many young people must endure during adolescence. These conferences are a way to help fill the void left by a society that appears no longer to know how to equip its youth for adult life.

I feel fortunate that all three of my children have had the opportunity to experience meeting others on a deeper level. The Youth Conferences played a very important role in revealing to them the possibilities for relating to and caring about other human beings. Just knowing that there are adults who live lives of service, who put the needs of others before their own, gives them a sense of hope for their generation. If, somehow, the message contained in the wisdom of earlier civilizations could be incorporated into our culture, could become a part of the curriculum of our lives, we would have something of substance and value with which to equip our adolescent children for the journey into adulthood. Rites of passage, ritual, markers on the path, all need our conscious embrace. There is a lot of good, solid work being done by our generation in this realm, but the message needs to be spread around the globe for all to hear.

Ritual and ceremony are an affirmation of life and growth. Rites of passage recognize the importance of conscious transition. They are a gift from the community which supports and affirms each separate individual.

The circle of dancers grows tighter around Least Bear until he can no longer stand. Hands reach out to him and he is raised into the air, buoyed by the rising chant, the singing and drumming and the good will of all the people. He floats for a long moment, utterly reliant on the circle to keep him afloat. Least Bear's birthday moon, The Freeze Up Moon, shines bright in the sky. The chanting begins to lessen in tempo. The singing gradually fades. The drums slow their beat. The arms holding Least Bear high up in the sky gently waft him down to the earth. The ceremony is winding down. Least Bear belongs now to the world of men. He has crossed the threshold on his 14th birthday and is reborn to new tasks.

Notes

[1.] *The Book of the Vision Quest, Personal Transformation in the Wilderness,* 1992, Steven Foster with Meredith Little; Simon and Schuster, New York
[2.] *Iron John, A Book About Men,* 1990, Bly, Robert; Addison-Wesley Publishing Company, Inc. Reading, MA

Lee F. Nagel

A promising career as a post-hippie yogi roofer was brought to an end by the uncompromising winters of upstate New York. When mashing my fingers with a hammer did not register in my cold benumbed brain, I decided it was time to look for an indoor job. Paying work had become important because in only a few months I would be starting a new chapter in my life with the birth of my first child. As luck or whatever would have it I immediately fell into work at a newly opened inpatient psychiatry unit in a community hospital. It was in this setting that I began to use my previous training in yoga, meditation, and psychodrama; creating ways to help people in serious emotional pain.

As my family grew to include four children it became important to keep the spirit alive in work and family life.

24
The gathering

I stand motionless on the ridge watching the setting sun, dwarfed by the blood red sky. Below me my son, Moses, and his mom talk by the edge of the pond in which I can see the slightly rippled reflection of the darkening clouds. I try to slow my fiercely beating heart with a few deep breaths, reaching for a calmness I find elusive. Wrestling with impatience I wait, giving them time to complete what they have begun, knowing that they will never again be together in quite the same way. Finally, just as the last golden sliver of the sun disappears behind the distant mountains, transforming the day into the softness of twilight, they turn and slowly, silently walk up the sloping field. When they are only ten yards away, I call out to Eva to stop and let the boy come across alone. She understands and halts as I notice the tears on her cheeks. Her obvious pain almost distracts me from my purpose. Still, I wait in silence. Moses hesitates for a moment at his mother's side, looking at her. Then he turns and crosses the space to join me without looking back. Together we turn away and head down the back of the ridge towards the Gathering.

I don't get a chance to say much during our short walk. Moses' entire body is twitching with excitement. He fills the air with a rapid-fire oration about the promise of this moment, straining to describe his exquisite sensation of the dawn of freedom, nearing the end of youth's captivity, about to enter the 'real world' with its adventures and dangers.

★

Two months ago, Moses turned eighteen. One morning during my commute to the office, drifting on the earnest voices of NPR's Morning Edition, my mind suddenly lurched with the realization that in a very short time he would graduate from high school and most certainly leave home. Moses was my first child to reach this milestone and I was unprepared.

The truth is I didn't want to face this transition. See, if I have a son old enough to pack his bags and set off into the world, it's pretty clear that I can no longer be that youthful knight-errant whom I still imagined myself to be.

After coasting through those idyllic early years, Moses and I had fought side by side and face to face the battles of his adolescence. The episodes of painful conflict and confusion have thankfully faded from memory and I mostly retain the excitement of our exploration and growth. At times I had been brilliant, hitting just the right combination of understanding pal and judicious parent. At other times I found myself uttering those senseless and embarrassing phrases, accurate echoes of my parents' voices, that I had vowed never to repeat. I still remember those desperate attempts to control or guide his path with words I knew would only elicit scorn. Now, like fierce competitors nearing the end of a long and draining match, most of the tension had eased and we felt a wearied sense of mutual admiration and respect. Rather than let him slip away after his graduation, I wanted to mark his coming of age and bear witness to this transition, a time that has been observed by men of every era. In that moment when a boy becomes a man and his father becomes the elder, the entire world shifts a bit. As a culture and a species we once again move past another milepost on our journey into the future. In that instant the load borne by the brotherhood of men, the responsibility we carry for our tribe, our community, and for the earth itself, is shared by one more.

My transition was never acknowledged nor was I officially welcomed into the community of men. Perhaps that has contributed to my struggle to be a man, to join with men, and to trust the vision and power that have come with maturity. I was determined to support Moses in his journey towards manhood. Perhaps this could be accomplished by highlighting the moment when we publicly recognize him and welcome him as one of us. I knew that men had done this for thousands of years through ritual and mystery. Native American boys might seek a vision alone in the desert, while Aboriginal youngsters would take a walkabout to experience their independence and seek wisdom. The Jewish bar-mitzvah at the local country club has evolved from a sacred ritual of promotion and acceptance. For Moses I pictured a circle of men, important men in my life, men who had known Moses. My imagination filled with flashes of dramatic moments of the past. I saw fire and smoke, and men gathering for this purpose wearing simple cotton, wearing skins, maybe wearing nothing at all. I heard the beat of drums and the ancient incantations carried by a portentous air. And I saw men looking each other eye into eye, searching for the truths they had learned, and speaking from the heart, allowing this youngster his first glimpse of the fellowship and wisdom that we share.

★

As we near the sacred space, actually a field on our land where we have often played football or soccer, I call out to announce our arrival. Moses falls silent, suddenly filled with the realization that he is about to enter into the unknown. I share his rush of thoughts and feelings. Would I perform adequately? Was I ready to be the father of a grown son? Would Moses embarrass me, or worse, act disgusted and scornful? The grass is cool and wet from the evening dew. The light has faded, revealing only shadows and rustlings. Where had everyone gone? Curling slowly upward in the heavy air, the smoke from the fire is the sole indication of a presence. Next to the fire a small domed hut covered in khaki canvas can be perceived through the mist. We stop in some confusion and then, one by one, eight naked men emerge from the sweat lodge into the gathering dusk of a late Spring evening. They silently form a circle near us and the Leader asks me my business. The unprecedented strangeness of the scene makes me fear I have forgotten my lines. Then I remember that there is no script, this is really happening. I take a deep breath and ask myself what my business is. I speak: 'I bring my son Moses, my first born, to be accepted into our community of men.' I step forward and the circle parts, allowing me to join. Moses is left alone outside. Now he is asked his business. My breathing stops. Will he be able to respond? Will he feel tested, angry, and reject the whole thing? He speaks. 'I come wishing to be accepted.' As one we nod and make a space. There is an awkward moment of silence as we all freeze on the edge of time. Then Moses takes a step forward, we all spontaneously exhale in relief, and the circle is completed.

★

For the last few years I, with many other men in our culture, have begun a vague and often unconscious search for a connection with other men. In that halting journey I have found brothers and we have shared what we have learned in our extended adolescence. We have tried to find the time apart from earning a living and tending to our families to be together. We have tried to go beyond playing or watching sports together to create an intimate fellowship where we can speak of dreams, fears, or frustrations with those who can truly understand.

I went with my vision of a ceremony for Moses to my friend Ed who has also been on this search. In days too busy with meetings and work, Ed and I met twice for an early breakfast to plan a rite of passage which would freeze time for a moment and honor just what was passing. Out of his concern for Moses and me, and with excitement about marking a transition that all of us are approaching with our sons, Ed agreed to become Honorary Uncle and take responsibility for leading the ceremony.

Ed insisted that Moses and I agree on the membership of the Gathering, inviting men who were important to each of us. We were urged to resolve any conflict or disagreement with these people before the day of ceremony in order to be able to focus on the ritual without distraction from the past. I had coffee with a friend and let him know of a resentment I had carried since a long trip we took together a year earlier. Awkwardly we worked through the left-over feelings and cleared the air. In his position as leader Ed spoke to each participant and by his instruction and tone conveyed the solemnity and sense of meaning we were trying to infuse into the ceremony. We were all urged not to talk about the upcoming event to anyone, and to pay attention to thoughts and feelings that arose for us as we anticipated coming together for this purpose. As the weeks passed I felt the sense of mystery deepening throughout the community.

★

The Leader speaks out, inviting the spirits of all men in history to join us and guide us in our endeavor this night. As the light finally fails and we see each other in the flickering shadows of the dying fire, I am trying to feel the eternal connection we have as our birthright, the chain of men stretching across the ages. Unexpectedly the circle breaks up and Moses and I are surrounded by the group. They silently undress us and bid us to enter the sweat lodge. It is still very warm inside, especially as we enter naked from the cool night outside. We have been urged to let the heat and smoke sweat away any resistance to openness and honesty that might exist between this father and son. My chest aches as I experience eighteen years passing in a flash. I remember this tiny ball of energy and curiosity that forever changed the priorities of my life. Now I am sitting with this young man to whom I have given so much and yet for a moment it seems totally inadequate. I fear I have never provided him with the essentials and, instead, have burdened him with expectations and prejudices that will impede his own growth. We talk quietly for a few moments as I try to express myself and let him know that I realize it has not always been easy to be my son. He is wonderfully accepting and tries to release me from guilt with a laugh. He tells me it has not been so bad; better, he is convinced, than most. Then we meditate silently. It is when we become still that I realize that we are surrounded by a powerful rhythm of drums and voices. Outside the men are dancing around the lodge, weaving a fabric of sound so primitive that the beat resonates with my heart, with the blood rushing through my veins, and seems to come up out of the earth itself. Again the strangeness of it all is disorienting and rational thoughts cease. For a moment I can really feel the presence of our ancestors. Only for a moment though and then I am wondering what will come next.

Time has lost its linearity and I can't even guess how quickly it is passing, but after a while there is a commotion at the door and, as I slowly and dreamily raise my eyes, the men of the gathering are entering the small, low space. Some carry hot rocks on shovels to add to the warm rocks in the center pit. Naked bodies crowd against naked bodies until all find a place in an intimate circle. The atmosphere is filled with smoke and sweat sweetened with the smell of burning sage, thrown onto the hot rocks to purify the sacred space.

One by one we share a story. Most speak of their memories of crossing the line as Moses is doing tonight. Others relate a special moment when they received a gift from their fathers, much as we fathers were offering a welcoming gift to Moses. Moses' uncle speaks first. In the course of a few minutes I learn more about a man who has been in my family for several years than I had known before. I cry with him during his tale. I cry a few more times before all have spoken. I laugh a lot too. I mostly marvel at the different experiences, yet similar struggles, of men. Now I realize how little I knew these men whom I consider my closest companions.

After all have spoken the Leader turns to Moses, who has listened quietly from the dark stillness of his place in the circle. Did he wish to speak, to add anything of his experience to the Gathering? By his silence I imagine that he is overwhelmed by the intensity of the experience. But, actually he is only gathering his thoughts. He does not seem to be plagued by the doubts and fear of failure that I know so well. Perhaps he believes that men do speak to each other regularly in this intimate way, and that he is only now being accepted into that private men's world. After a few moments he begins. He offers gratitude for what has been given. He offers appreciation for what he believes to be an unusual effort by adults to do something of meaning. He recognizes from our tales that he can expect a richness of experience as he sets off on his own. He pauses for another moment and I think perhaps he is done. Then he raises his head and slowly gazes around the circle, taking each of us in with his eyes. With a directness that touches each of us he says that he has listened and heard all we have said, that he has given it weight in his heart, considered all the teachings significant. But he adds, he hopes we will understand that in his turn he will have to do what feels right to him. We should not be surprised if his path takes him to a different place. He believes from what we have done for him this night that we will understand. Then he sits back in his place.

I feel a stab of discomfort. Isn't this last comment just a bit arrogant? I cautiously look around the circle to check the reactions of others and notice that most of my colleagues are smiling and nodding their heads. In that moment I really get it. I breathe and finally feel I can let go. Moses has accepted our offer to join us and at the same time has declared his independence, showing us all the paradox inherent in being a man.

We sit quietly for several minutes, letting the richness of the ceremony sink into our souls and then Ed leads us out into the starry darkness. By the light of the night sky he produces a knife and asks Moses to approach him. I am not prepared for this moment and again my fears rush in. When Ed raises the knife I am ready to protect my boy, even though he stands placidly and trustingly before the leader. Ed takes several strands of his abundant hair and severs them from Moses' head. For me the lesson of acceptance is driven home as I am able to breathe evenly again. Then we stand together in a circle and close the ceremony with a short prayer.

★

Well, that's about it. We asked Moses to take a walk alone and let the experience linger while the rest of us adjourned to the house to eat and have some tea. There I found my wife and daughters. They seemed like creatures of a different species and it took about an hour before this difference was lost in the well-established patterns of our relationships.

Looking back to that evening three years ago I think I can discern a real change in myself and the way Moses and I relate to each other. Something was released in the smoke, something washed away in the intimate tales shared in that sweltering dark place. I have come to feel more solidly rooted in the middle age of my life with its bittersweet mixture of power and loss. Moses and I have definitely graduated to a relationship more respectful, tolerant and open; a relationship I look forward to sharing with him for the rest of our lives.

★

It is very late on the night of the Gathering. I am again on the ridge above the pond where Moses and I started our journey earlier today. So much has happened in these few hours, and yet the stars seem unaltered, measuring their time in eons. I am struck by the paradox of change versus constancy that underlies everything we did today. It may be that change is the only thing we can be sure of, but in other important ways we continually echo all those generations that have preceded us. Tonight I helped to bring a man into the world. I wonder what grandparenthood has in store for me.

25
Image and inspiration in human becoming: searching for the Goddess in an evolving world[1]

Signe Eklund Schaefer

The long arm of culture reaches into every home in America, through television, books, newspapers, magazines, and our educational system, dictating our parenting practices and attitudes and telling our daughters who they should be.[2]

Images play an important role in our becoming, and I would like to look in particular at how they influence the attitudes, behavior and sense of self of young girls as they head toward adulthood. Much of what I share could also be said about boys, but I am focusing on girls because they are so obviously at risk in our modern materialistic world.

Where do the images we hold about being girls or women come from? It seems to me that whether positive or negative, they come from two basic directions. Many come from the world around us—either from the culture at large as expressed through TV, movies, music, advertizing, etc. or from family members, peers, teachers and the other real people in our lives who act as role models for our behavior and attitudes. Often these images from outside become hardened, fall into stereotypes that work in subtle but powerful ways to shape our development. The other primary source of images influencing our becoming is from our inner longings, our individual yearnings for self-definition and expression. Colored, of course, by what comes to us from outside, they nevertheless have an individual core that shapes itself into mental pictures of what we hope to become; sadly, these aspirations are often at odds with what we meet in the world. This experience of conflict can grow into a feeling that one does not fit in as one is, that one is somehow unacceptable. As parents and teachers, I think it is very important for us to look carefully—individually and collectively—at how our attitudes and behavior, our words and our deeds are shaping the young women who will find their way as adults into the Twenty-First Century.

One of the first generalizations that can be made about the images coming from the outside is that, taken together, they form a mixed message.

On the one hand, there are traditional pictures of woman as server, nurturer, an agreeable and demure presence supporting others from the background. This is the image of the secretary with pen and pad in hand or the at-home-Mom waiting with milk and cookies. Quite contrasting views have emerged in the last 30 years under the influence of the Women's Movement. Girls have been encouraged to believe that anything they dream is possible. Media heroines fight for their rights and move toward the world's definition of success, which is all too often based on traditionally male roles and behavior. The word 'feminist' conjures up many contrasting pictures: for some a tough militant career woman who is angry and unappealing, for others a strong, independent, fulfilled and caring individual. The entertainment industry portrays women in an aura of throbbing sensuality. 'Models' surround us: tall and impossibly thin with perfect hair and skin, these figures live only as image, in advertizing stereotypes. They abound in magazines, billboards and in the catalogues that accumulate on every kitchen counter; but they are not images of real women like the ones we meet on the street or in the mirror. Life has been air-brushed out of them along with wrinkles, blemishes and cellulite. Nevertheless, they define beauty and sex appeal in incredibly powerful ways, leaving real girls and women, whose lives and bodies are generally at odds with these media images, seeing themselves and being seen by others as somehow deficient.

The Women's Movement has brought into focus how much our culture is shaped by masculine ways of thinking. There is nothing intrinsically wrong with rational analysis, logical penetration into an issue, self-assertion or product orientation; but, in the absence of a sense for the whole, an appreciation of process, an attitude of service, or the ability to nurture, those former qualities can make for a one-sided relationship with nature and other human beings. The former qualities can be seen as more masculine ways of relating to the world, the latter as more feminine. Neither masculine nor feminine, as I am using them here, are qualities belonging only to men or women. We all can exercise these different ways of being, but our culture has for many centuries valued masculine traits more. Our competitive, materialistic, individualistic western society is the product of masculine striving for control.[3]

In recent years, feminist researchers have begun to question the prevailing standards for success which have tended to find women deficient. They have questioned automatic definitions of human development based on male behavior. More and more studies point to differences between how girls and boys, or women and men, relate to themselves, to others and to the world.[4]

As a generalization, boys exhibit greater visual and spatial skills than girls. They are more interested in physical activity than communication and are fascinated with material things and how they work. They seek to discover logical principles and tend to follow laws and work with strict conceptions of what is fair. Girls are generally more people-oriented; they value the give and take of relationship and tend to base decisions on how something will affect others. Interdependence is obvious and appreciated. Girls generally have greater verbal abilities than boys; they certainly talk more.[5]

With findings like the above, we may feel an immediate sense of discomfort. Even if the phenomena are true, how much is environmental influence? How much is gender related? How much is individual difference? Recent research suggests that within hours of birth, girls are more sensitive to noise, to touch, to warmth and cold. Within two to four days, they stay interested in faces longer than do boys. Even as toddlers, girls talk more; and the questions they ask are as much for contact as for information. Boys, on the other hand, ask for a specific answer and speak to inform.[6]

A group of elementary school children was given a lesson on bicycle assembly and then asked to draw the parts of a bicycle. The boys' drawings were technically correct and well-labelled. So were the girls'; but their's also included themselves riding their bikes, their dogs running along and the sun shining.[7] Until recently, drawings like this would have been seen as soft, as not quite objective enough. But why not? Are the girls' drawings any less accurate for placing the subject within a life context?

Many readers will have read Deborah Tannen's *You Just Don't Understand* [8] which addresses the differences in communication patterns between women and men. Women use language to share intimacy, to offer support, to build consensus and community. Men are more likely to speak in order to solve problems, to offer advice, or to establish their identity. I recommend this book to anyone who has not read it; it is filled with recognizable anecdotes of how, with the best intentions, men and women experience breakdowns in communication because of the ways we use language. We must always take care when making generalizations about gender, yet recognizing the validity of differences can be a great help in fostering mutual appreciation and respect.

I am intrigued by recent research into male and female brains. With advances in technology, it has become possible to track how women's and men's thinking use different parts of the brain for the same activities. Women's brains appear to be structurally more complicated, more differentiated and mobile. Some researchers feel this may be related to differences in language ability and to a greater sensitivity to read feelings.

These brain studies offer physiological evidence for some challenging statements by Rudolf Steiner about the different possibilities for development offered by male or female bodies. Steiner gives a picture of women being less deeply incarnated into physicality than men. He imagines a kind of ideal human form and suggests that the female body hovers slightly above this while the male body descends beyond the ideal into greater density. This extends even into the structure of the brain. Consequently, Steiner says, the female brain exhibits greater flexibility; it is softer and more finely differentiated, and therefore more inclined to receive what is new, more easily trained for spiritual activity. The male brain is more rigid, more firmly structured, more able to follow straight trains of thought.[9] Many women, myself included, have found Steiner's words confirming and gratifying; they must, however, be considered within the context of his general picture of the human being reincarnating in one life as a woman, in the next as a man because of the yearning of the undivided 'I' to express itself in ever more whole and balanced ways. Clearly, with such a view of alternating genders in each succeeding incarnation, there can be no place for gender chauvinism, although we can each ask why we are living this particular life, at this time in history, in a female or a male body.

From quite different directions, we find evidence of innate differences between boys and girls, men and women, differences that are not only due to outside influence. But what are we to do with such information? Many feminists resist this kind of research for fear that it will be misinterpreted and misused to further oppress women. They want to focus on equality rather than difference. For me it has always been important to acknowledge both: to allow equality of opportunity for development and to appreciate and respect the different gifts and limitations. Beyond all this, it is vital to remember that each individuality is unique; gender is one aspect of who we are, and even within our gender, we all use and manifest feminine and masculine qualities.

I now want to return to the way images and attitudes can work into us, too often with narrow interpretations of possibility and one-sided values. In a very helpful book called *Reviving Ophelia*, Mary Pipher, cites many examples of how our culture and our schools treat girls differently from boys. She discusses the results of a study by the American Association of University Women (AAUW) published in 1992 called, *How Schools Shortchange Girls:*

> In classes, boys are twice as likely to be seen as role models, five times as likely to receive teachers' attention and twelve times as likely to speak up in class. In text-books, one-seventh of all illustrations of children are of girls. Teachers choose many more classroom activities that appeal to boys than to girls. Girls are exposed to almost three times as many boy-centered stories as girl-centered stories. Boys tend to be portrayed as clever, brave, creative and resourceful, while girls are depicted as kind, dependent and docile... Analysis of classroom videos shows that boys...are asked more abstract, open-ended and complex questions. Boys are more likely to be praised for academic and intellectual work, while girls are more likely to be praised for their clothing, behaving properly and obeying rules...[10]

In both direct and indirect ways, girls are encouraged to behave, to be quiet, to look good, to control themselves while boys' behavior is very often viewed as 'boys will be boys'. At the onset of puberty, the years of conflicting messages meet with an inner confusion that is especially difficult for girls. All teenagers withdraw into themselves, but, as Mary Pipher says, for girls the change is like planes and ships disappearing into the Bermuda Triangle.[11] Pre-adolescent girls are generally eager, adventurous, open and enthusiastic. Then all too many seem to lose all confidence, optimism and resiliency. Amazingly, their IQ scores drop (which certainly says something about the objective validity of these tests!) and their performance in math and science plummets. Of course, there are exceptions, but too many girls retreat not only from their parents, but also from class involvement, from intellectual engagement, and often tragically from their own bodies.

With adolescence, the cultural pressures begin to take a terrible toll. Girls become painfully aware of their appearance. In the midst of so many changes of body and soul, they are inundated with materialistic, aggressively sexual, empty but enticing images of women. Inevitably, their body image suffers: who would not feel fat compared to Barbie or the models that populate magazines and newspapers, or the actresses gyrating on music videos? Girls of this age become self-critical to the point of self-hatred, and in our competitive world, they can even feel isolated from their peers.

The chapter by Olivia Dreier explores the problems of body image more thoroughly. It is interesting to note here that in analyzing 48 issues of popular women's magazines, researchers found 63 ads for diet foods, while in the same number of men's magazines, there was only one. There were 96 articles about body size and shape in the women's magazines, but only eight in the men's.[12] Everywhere girls are being flooded with degrading images, are being told that what is most important for fulfillment in life is the right pair of jeans, the right cosmetics, the sex appeal of a thin body. And the women in these images are compliant, powerless, possessed.

Unfortunately, it is not only the media that exerts these pressures. We have all been conditioned to some degree, and we can also, quite inadvertently, pass on negative messages. How often do we complain about our bodies in front of our children? Or comment on someone else's? What standard are we using here? Have you ever refused food you wanted, even when you were hungry, in order to preserve an image? In what ways do we signal the importance of physical beauty? Have you, as a woman, ever tried to hide or minimize an accomplishment in order not to stand out or to appear too smart? Have you ever commented negatively about a woman who has achieved prominence or academic success, perhaps criticizing her appearance or her ambition? Do your children see you being polite rather than honest, or silent in the face of justifiable frustration?

Many subtle attitudes work powerfully into our own sense of self and through us become sources of imitation for our children. The pressures on children, the available negative sources for imitation, are much greater today than even ten years ago, certainly than when I was a child. Decisions—whether about likes and dislikes in clothes, in food, in activities, or about drugs, alcohol and sex—come ever earlier. The messages influencing these decisions are mixed: be independent but also fit in; be sexy but don't have sex; 'just say no' but be cool and popular.

It is sad and ironic that social conditions and conditioning seem to have become more problematic in spite of the advances brought on by feminism.

We are all exposed to ongoing portrayals of women as sexual objects, to more graphic sex coming right into our homes through TV and videos, and to more violence against women. The Women's Movement arose, in part, in resistance to just these phenomena, so why are things worse? This question connects to what I see as a continuing societal resistance to attend to a deep yearning in many modern people for an expanded definition of what it is to be human. The push for women's rights and opportunities is not enough if the world stays basically as it is. There is a whole part of our human nature that has been undervalued for too long and so we are jeopardizing the earth, ourselves and our children with misguided self-interest, competition and materialism. We need to awaken a feminine dimension in and for us all. This links back to what I referred to at the beginning of this chapter as the second source of image and inspiration guiding our becoming.

A phrase of Rudolf Steiner's that has echoed in my thinking for many years is, 'Everybody resembles the God he (*she*) understands.'[13] I believe that increasing numbers of women and men have come to feel that something has been missing in descriptions of God, in portrayals of human beings, in the outer images available for resemblance. As images of God with a long white beard became ever less satisfying, some people determined that 'God is dead.' This view, however, leaves nothing to identify ourselves with. And so in recent years, many have begun searching for the Goddess, for an expanded image of the divine world and of our human becoming that encompasses a feminine archetype. I do not see this as a wish to replace God with Goddess but as an expression of a need to understand further dimensions of human development.

Particularly since the 1960's, there have been many studies in mythology, archeology and history that explore a time before what we have usually understood as the beginnings of civilization, before what have come to be known as patriarchal times. This work leads back over 5000 years into the world of the Goddess, into apparent matriarchal cultures that were peaceful, egalitarian, stable for long ages, and highly civilized. Matriarchy here refers to a state of consciousness, not a time when women exerted power over men. It was a time before a real consciousness of division and the exercise of power of one group over another. Riane Eisler refers to this as a time of partnership in contrast to the later dominator mentality that came in with the patriarchal assault.[12] Here the Great Mother Goddess was the guardian of birth and death, the healer, the keeper of the flame, the bringer of civilization through activities like spinning, weaving and baking, as well as the inspirer of religious ritual. She had many names: Ishtar, Isis, Demeter, Spider Woman, and perhaps the most encompassing, Sophia, the being of Divine Wisdom. She was the Cosmic Mother of All, bringing an integrating, if non-individuated, knowledge of the spirit to human beings on the earth.

As time passed, however, her world was gradually destroyed. Human consciousness was evolving, human beings were acquiring new mastery over the natural world; the individual, and not only the blood group, was becoming ever more important. This story is told in many myths of the 'son' who does battle with his mother, or the hero who destroys threatening, smothering monster figures most often portrayed in female form (the Sphinx, Medusa, the Amazons...). Archeological discoveries in this century support the same story, with their records of matriarchal cultures like Catal Huyek in present-day Turkey or Minoan Crete succumbing to takeovers by tribes from the north.

This story of a shift from unconscious unity of human beings with each other, with nature and with the spiritual world to a time of growing power struggles, mastery over the forces of nature, and individual accomplishment is a familiar one. Although in these years of the patriarchy we have developed very important qualities of self-knowledge, rationality, and freedom, we have in fact gone so far that we now experience great imbalance. Individual power and greed have gotten out of hand and the forces of isolation and alienation continue to grow. We are plundering Mother Earth, and destroying our own children. We are challenged to make new, now conscious, reconnections with each other and with the natural and spiritual world. While there are those who would go back to what feels like a more idyllic world of the ancient Goddess, I do not believe this is possible. Rather, we must use the self-consciousness and clarity of thinking that have been the gifts of these past 5000 years of development to go forward toward new ways of coming together, new ways of knowing the spirit.

Rudolf Steiner also speaks of a need for modern people to fulfill a new Goddess myth. In a lecture series called *The Search for the New Isis, Divine Sophia*, he speaks of our modern estrangement from a living connection to the wisdom of the world.[15] He describes how we have lost the capacity to understand in an integrating and holistic way. Rather we gather data, we weigh and measure, we are beguiled by statistics and think we know. Yet he says, until we come again to a living appreciation the New Isis, of Divine Sophia as Cosmic Mother Wisdom, we will be unable to truly understand the weaving spiritual truths within and around us.

Rudolf Steiner also tells a New Isis myth. It is a strange and prophetic story of a veiled Goddess figure. She is the Goddess showing her face as human soul, asleep to her real responsibilities and confused about her offspring and its needs. Because she does not understand her offspring's true nature, she drags it about until it falls into fourteen pieces through the power of the world. A visitor who believes he is the father and whom the New Isis, through illusion, believes to be her benefactor, uses his technological know-how to reassemble her broken offspring fourteenfold, each one bearing an image of this visitor's face. The New Isis dreamily experiences all this without understanding what has happened, until finally, with the help of elemental spirits of nature, she can recognize her offspring restored to its true form. As the story progresses, the New Isis discovers that she is still wearing the cow horns of ancient Egyptian clairvoyance placed on her head by her son Horus, even though she has become the New Isis. This self-knowledge summons a visitor again who places on her head, on top of the cow horns, a crown of paper filled with scientific writings. Only when she can understand the Spirit of Humanity working in earth evolution and in human destiny, is it possible for the ancient clairvoyance of the cow horns to grasp the paper crown and for both to be transformed into a golden crown of genuine substance.[16]

First told in 1918, this is a story for now and for the future, calling us to recognize this female figure who has been exiled, veiled, by our materialistic culture. The images speak powerfully of modern life: soul dullness, the confused mother, the unknown father, the illusionary appeal of technical skill, the neglected child, cloning, computer paper, the need for a new relationship to the forces of nature, the availability of, yet lack of connection between, ancient forms of clairvoyance and modern scientific knowledge unless they are integrated through a new understanding of the Logos. The New Isis myth is a story of the human soul gradually waking up to what it means to bear (in every sense of this word) our spirit child, our true self.

Awakening is what our daughters—and our sons—are seeking. They long for images of wakefulness, for the promise of wholeness and connection. Even as they head straight into the darkness of much of modern culture, they also challenge us with concerns for the environment, with a new volunteerism for many social needs, with commitment to inclusiveness in our multi-cultural world. How can we help them pierce the disorienting veils of modern life and discover who they can 'resemble', what they can 'understand'? And how can we ourselves learn from what they are bringing that is quite new and needed in our troubled times?

If we are to offer and manifest more hopeful and helpful images of human becoming, we cannot fall back on the ways of the past; neither looking nostalgically to women's traditional roles, nor touting the superwomen who can succeed in a 'man's world', will prepare our daughters to meet what a healthy social future requires. A status quo world with more women doctors and lawyers, doing business as usual, is no real improvement. The Women's Movement has brought to consciousness something much more profound: we need to change the world! It needs a more awakened feminine activity in all of us—greater relationship capacity, an openness to a spiritual dimension, an appreciation for process as well as product, a sense for the interconnectedness of all aspects of life.

These more feminine virtues have been undervalued for too long—by women as well as by men. Do you ever, for example, put down traditional women's work such as teaching school, or being *just* a homemaker? These should never be an individual's only option, but they also need to be revalued. How else can we—as a society—assume the responsibility for raising, for educating all our children? And beyond the sphere of the home, can we develop new models of service and of leadership, new ways of working together that are cooperative, non-hierarchical, and based on consensus rather than power? Can we create new products that serve life, rather than destroy it in the name of profit as progress?

Much is happening today—there are many worthwhile efforts toward new social forms and greater balance. I wonder sometimes whether we share with our children the good works we see, or even our own strivings. There is so much bad news that surrounds them. We cannot cloister our girls or keep away all the negative cultural influences, but we can offer counter images. Our children need life-giving examples of adults striving, growing, facing difficulties and making constructive changes for a more balanced world.

And we can also let our children practice building confidence. In age-appropriate ways, we can challenge and encourage them to rely on their own inner resources, to trust in their ability to think for themselves and so be able to say 'no' *and* 'yes' to what life offers. We need to let their voices be heard, not silenced, in classes and at the dinner table. We do not need to agree with everything they say, but to signal that their having views has value. I do not mean we should make them act independently too soon or drop our protection where it is needed; but as they grow older, we must loosen our hold and develop an active trust in their destinies. Can we applaud their achievements without pushing our own goals onto them? Can we prepare ourselves to be receptive when they wish to go wilderness camping, to make a school exchange, to volunteer in a homeless shelter? So much in the world rewards their compliance, but they also need encouragement and support for their risk-taking.

As parents, we have the task and the joy of helping them discover who they are and how to find their unique places in the world where they can serve and belong, partake and make better. Central to this will be our own striving to be authentic. They do not need us to be perfect, but they do need to experience that we take our development seriously, that we keep trying to know and believe in ourselves as well as in them. We give them very much if they can feel and trust in our willingness and our gratitude to be growing together with them in our evolving world.

Notes

[1.] This chapter is based on a talk given as part of a conference called 'Who is Raising Our Daughters? Women Coming of Age for the 21st Century'. The conference was sponsored by the Center for Life Studies of Sunbridge College in Spring Valley, New York and was held April 7-8, 1995.

[2.] Jeanne Elium and Don Elium, *Raising a Daughter* (Berkeley: Celestial Arts, 1994), 52.

[3.] For my discussion of feminine and masculine qualities in individuals and in social development, see Margli Matthews, Signe Schaefer and Betty Staley, *Ariadne's Awakening* (Stroud: Hawthorn Press, 1984).

[4.] See Carol Gilligan, *In a Different Voice* (Cambridge MA: Harvard University Press, 1982) and Mary Field Belenky, et al., *Women's Ways of Knowing: The Development of Self, Voice, and Mind* (New York: Basic Books, 1986).

[5.] Elium and Elium, *Raising a Daughter*, Chapter 2.

[6.] Ibid.

[7.] Ioannis Miaoulis, 'What makes girls shun science?' *Tufts Alumnae Magazine*, Winter, 1995, 19.

[8.] Deborah Tannen, *You Just Don't Understand: Women and Men in Conversation* (New York: William Morrow, 1990).

[9.] See Rudolf Steiner, *The Manifestations of Karma* (London: Rudolf Steiner Press, 1968), Lecture 9; *The Christ Impulse and the Development of Ego Consciousness* (New York: The Anthroposophic Press, 1976); and *The Reappearance of Christ in the Etheric* (New York: The Anthroposophic Press, 1983), Lecture 4.

[10.] Mary Pipher, *Reviving Ophelia* (New York: G P. Putnam's Sons, 1994), 62.

[11.] Ibid.,19.

[12] Quoted in Elium and Elium, *Raising a Daughter*, 61 from Carol Travis, The Mismeasure of Woman (New York: Simon & Schuster, 1992) 32.

[13] Rudolf Steiner, *The Gospel of St. John* (New York: The Anthroposophic Press, 1984), 191.

[14] Riane Eisler, *The Chalice and the Blade* (San Francisco: Harper and Row, 1987).

[15] This lecture is printed in Rudolf Steiner, *Ancient Myths and the New Isis Mystery* (New York: The Anthroposophic Press, 1994).

[16] This is a condensed version of the New Isis Myth. I encourage readers to see the complete original as told by Rudolf Steiner, Ibid., Lecture 3.

Patti Smith

Patti Smith and daughter Shannon

Change has been an intimate part of my life. Growing up the child of a U.S. Navy pilot and his dutiful wife, I moved every three years. The stress and challenge of making new friends, catching up in school and getting accustomed to new homes and neighborhoods made me conscious at an early age about the impact of change.

During adolescence, moving was especially painful. In retrospect, I can trace back to sixth grade events, that led to the silencing of my voice, such as when Mrs. Vogt threw a dust pan at me because I could not read aloud well. Drama became my salvation. A safe harbor where I became an instrument for the voice of others. My confidence, stellar on the stage, evaporated after each performance.

After giving birth to my first child, a daughter, I studied the patterns and rituals of a male dominated society that habitually affect our daily interactions. I wanted to find ways to prevent the silencing of her voice. Like all mothers, I thought I could shelter her from life's hard blows. I wanted to find an education that would recognize the importance of the human soul and spirit. Since the arts had been a safe harbor for me, I wanted her to be exposed to them. I discovered Waldorf education with its skillfully crafted curriculum, respect for the arts and the human spirit.

I am still a champion of change. In midlife, the change is not about new homes and new friends, it is about living with new ideas, in spite of old habits that are difficult to change. Courage is the virtue that demands cultivation; a whispering soul developing a firm assured voice that can dare to share thoughts with others. This is difficult. It is much easier to quote the wisdom of others, who surely know more than I do. I dedicate my article to my daughter, that in reading it she will appreciate the struggle.

26
Raising our daughters: the heart of the matter

The past

The changes that occur in the flow of evolution can be traced by examining the language of a people. For example, the word, 'courage'—'cor' comes from the Latin meaning 'heart' and from a common Roman word meaning 'age'. The word originally meant the heart of an age. In 1300, courage was closely linked to the act of speaking and generally meant 'to speak one's mind by telling one's heart.' Courage, at that time, aligned speaking with mind and heart—intellect and love were combined in the meaning of the word. By 1500, 'courage' commonly meant the quality of mind which shows itself in facing danger without fear, and with bravery or boldness. Consequently, 'courage' was cut off from the heart, the seat of feeling. The symbiotic relationship of heart and mind was severed. Courage was no longer a quality of mind revealed through the absence of fear, but became verb-like, 'take courage', and was associated with warriors, conquering, and committing heartless actions. (Rogers, 1993).

The change in this one word is symbolic of the change that was occurring in the world at that time. Market economy and materialism were the warriors conquering the human psyche. The heart, which is not marketable, was easily forgotten. Ownership of material things became the defining factor of power and success. It was a time of tremendous productivity and transformation of the physical world. It was not a time of care and concern for things that did not bring power or success. It was a time of oppression of women and indigenous populations.

We are standing at the threshold of another Renaissance; now, one thousand years after the embryo of the modern world was being formed, the womb of another age is being prepared. Mankind now has the opportunity to become Humanity. 'Courage,' as a heartfelt gesture of 'speaking your mind by speaking your heart,' re-emerges as a valuable and necessary possession, not bought and sold in the marketplace, but cultivated and developed in the interior storehouse of the human soul.

The Woman's Movement, the Civil Rights Movement and the Ecology Movement are three seeds of the new age. Women, minority populations, and the earth herself are demonstrating that there are other aspects of experience that are valuable. Against great odds, and with great courage, advocates from all three of these constituencies are forcing paradigms to change. Any of the three movements could be used to illustrate the change in consciousness that is occurring; this chapter will focus on the changes that women, and therefore our daughters, bear.

In a 1910 lecture, philosopher Rudolf Steiner spoke strongly about the materialistic trends that were firmly in place even then, and he said that it would be increasingly difficult for women to experience fulfillment in their daily tasks.

> The truly human element—that which spoke to the heart and soul, that which spoke to the human being in his yearning and hopes for eternity, that which gave him strength and certainty in life—this element was the same for both men and women. It arose from an origin other than psychological research or from the laboratory. One could attain the highest heights of philosophical and religious development without any kind of academic education at all. One could do this at any time—even as a woman. Only because the materialistic age has made so-called positive science with its so-called facts the basis of higher problems—only because of this is it so that, alongside the general inclination arising from practical life, another inclination, one of the heart, a longing of the soul had to arise and drive women even to look at the mysteries offered us by the microscope, the telescope, and the research of biology and physiology. For, as long as people thought that decisions could not be made by means of a microscope concerning life and immortality of the human being, so long as people knew that these truths had to be drawn from quite other sources, there could not be the clamouring for scientific studies there is today. We must be aware of this: that the trend of our age had generated this desire for academic education and that the women's question itself has come up in our time through the whole nature of our culture.(*Women in Society*, p.13.)

Women struggle to find an appropriate place in an ever changing fast food society. No longer do clothes need to be made at home; meals can be ready instantly, and neighborhoods are barren of children and other women during the day. How does a woman spend her time meaningfully? Where is she to find a sense of value? Women who stay at home think of themselves as 'just moms.' Steiner's quote warned of this dilemma and suggested that women would need to struggle both within themselves and within society to change the focus of what is considered meaningful in the workplace, the home and society.

The present: facing the struggle: dealing with images and their effect on us and our daughters

We are subjected to thousands of positive and negative images every day. Images which can be reflected, magnified, distorted, overexposed or superimposed. As we are exposed to images they become magnified in our mind—they become bigger than life. The inner manifestation of an image is the reflection that becomes imprinted in our being. If we get overexposed to images, they become so familiar that we hardly notice their ongoing effect on us. When images coming toward us are more powerful than the images that already exist, our identity is either distorted or transformed, depending on whether the images were negative or positive.

Commercialism, the child of materialism, flourishes in our multimedia society. It is a force that keeps the heart smothered as it preys on selfish desires in each of us. It is used with great effect to saturate women and men with images that cripple. We are constantly led to believe that we need more 'things' to survive, and that we have the right to acquire those things in any way necessary. Not a heartfelt thought! *The Beauty Myth* describes the calculated marketing plans at work to destroy women's sense of self. Open any magazine, you will see pictures of emaciated girls in tight jeans with bewildered looks on their faces; images that reflect weakness, physical deprivation and need. What happens to us and our daughters when we are exposed to such pictures all the time?

What images are bigger than life in the lives of our daughters? What do those images reflect? As adults, we need to be active and courageous in our efforts to provide positive role models for youth. Our behavior can mirror images that are worthy of imitation or not. We can magnify positive images and deeds. We, as victims of overexposure to certain images, can deliver unconscious negative images to our children. If we work to establish courage within ourselves and establish a positive identity about our womanhood/manhood, we provide images that permit our daughters to love themselves, in spite of the images coming towards them from outside by media and peers.

Kindergarten teachers make an interesting choice. They are generally strong able women who make a conscious choice to work with young children. They recognize that this choice will alienate them from the power structure of the education system, and that they will not become rich in material possessions. As a kindergarten teacher, I valued the wonder of being with young children. I hope this commitment to children has influenced my own children in their search for what is valuable.

Growing up: life phases and images

Looking at childhood developmental stages and the effect of images bombarding children from the world, concerns arise. From birth to age seven, children are involved with the physical growth of their bodies. More physical growth occurs than at any other time in life. Children are egocentric and want our attention, but that need for attention often focuses on what they DO. 'Look, Mommy, see what I made?' 'Look, Daddy, see how fast I can run?' Children learn by imitating adults. It is the only time we have the opportunity to oversee the environment of our children and what images are coming toward them. What messages are they receiving from us at this most impressionable age? What do they learn from our gestures, our choice of words, and the kinds of activities we engage in with them?

From seven to fourteen, there is a shift; they are still growing, but feelings enter their lives in new ways. This is a time of the feeling explosion. Children develop relationships with friends outside the home. We share influencing them with others, as the likes and dislikes of friends become more important to put into action than the wishes of their parents. They look at us differently, and they are more judgmental. Puberty comes. Love takes on new possibilities. A changing physical body causes a new kind of self-consciousness. They can physically provide for themselves, so our task is to help them traverse the landscape of feelings. Contradictions in themselves and in the world surface. Mixed messages cause stress and disharmony; the truth is masked. It becomes difficult for young people to establish criteria for decision making.

At puberty, as a friend of mine once said, they begin to build altars to themselves. What goes on the altar, the symbols that make them feel good, significantly affect how they address teenage years. Which 'icons' do they bring to their altar, and why, is our concern. Do the images echo the heartlessness distilled from the world around them? Do the images help them to develop a healthy understanding of what it means to be a woman? What can we do to influence the altarpieces?

I have a friend, a kindergarten teacher, who is accustomed to making her classroom very beautiful and flower filled. As she prepared to celebrate a festival in school one day, she bought one extra rose for each of her daughters (both teenagers). She said that they do not get excited about celebrating festivals with her anymore, but that she continues to put a rose in each of their rooms on celebration days. She brings to their altar an image of beauty, and importantly, her love and care. The rose sits on each dresser with half undressed rock stars taped to the wall behind.

From fourteen until adulthood, new forces influence adolescents. Not only the doing and growing of the young child, or the feelings and confusion of early puberty, but the forces of identity: 'who am I and what do I want to be?' penetrate the thinking in a way that was not noticed earlier. These forces stream differently into males and females. Puberty dawns in young women, first in the heart area as their breasts begin to grow and in their womb at menstruation. In young men, those forces penetrate their extremities. This difference is very important. The boys find their identity in what they do, what they master. Power and control of physical things interest them. Testing themselves physically is paramount. Feelings, however, are taboo. They are secret, even to young men, locked away in their treasured chests. They are at home in the physical world. They are comfortable with discussions of facts, wars, and sports. The conditions of the time are advantageous to the constitution of boys. Their soul needs, however, are not being met.(Steiner, *Soul Economy and Waldorf Education*, pp. 223-243).

Girls have a different experience as the forces of identity enter and lodge in their hearts. They develop knowledge of themselves and the world through a sense of connectedness. Relationships, who they are to others, and who others are to them, are paramount. Relationship and relatedness are priorities for girls and surface as such in studies that have been done concerning school girls. (Brown and Gilligan, Belenky, Clinchy, Goldberger, Tarule). Young women do not embrace the world of facts with the same vigor as young men:

'What do they think of me, and what do they want me to become? Everything I say about myself is what other people tell me I am. You get a pretty good idea about yourself from the comments other people are saying about you.' If one can see the self only as mirrored in the eyes of others, the urgency is great to live up to others' expectations in the hope of preventing others from forming a dim view. Thus, women of received knowledge, listen carefully and try hard to live up to the images that others have held up to them. They are especially at the mercy of authorities' judgements If someone in a powerful position tells a woman she is wrong or bad or crazy, she believes it. (Belenky, Clinchy, Goldberger, Tarule 1986, p 211).

Contradictions are blinding at this age. Adolescents point out contradictions all the time. They observe boys being called on more often in class. Young women witness their answers being overlooked or considered incorrect, because of the lack of specificity. (Gilligan, 1991). The overwhelming message young women receive is that what they understand is neither relevant nor important. They become quiet. When they do speak it is through a veil of words, codes, such as 'like', 'um' and 'yeah know' which become substitutes for real thoughts and feelings. Girls learn to suppress. They begin to regress. In their desperation to relate to the world, they become more and more distant from the voice calling to them from inside. They long to fit in and to be accepted. The images coming toward them become their barometer of acceptability and safety.

As I struggle to write this article, I am painfully aware of this problem. Expressing ideas and opinions puts me in jeopardy of criticism, rejection, being disliked, not pleasing my audience. These feelings are all too familiar to me. I hear the voices inside me, some of fear, some of courage, one saying of course you can write this, the other saying: Who do you think you are, what do you know about this, no one will read it anyway. I persevere because it is the activity of struggle that helps me to find my voice. Equally important, it is that silent struggle in me that affects my daughter and her ability to strive to find her voice.

Waldorf Education: exemplar of change

We can influence what happens in our homes. We choose the images that hang on the walls and in the case of the middle class, where we live: the neighborhood and landscape. We establish limits, rituals, and the 'being' of our homes. When we walk out of our doors and enter the world, our influence wanes. We have no control over the images on billboards, on television or in magazines. School, spanning a vast amount of time in the formative years of child development, can be a haven of positive images and healthy development, or a hell of self-devaluation and fragmented development.

Waldorf education is designed to meet the challenges of our time. Rudolf Steiner, realizing the overemphasis of masculine thinking, specifically designed an education that would help to develop the voices of both young women and men, an education that would help to expand dimensions of thinking and emphasize the need to develop new capacities. Steiner recognized the importance of creating teaching and learning practices that enabled the student to learn both the art of science and the science of art. Steiner recognized the difference in learning styles in boys and girls. Waldorf schools are known for curricula that weave art and science in every lesson. For example, teachers use stories to introduce mathematical concepts in the early grades.

In later years, students are reminded of the past to help them interpret and understand the conditions which exist today in all societies. The education recognizes the need for students to have a relationship to the past, present and future. Moreover, the education deeply values the quality and beauty of presentation of work. Students develop creative aspects of themselves alongside the more cognitive capacities. Math, for example, is learned by both memorizing the times tables and by counting out stitches in knitting projects. Practical application of concepts that are being learned is essential in the curriculum. This method insures that students always know that what they are learning has a relationship to what is happening in the world. In discussing the need for versatility in education, Steiner gave the following example of the teaching of history:

> Both masculine and feminine forces were at work during actual historic events, though in different form than from today. Today all historical events bear a decidedly masculine quality. Girls who have reached sexual maturity show little inclination towards such an approach. Boys find it more possible to relate to this teaching through judgement, and through holding on to what can be ascertained and established. But there is another way of teaching which does not only record events that actually happened, but shows how impulses which led the past have become current ideas of the present and how impulses continue to lead the present times further.

It would not be right to teach girls in one way and boys in another. The minds of the young men would simply flow back into past times to become more rigid than they already are. If only history of the technique which relates to girls is taught, the students would be tempted to fly off into futuristic speculations. If both attitudes are alive in a lesson, we shall at last achieve the right approach to history for those who have reached the age of sexual maturity' (Steiner, *Soul Economy and Waldorf* Education. pp. 239-240).

It is interesting that Steiner made these statements about males and females long before the needs of women in education were studied. Only in the last twenty years have educational studies made distinctions between males and females. Until that time, data were not disaggregated to show male and female groupings because women were not included in most studies. There was no consideration that men and women may have different learning styles. Only recently have teaching methods and testing rubrics been acknowledged to give advantage to young men since the tests are based on the method of knowledge most conducive to their way of learning.

The androcentric form of knowledge and science accepted in the Twentieth Century United States is based on the theory of knowledge called positivism, which includes the following assumptions: scientific explanations should be reductionist and atomistic, building a complex entity from simple components; one can and should be objective (value neutral) in scientific research (Jagger 1983:356); and reason and emotion can be sharply distinguished (Jagger 1985:2). This form of androcentric knowledge tends to be dualistic and dichotomous, viewing the world in terms of linked opposites: reason-emotion, rational-irrational, subject-object, nature-nurture, mind-body, universal-particular, public-private, and male-female. It contains an individualistic conception of humans as separate, isolated individuals who attain knowledge in a solitary, rather than social, manner. Standardized tests are clearly based on this model. (*Gender/Body/Knowledge: Feminist Theory and Standardized Testing*, Phyllis Teitlbaum)

Waldorf schools do not subscribe to standardized tests, but seek to develop alternative methods of assessment. Portfolio-based assessment is developed in many Waldorf schools where students not only handwrite their lessons in main lesson books, but make sure that each lesson is artistically presented. This sensitivity to creativity and beauty has the potential to give young women the opportunity to find their voices. It takes exceptional people to teach in such an environment, because the danger is to revert to techniques and habits that were learned in one's own schooling. Waldorf teachers themselves require schooling beyond the traditional, which enables them to create education that develops the capacities of a thinking heart.

Why is feminism such an explosive topic?

This article began as a speech at a conference, 'Who is Raising Our Daughters? Women Coming of Age for the Twenty First Century?' There was much commotion about having a conference about girls. 'Well, the boys are in trouble, too,' many stated. Why are we so uncomfortable about taking some time to address the specific needs of girls? There is similar discomfort about African-American studies. 'Well, we can't only study Black writers,' a teacher states. 'Why?' the student responds, 'for years we only studied White males. Did that bother you?' Changing patterns, redefining the knowledge base, is not comfortable. Bearing the future means being able to change things in ourselves as well as cultivating the courage to make societal changes. Working to change small habits is a useful place to begin (Steiner: *Practical Training in Thought*. See also Schaefer article on inner development).

It also means that since the pendulum has swung too far to one side, we have to take some action to establish equilibrium. No wonder we hear so much about equity. Equity means that we look at what is needed and we distribute to an individual, a people, or a gender in this case, that which is necessary to enable fairness. For example, you and I both need medicine. I need vitamin C and vitamin B. You only need vitamin B to survive. Do we give equal amounts of B and C to each of us, or do we give each of us what is needed ? (Edmund W. Gordon, Ph. D., at a speech on the *Bell Curve* at Rutgers University. 1995). Young women need extra help to find their 'voice' and we need to swing the pendulum to make this possible. Yet, as soon as it is announced that there is going to be a conference on daughters, complaints are raised about excluding the sons. How interesting, given that all social, economic and political structures are designed to suit the needs of men. In the words of Yale scholar Catharine McKinnon:

Virtually every quality that distinguishes men from women is affirmatively compensated in this society. Men's physiology defines most sports, their needs define auto and health insurance, their socially designated biographies define workplace expectations and successful career patterns, their experiences and obsessions define merit, their objectifications of life define art and beauty, their military service defines citizenship, their presence defines family, their inability to get along with each other, their wars and rulership define history, their images define god and their genitals define sex.

(Wolfe, *The Beauty Myth*, p. 36)

The future: what can we do to achieve equity for our daughters?

In the 1960's there was a rebirth of the Women's Movement. This cultural movement has enabled many changes to occur: some to the advantage of women, and also much backlash, as we learn in Susan Faludi's (1992) book *Backlash*. Feminism has become a confusing term. Many women do not want to associate themselves with the movement—which conjures up images of bra burning radicals, or workaholics without children bemoaning women who stay at home and have babies. Neither of these images represents the truth of feminism, which is a movement for more inclusion, more possibility and greater interest in the 'other'. Trends and counter-trends make it difficult for us to discern where to make needed changes. What is clear, however, is the need to work within ourselves to distinguish between the lie of the multimedia society and the truth of bringing '*courage: the heart of an age,*' back into the world. It is time for a more balanced society, and it is necessary to change some of our habits.

The suggestions listed represent gestures and actions that will support the healthy development of young women. In responding to young women, young men will also be positively affected. As Steiner said, we no more want the girls with their heads in the clouds all day than we want the boys absent from what is cooperative and relational. Our sensitivity to girls, will awaken the hearts of young men.

Listen to women, notice and value women's perspectives. How many times have you noticed that a woman makes a suggestion at a meeting that is passed over. Ten minutes later, the same suggestion is made by a man and suddenly it is a good idea which receives attention. Just recently I was facilitating a workshop on gender. The group had 30 women and 6 men. We divided into groups to investigate some questions about gender, and at the end, each group reported to the entire group. Five of the six reports were given by the male in the group. At the end of the session, one woman pointed out what had just occurred. We (both women and men) are so accustomed to letting the men speak that it happens unconsciously, even in situations where we are addressing gender!

Be conscious about the amount of attention given boys and girls in classrooms, homes, and workplaces. Boys are often allowed to speak out of turn. Girls are often overlooked, ignored, because they tend to chatter. Encourage conversation from girls. Do not interrupt them. Validate answers that are relational rather than factual. Ask girls to define the relationship they observe between events. Respect answers, accept answers. Thank them for their insights.

Provide appropriate 'spaces' for young women. Boys tend to take up more space both inside and outside (Thorne, 1993). Some schools are creating special places for young women by encouraging after school support groups. At a small conference earlier this year, this topic of support groups for young women was discussed. Junior high or high school were suggested as appropriate times for such groups to begin. We were not sure by whom or how the group should be facilitated. We were certain that groups in various configurations should begin.

Work toward changing the status of women in society. Women should be a presence in government, church, school, and the home; they should bear meaningful positions and draw equal wages. If students see only males in respected positions, a message prevails. Women are absent from positions of power and influence in government, as seen in the recent 50th anniversary of the United Nations. There are few women church leaders. Women's leadership in business is growing, but we still see few women representatives of the business community. Statistics show that women make far less money for equivalent work. Most of the poverty in the world is experienced by women and children. Certainly this is not because women are of inferior ability. How confusing, especially for women who want to become homemakers. Given the recent degrading of welfare mothers who wanted to stay home with their children until they are three, it is difficult to feel a sense of value and purpose in the role of homemaker. Feminism is not only about women getting into the workplace outside the home, it is about valueing the home as a workplace.

Help young women to identify and express their feelings, even anger. The old saying, 'Well, boys will be boys' has allowed us to overlook certain behaviors in boys. 'Now be nice and sit still' has had a certain impact on the behavior we expect from girls. Help young women to articulate their feelings, and help them to find constructive outlets for those feelings. This will decrease the likelihood of self-destructive behavior such as self-mutilation and starvation (See Olivia Dreier's article).

Deal with love and sexuality. is filled with messages for our children. Boys are more comfortable with their physical bodies. Young women, on the other hand, are painfully uncomfortable with their physical bodies. To further complicate things, girls need to be in relationship with others. Love, in a materialistic society, means physical contact. Too often, relationship equals sexual contact. We can redeem love to mean interest in the other, rather than satisfaction for oneself. It is important that adults exemplify this attitude of interest in others. Young people need to see adults who are willing to give their time to projects that do not offer personal benefits but that are advantageous to society. What organizations do we belong to? How do we spend our free time? Our children are watching us all the time. What values do they see are important to us? In the area of service, we can deeply affect our daughters. We can be living examples of love as service, as well as love as physical relationship.

Recognize language is a powerful tool in society. Through language our voice has audience, or not. As with the word courage, we can trace the history of human consciousness through the use of the word. For example, using the word humanity rather than mankind we really do acknowledge a more inclusive audience. In the words of my friend and mentor, Ruth Pusch:

> Human is a word to cherish; after all humus is the organic part of the soil. And with it we should cherish humane, humble, and humanity (wish we could include humor!). Human was used as a word for centuries, as far back as the 15th century, when it fell out of favor. Humanity and humane were used, too, from 1400. It is somehow a pleasure to widen and enlarge a modern word, for so many have become shorter, dryer more lifeless...
>
> Why are we hearing so much argument these days (let's not call it battle cries!) about the use of man/human. What is this fanatic feminism?
>
> Hear the telegraph that came to Ann Walter Fearn (1865-1939), who became famous for her medical work with the Chinese government on child welfare and refugees from war, from her father: 'No disgrace has yet fallen upon your father's name. Should you persist in carrying out your mad determination to study medicine, I

shall never again recognize you as my daughter.' Ann was 24.

Talk about fanaticism! We all know these stories, it is not a fad or fashion that women are still looking for recognition of their abilities. It's a pity that there are so many loud shrieks, but some are caused by pain. A lot of us are quiet and begin to speak gently about the need in all men, in all women for something much more precious than equality. Florence Nightingale was probably not the first to realize that a new culture of compassion and cooperation, replacing that of war and greed, would arise only when those soul qualities are truly recovered. I believe we all want to rise up towards a future humanity, in which we're not just men and women but marvelous, magnificent 'humanity' (Unpublished letter).

Speaking of language—a female hero is a heroine, not to be confused with the addictive drug heroin. Or perhaps there is a subtle reason for such an association. The definition of heroine is revealing: a mythological woman or legendary woman having the qualities of a hero. The standard is of course the Hero. Why isn't a hero described as a man having the qualities of a heroine? Heroin is a trademark for a dangerous addictive drug. Was it an accident that this trademark name was chosen for such a lethal substance? Or is there something so displeasing in strong women that this association exists. We can't even say, 'She is a real heroine,' without the addictive image of heroin entering into us. Strong women, women of courage, do suffer a mixed identity in society.

This effort, to be conscious of how we include women in speech, and therefore in thinking, is powerful. It gives a message to the long silenced voices that it is time to speak. The resistance to this notion is amazing. Instead of seeing inclusive language as an opportunity for human development, pundits pontificate about why it is just another ridiculous ploy of feminists, that surely everyone in their right mind knows that 'man' includes everyone. This deed, to change speech, requires that we constantly re-evaluate our consciousness and work to change our conditioning. This deed is another rose upon our daughters' altars.

Describe beauty as a quality, rather than a physical look. Our materialistic, market based thinking has degraded beauty. Women, in particular, define themselves in accordance with these market images. Eating disorders plague young women as the pressure to be thin overcomes them. Girls as young as second grade refuse to eat lunch because they do not want to be fat. Beauty means false nails, false teeth, dyed hair; beauty means, 'I hide me behind man-made materials.' We can raise that image and resurrect a deeper meaning of beauty. We can value ourselves and speak of beauty in many contexts. Men can be careful about how they describe women: 'What a babe' (not a full grown person), or 'What a hog' (not a human).

Seek out positive role models for young women to emulate. We can direct our daughters to women who exemplify qualities that our daughters seek to develop. My daughter is searching for her spiritual identity. She has found a Native American teacher whom she trusts. How fortunate that she has the opportunity to be associated with a woman who has the courage to live a modest life, and who is determined to share her understanding of Native American culture and spirituality with young people all over the country. Adults need to encourage such positive relationships and provide support to our daughters to continue such relationships, even when they take our children on a path that is not the one we would have chosen for them.

Bear in mind that it is confusing for young men to develop as caring, heart-feeling individuals because of the dominant role they have inherited from society. It is difficult for young women to know what they are supposed to be: scholar, whore, beauty queen, mother, sex goddess, doctor or army general. It is our responsibility as adults to make conscious efforts to place positive examples before our children. It is our responsibility to speak and act individually and collectively to bring equitable opportunities to women. We can achieve this difficult task if we are on a path of self-development, constantly reflecting on the impact of our deeds.

Conclusion: the heart of the matter

In order for us to meet the needs of the time, we have to recognize the difficulties which the present conditions of society place on our young people. Many of us are genuinely seeking ways in which we can work to understand and change the conditions facing our daughters. This earnest search, in itself, is at the core of self-development, and will impact on the needs of the time. The heart of the matter is that care, concern, interest, and reflection are the deeds and needs of the soul. How do we nurture the soul to enable the quest for change to grow in us?

The arts are the food of the soul. Through developing ourselves as artists of life, training ourselves to see multiple levels of beauty, we cultivate the ability to bring 'heart' into images. Materialism causes us to concentrate on our physical needs—for instance, working out. But we can also imagine that our souls need workouts. The calisthenics of the soul are the arts. Poetry, painting, modeling, singing, meditating and thinking, all strengthen the muscle of the *inner* heart. In order for the heart to bear the future, it must be made strong.

Materialism has been a useful force in modernizing our world. Ecologists, feminists, civil rights activists, however, would tell us that the world needs new emphasis, new direction. The reality of the soul and spiritual aspects of all living things need to be acknowledged. This message is what our children are seeking. They are starving for images that reflect a world view that transforms the material into the spiritual. In the spirit, there is not dominance. There is the power of love, not just sex for physical pleasure, but for a heartfelt experience, a deepening of human relationship; not just bodily beauty but the recognition of the deep inner beauty that lives within each creature; not just factual knowledge but knowledge that allows the voice of each individual to express ideas and ideals.

Our daughters await images that acknowledge the spark of the divine in all living things. They have difficulty identifying with the values (and lack thereof) that presently exist. Many of them cannot imagine themselves as productive contributors to this world. Suicide is an option for an increasing number of young people. They are desperate for deeper meaning and purpose. They are looking to each other. They should be able to look to us. We have much changing to do.

Our daughters long for trust and responsibility. They want to believe in something. They want someone to believe in them. If we, the adults, work to transform ourselves, we place our struggles as roses on the altars of our daughters and sons. Working to transform our consciousness, to trust our voice, to bear responsibility for a changing world, we transform the images of a heartless, material society, and we become living examples of courage. Can we be inclusive in our use of language? Can we embrace people from many cultures? Can we be less selfish about our needs and more caring of the needs of the being of the Earth? In bearing the future, we conceive a world with new meaning, bringing to birth restored courage. We allow courage to enter into the world as the spoken word of a thinking heart. We prepare the world to embrace our daughters in a new way, one which welcomes their valuable voices.

Notes

Belenky, Mary Field, Blythe McVicker Clinchy, Nancy Rule Goldberger, and Jill Mattuck Tarle. *Women's Ways of Knowing: The Development of Self, Voice and Mind*, New York: Basis Books, 1986.

Brown, Lyn Mikel, and Gilligan, Carol. *Meeting at the Crossroads: Women's Psychology and Girl's Development* Cambridge: Harvard University Press, 1992.

Faludi, Susan. *Backlash: The Undeclared War Against Women,* New York: Crown Publishing, 1991

Rogers, A. 'Voice, Play, and a Practice of Ordinary Courage in Girls' and Women's Lives' in *Harvard Educational Review: Vol. 63,* 1993

Steiner, Rudolf. *Practical Training in Thought,* Spring Valley: Anthroposopical Press.

Soul Economy and Waldorf Education, Anthroposophical Press: Spring Valley, 1986

Women in Society, London: Rudolf Steiner Press, 1985.

Teitelbaum, Phyllis. 'Feminist Theory and Standardized testing' In *Gender/Body/Knowledge: Feminine Reconstructions of Being and Knowing,* ed. Alison Jagger, and Susan Bordo. New Brunswick:Rutgers University Press.

Thorne, Barrie. *Gender Play: Boys and Girls in School,* New Jersey: Rutgers University Press, 1993.

Wolf, Naomi. *The Beauty Myth,* New York: William Morrow Co., 1991

Gertrude Reif Hughes

Professor of English and Women's Studies at Wesleyan University in Connecticut. Author of *Emerson's Demanding Optimism*:

The essay I wrote for this book has a long tap root in my biography and a central place in my heart. It combines two of my academic specialties—Emerson's writings and Women's Studies—with a lifelong love of anthroposophy. Students at Wesleyan introduced me to feminism in 1979, just when a dear friend and mentor had died and when I was about to lose, in rapid succession, my mother—through her death; my marriage—through divorce; and my four children—because they were reaching college age. Two young women in my course on Emerson and American poetry asked for a tutorial in the work of the poet, Adrienne Rich. I hadn't even heard of her, I'd been so busy raising children, building an academic career, and trying to stay married.

Thanks to those two students, I started to read feminist works on the dynamic relation between personal realities and political practices. Soon I was writing feminist literary criticism, teaching Women's Studies, and waking up to the many ramifications of making gender a conceptual category.

My mother had been a deeply committed anthroposophist. Since my childhood we had engaged in a continuous conversation about anthroposophy. Before her death in 1981, I told her about Rich and other feminists of the 1970s. Years later, I began to integrate feminist concerns with Rudolf Steiner's primary insight, which Emerson also had: individuality is our soul-spiritual core as human beings and the basis of any human community we can make.

27
Feminism or humanism? Women's studies meets Steiner studies

Talk about feminism is sometimes perceived as trivial, unspiritual, too focused on sex, interested in what divides instead of what unites. Particularly among people who incline towards a spiritual outlook, feminism can seem limiting instead of liberating. After a talk I gave recently about feminism and anthroposophy, a woman in the audience came up and confided that she wasn't a feminist. The idea made her uncomfortable. She felt that calling herself a feminist would negate her more important allegiances. It would make her less humane. 'I'm not a feminist,' she declared. 'I'm a humanist.'

The woman's remark made me think. I knew that I believed in a basic unity among human beings, yet here I was, advocating a feminist consciousness. Was I unwittingly provoking contention in an already embattled society? Does a feminist perspective prevent a fully human one?

Perhaps, I speculated, it is unwise to highlight the differences between men and women when more than enough anxiety already burdens human relations, inside the house and out. Where lives are paralyzed by uncertainty over what to eat, how to conduct children's schooling, how to secure self esteem for all individuals, and how to decide the baffling questions raised by technological opportunities and temptations, talk about feminism may seem provocative at best and divisive at worst. Maybe, I thought to myself, it is wrong to emphasize gender in a world where sex is more readily associated with violence than with love and where differences between people seem to provoke discord instead of making for an enriching variety. Certainly, harmony is needed, not more strife. As human beings we need to find what connects us not what divides, and feminism introduces yet another 'ism' in a world already rife with clashing interests. What is needed is more spirit not more flesh, more emphasis on universality, not more splitting into sects and factions.

As I pondered all this over the next several days, I began to wonder how it is that the mere announcement that one wants to emphasize women's lives, women's questions, women's contributions can cause such anxiety. For it certainly does, and not only in spiritually minded circles. It doesn't matter whether you speak up at a committee meeting to ask, say, if more men or more women took part in some event that is under discussion, or whether you bring up some question about gender at a social gathering. Express an interest in women and your comment will usually be received— with or without uneasy joking—as an attempt at special pleading or factionalism. The same can't be said for efforts to raise consciousness on related topics like racial or religious difference or class divisions. Talk about those topics can certainly make tempers flare and cause painful confrontations, but talk about gender difference is more than just controversial. It is somehow unacceptable. A feminist viewpoint is expected to justify itself each time it is offered.

While I contemplated the simple if sad fact that feminists repeatedly have to earn the right to speak out, an even simpler fact emerged: If one can't pay explicit attention to 51% of the human race and still count oneself a humanist then 'humanism' must be conceived very narrowly. Whoever feels that feminism inhibits humanism must also feel, probably without knowing it, that women are not really human. Or, to put it another way, if feminism conflicts with humanism then what passes for humanism must be masculinism in humanist clothing.

What other phenomenon, I asked myself in exasperation, is so underrated, so overlooked, dismissed, or ignored and with so little apology, so few qualms. What other presence in daily life is routinely allowed so little recognition? My silent outburst turned out to have an answer: Spirit. Spirit is about as prevalent as femaleness and about as neglected. Like women's rights, spirituality is not discussible in polite society. A person who wants to mention divinity or morality, routinely prefaces the remark with a disclaimer like, 'At the risk of sounding moralistic...' or 'This may sound a little pompous but...' Like women, spiritual beings may be worshipped or feared but they are not accepted as a normal part of everyday life. In our culture, spirit, like femaleness, has peripheral status.

The mere act of consciously making gender or spirit a category of one's thinking about the world, creates profound changes in how the world looks and what one thinks ought to be done in it. At this point in my deliberations, I realized that as a college professor who teaches women's studies and as a woman who is committed to a spiritual path and to studying Rudolf Steiner's work, I am in a very good position to compare the far-reaching results of raising consciousness about either gender or spirit and to find where, if at all, they overlap.

Take gender first. By making gender a category of analysis, a feminist consciousness recognizes the rights of women and discovers areas of life in which these rights are not taken seriously. At its most effective, a feminist consciousness notices and tries to change the 'invisibility' of women and all that is designated female or feminine—whether it is found in actual men and women, or in supposedly gender-free ideals and practices. A historian asks, 'Where were the women?' Suddenly domestic life, not just officialdom, becomes an arena for serious study. Parlors count as well as parliaments, feeding nations not just warring with them, raising the young not just raising taxes. Letters, recipes, memoirs, and diaries of 'obscure' individuals—that is, those with no public standing—become a legitimate part of 'the' record, and history takes on a very different look.

An economist asks, how is housework different from paid labor? Indeed, it qualifies as paid labor when 'domestic' workers perform it outside their homes; what makes housework wage-worthy under those conditions and not when it is done by someone who lives in that home? Making gender a conscious category allows the question, 'What counts as work?'

Insurance companies and employers who grant sick leaves need to know what counts as illness as well as what counts as work. Such questions pertain crucially to childbirth and childcare, areas of life that, under present social arrangements, usually affect women and children more closely than men. Should employers make workplaces safe for children as well as for adult workers? Is childcare a business expense like travel costs? Is childbirth illness? If not, does it qualify for health insurance and corporate leave? If so, does medical insurance cover births presided over by individuals without medical degrees? Can adoptive mothers have maternity leave or should it go to birth mothers? And how about fathers?

In a similar way, what I will call spirit-consciousness identifies the absence of a regard for spirit and recognizes the difference that taking spirit seriously can make.   As soon as the sheer reality of spirit becomes a category, a viable concept in everyday life, its unacknowledged omission from ordinary cultural concerns and practices becomes noticeable and, as with gender consciousness, enormous changes in daily life can occur. All the activities based on the work of Rudolf Steiner, from Biodynamic farming and gardening to Waldorf schooling and from anthroposophically extended medicine to the most basic questions governing the conduct of life, make outstanding examples of how a spirit consciousness changes all kinds of cultural practices.

Farmers and gardeners, for example, notice that it makes a difference whether you think of the earth as a living being or just as dirt. Decisions about how best to enhance the land's fertility become not just commercial questions but topics for serious scientific research and development; the use of pesticides is closely studied; organic waste materials are treated differently from inorganic ones. Spirit consciousness changes the practice of medicine, too. The relation of patients to sickness and health becomes rich with both mystery and complex possibilities for meaning when physicians, nurses, psychotherapists, and other care-givers think of their charges as beings of body, soul, and spirit. They see that the physical bodies of their patients may express inclinations and decisions that have their sources in a body-free, spirit existence where definite intentions have been conceived in urgent, if now unremembered, activity. When spirit is considered real, intimate, subtle relations between humans and their environments—natural, physical, or psychological—can be taken into account. Then correspondingly subtle diagnoses and treatments can start to result, and hitherto neglected areas receive new interest. Nutrition, childbirth, geriatrics—a spirit consciousness sheds light on those relatively neglected areas of medicine and shows their importance.

In schools, teachers change their classroom practices when they think of their students as beings whose feelings and intentions can be educated as well as their minds. When one pictures the learning processes of children and young people as a gradual incarnation by a spiritual being into a physical body, virtually every school subject and every teaching technique gets a revitalizing new impulse. Qualities are as important as quantities, and artistic work comes into its own. Instead of being reserved for enrichment or relief, music, painting, or movement turn out to be the most appropriate and effective ways to study and learn a knowledge discipline experientially, be it history or physics, arithmetic or grammar. Spirit-aware parents and teachers see that a curriculum shouldn't just fit children for the society into which they are born but should fit them to take up their earthly missions.

As everyone knows, whatever we imagine a human being to be, that idea generates how we live with one another. Fewer people, however, know that it takes both spirit consciousness and gender consciousness to form a viable idea of what a human being is. My Women's Studies students and colleagues rarely acknowledge spirit as a category. My fellow anthroposophists often overlook questions of gender or actively dismiss them. Without gender consciousness certain important discrepancies disappear from view, discrepancies between a woman's access to resources and a man's, between a woman's rights and a man's, and between a woman's sheer individuality and a man's. And of course where such discrepancies are erased they can be disregarded. As with gender, so with spirit: without consciously taking into account the spiritual dimension of earthly life, including how our spiritual origins and destinations shape the course of our lives, and without a sense for the unique, soul-spiritual core of each single human being, we see ourselves and each other as interchangeable parts in a machine or members of a herd whose behavior, however complex and magnificent, is essentially predictable and therefore controllable. For views that neglect the reality of spirit, just as for those that neglect gender, deny human individuality.

Individuality is the crux, it is the crossing point where gender consciousness and spirit consciousness coincide and strengthen one another. Rudolf Steiner recognized a spiritually radical yet socially harmonious individualism, 'ethical individualism,' he sometimes called it. He saw individuality as the key to human relations of difference and of equality. His passages on ethical individualism articulate a fundamental dynamic that I call the paradox of 'shared uniqueness'; in other words, uniqueness is the primary trait that we all share.

In presenting uniqueness as a social problem—a problem in doing justice to both difference and equality—Steiner highlights the issue raised by the woman who declared that she could not be a feminist because she was committed to being a humanist. In a chapter of his book, Die *Philosophie Der Freiheit*[1], entitled 'Individual and Genus' he avoids making individual the opposite of society, contrasting individual with type instead. He says that when human beings view each other generically, as types, they cannot hope to understand one another. To illustrate this, he uses misunderstandings and inequities that are based on gender; so it seems as if, like the woman who preferred humanism to feminism, Steiner too would find feminism an impediment to social harmony. He writes:

> The tendency to judge according to the genus is at its most stubborn where we are concerned with differences of sex. Almost invariably man sees in woman, and woman in man, too much of the general character of the other sex and too little of what is individual (p. 200).

Here Steiner seems to perceive exactly the situation feared by those who suspect feminism of being divisive: that emphasizing gender exacerbates the already deplorably prevalent anti-humane tendencies in social life. But as he continues, he makes gender a category in his analysis, and significant insights result. In considering the social dangers of erasing a person's individuality by highlighting the person's sex, Steiner finds that women are particularly liable to this kind of erasure:

> A man's activity in life is governed by his individual capacities and inclinations, whereas a woman's is supposed to be determined solely by the mere fact that she is a woman' (p.200).

In short, women somehow have more gender and therefore less individuality than men!

Steiner shows how crucial individuality must be as the defining concept of humanness, but also that, ordinarily, individuality is more readily accorded to men than to women. Women are more often seen as members of the group 'women' than men are seen as members of the group 'men.' As a result, a woman's gender more often obscures her individuality than a man's obscures his.

With the help of Steiner's analysis of individuality, in which he opposes individualism to stereotyping rather than to community, it becomes clear that feminism and humanism don't oppose one another. They are not mutually exclusive; it's impossible and unnecessary to choose between them. Rather, feminism makes it possible to understand what is at stake in calling oneself a humanist in a masculinist world—nothing less than learning to accord equal yet distinct individuality, humanness, to every woman or man whom one meets. A feminist consciousness calls for attention to women's individuality despite prevalent cultural tendencies to erase it; and a spirit consciousness recognizes that a communally responsive individuality is the soul-spiritual core of every human being, despite widespread notions that human beings have no core other than their central nervous system. Is it, then, more humane to be a humanist than a feminist? No. In fact, if Steiner's 1894 analysis of the situation applies now, at the turn of the next century—and it still seems all too accurate—you really can't be a humanist unless you're a feminist too.

Notes

[1] The book has various titles in English: *Philosophy of Freedom*, *Philosophy of Spiritual Activity*, *Philosophy of Freedom as Spiritual Activity*, and *Thinking*

As A Spiritual Path. All are available from either Rudolf Steiner Press in Great Britain or Anthroposophic Press in the U.S. Page numbers refer to the Wilson translation.

Other books from Hawthorn Press

BIOGRAPHY AND SELF DEVELOPMENT SERIES

WORKWAYS: SEVEN STARS TO STEER BY
Biography Workbook for building a more enterprising life
Kees Locher and Jos van der Brug

This biography workbook helps you consider your working life, and make more conscious choices, at a time of great change in our 'workways'. Background readings, thirty seven exercises and creative activities are carefully structured for individuals or self-help groups.
21st June, 1997; 297 x 210mm; 224pp approx.; hb;
ISBN 1 869 890 89 2

LIFEWAYS / PARENTING SERIES

ALL YEAR ROUND
Ann Druitt, Christine Fynes-Clinton, Marije Rowling

Brimming with seasonal stories, activities, crafts, poems and recipes, this book offers a truly inspirational guide to celebrating festivals throughout the seasons.
200 x 250mm; 288pp; colour cover; fully illustrated; limpbound
ISBN 1 869 890 47 7

BETWEEN FORM AND FREEDOM
A practical guide to the teenage years
Betty Staley

Betty Staley offers a wealth of insights about teenagers, providing a compassionate, intelligent and intuitive look into the minds of children and adolescents. Issues concerning stress, depression, drug and alcohol abuse and eating disorders are included.
210 x 135mm; 288pp; illustrated; ISBN 1 869 890 08 6

CHILD'S PLAY 3
Games for life for children and teenagers
Wil van Haren and Rudolf Kischnick. Translated by Plym Peters and Tony Langham

A tried and tested games book consisting of numerous ideas for running races, duels, wrestling matches, activity and ball games and games of skill and agility. It's clear lay-out, detailed explanations and diagrams and its indexing of games by age suitability and title makes *Child's Play 3* an invaluable and enjoyable resource book for parents, teachers and play leaders.
145 x 215mm; 96pp; paperback; colour cover; ISBN 1 869 890 63 9

CHILD'S PLAY 1 AND 2
Games for children and teenagers
Wil van Haren and Rudolf Kischnick

Child's Play 1 and 2 follows up *Child's Play 3* as a games book particularly for younger children, suitable for nursery, kindergarten and junior schools. Parents, teachers and play leaders will find this guide to be a handy resource for schools, camps, parties, family occasions and gatherings.
215 x 145mm; 192pp; colour cover; paperback; ISBN 1 869 890 77 9

FESTIVALS TOGETHER
A guide to multi-cultural celebration
Sue Fitzjohn, Minda Weston, Judy Large

This is a resource guide for celebration, and for observing special days according to traditions based on many cultures. It brings together the

experience, sharing and activities of individuals from multi-faith communities all over the world—Buddhist, Christian, Hindu, Jewish, Muslim and Sikh.
200 x 250mm; 224pp; colour cover; fully illustrated;
ISBN 1 869 890 46 9

GAMES CHILDREN PLAY
Kim Brooking Payne

Following on from ***Looking Forward, Child's Play 3*** and ***Child's Play 1 and 2***, Kim Payne's ***Games Children Play*** offers an accessible guide to games with children ages 3 upwards. These games are all tried and tested with children, and are the basis for the author's extensive teacher training work.
215 x 145mm; 256pp; paperback; colour cover; illustrations;
ISBN 1 869 890 78 7

INCARNATING CHILD
Joan Salter
'Our birth is but a sleep and a forgetting.' Joan Salter picks up on Wordsworth's theme and follows the soul life of tiny babies into child-hood and adolescence. A specialist in maternal and child care, she addresses physical, spiritual and psychological development as well as environmental factors. This book will be particularly valuable for those embarking on parenthood for the first time.

210 x 135mm; 224pp; illustrations and photographs;
ISBN 1 869 890 04 3

PARENTING FOR A HEALTHY FUTURE
Dotty T. Coplen

Here is a commonsense approach to the challenging art of parenting; an offer of genuine support and guidance to encourage parents to believe in themselves and their children. Dotty Coplen helps parents gain a deeper under-standing of parenting children from both a practical and holistic, spiritual perspective.
216 x 138mm; 126pp; ISBN 1 869 890 53 1

VOYAGE THROUGH CHILDHOOD INTO THE ADULT WORLD
A guide to child development
Eva A. Frommer

Human beings have a long infancy during which they are dependent upon others for the means of life and growth—such a book on child development is therefore vital. A deep concern for the uniqueness of each individual child permeates this book, while offering practical solutions to the challenges of raising a child at each stage of his or her development.
216 x 138mm; 152pp; paperback; colour and black & white photographs; ISBN 1 869 890 59 0

SOCIAL ECOLOGY SERIES

BATTLE FOR THE SOUL
The working together of three great leaders of humanity
Bernard Lievegoed

Bernard Lievegoed M.D. was a distinguished physician, psychiatrist, organisational development consultant and educationalist. *The Battle of the Soul* complements his more autobiographical, *The Eye of the Needle* (Hawthorn Press, 1993).
135 x 238mm; 144pp; ISBN 1 869 890 64 7

EYE OF THE NEEDLE
His life and working encounter with anthroposophy
Bernard Lievegoed

A man of wide ranging interests, Lievegoed combined his profound inner, spiritual research with his pioneering social, medical, educational and management work to produce a number of fascinating books. **The Eye of the Needle** illustrates the dynamics between the inner and outer worlds— and of Lievegoed's ability to work with these dynamics.
216 x 138mm; 103pp; paperback; ISBN 1 869 890 50 7

HOPE, EVOLUTION AND CHANGE
John Davy

The twenty-seven articles in this book reflect the author's work as a scientist, journalist and lecturer: articles on evolutionary questions, language, education, science, ecology, life after life and contemporary thinkers such as Schumacher and Elizabeth Kübler-Ross.
210 x 135mm; 274pp; paperback; ISBN 0 950 706 27 2

HOW TO TRANSFORM THINKING, FEELING AND WILLING
Jorgen Smit

This book aims to enable readers to follow a meditative path leading to deepening insight and awareness of themselves and the world around them. Practical exercises for illuminating and strengthening thinking are described, for developing inspiration and intuition.
210 x 135mm; 64pp; paperback; ISBN 1 869 890 17 5

IN PLACE OF THE SELF
How drugs work
Ron Dunselman

Why are heroin, alcohol, hashish, ecstasy, LSD and tobacco attractive substances for so many people? Why are unusual, visionary and 'high' experiences so important to users? How can we understand such experiences? These and others questions about drugs and drug use are answered comprehensively in this remarkable book by Ron Dunselman.
216 x 138mm; 304pp; hardback; ISBN 1 869 890 72 8

MAN ON THE THRESHOLD
Bernard Lievegoed

Concerned with inner training and development, ***Man on the Threshold*** takes an anthroposophical approach to its theme. Lievegoed, the distinguished physician, educator and industrial psychologist, is aware that humanity is crossing a major threshold and a redefinition of boundaries is needed.
210 x 135mm; 224pp; paperback; ISBN 0 950 706 26 4

MONEY FOR A BETTER WORLD
Rudolf Mees

This slim volume re-works our attitudes towards handling money and presents finance on a human scale. It discusses alternative ways of looking at money in our modern world and realistic methods of approaching borrowing, saving and lending.
216 x 138mm; 64pp; paperback; ISBN 1 869 890 26 4

MORE PRECIOUS THAN LIGHT
How dialogue can transform relationships and build commuity
Margreet van den Brink

Profound changes are taking place as people awaken to the experience of the Christ in themselves. The author is a social consultant and counsellor and offers helpful insights into building relationships. She shows how true encounter can be fostered.
216 x 138mm; 160pp; colour cover; ISBN 1 869 890 83 3

RUDOLF STEINER
An Introduction
Rudi Lissau

This portrait of Steiner's life and work aims to point out the relevance of his activities to contemporary social and human concerns. Under discussion are Steiner's philosophy; his view of the universe, earth and the human being; Christ and human destiny; the meditative path; education and social development and approaches and obstacles to his work.
210 x 135mm; 192pp; ISBN 1 869 890 06 8

SEVEN SOUL TYPES
Max Stibbe   Translated by Jakob Cornelis

The educationalist, Max Stibbe, describes the seven soul types of man, indicating the most significant inner and outer characteristics of each type. Recognition of soul types can be invaluable in communicating with others in social, educational or therapeutic situations and the author's insights are both fascinating and instructive.
216 x 138mm; 128pp; ISBN 1 869 890 44 2

SOULWAYS
The developing soul: Life phases, thresholds and biography
Rudolf Treichler

Soulways offers insights into personal growth through the phases and turning points of human life. A profound picture of child and adult development is given, including the developmental needs, potentials and questions of each stage. Drawing on his work as a psychiatrist, Treichler also explores the developmental disorders of soul life—addictions, neuroses, hysteria, anorexia and schizophrenia.
210x 135mm; 308pp; ISBN 1 869 890 13 2

THE ENTERPRISE OF THE FUTURE
Moral intuition in leadership and organisational development
Friedrich Glasl
Friedrich Glasl describes the future of the modern organisation as a unique challenge for personal development. Every organisation, whether a business, a school, a hospital or a voluntary organisation, will have to develop closer relationships with the key stakeholders in its environment - its suppliers, customers, investors and local communities. Our consciousness as managers needs to expand beyond the boundaries of the organisation to work associatively with the community of enterprises with whom we 'share a destiny'.
216 x 138mm; 160pp; ISBN 1 869 890 79 5

TWELVE SENSES
Albert Soesman

The senses nourish our experience and act as windows on the world. But our stimulation may undermine healthy sense experiences. The author provides a lively look at the senses, not merely the normal five senses, but twelve: touch, life, self-movement, balance, smell, taste, vision, temperature, hearing, language, the conceptual and the ego senses.
210 x 135mm; 176pp; ISBN 1 869 890 22 1

Orders

If you have difficulty ordering from a bookshop, you can order direct from

Hawthorn Press,
Hawthorn House,
1 Lansdown Lane,
Stroud,
Gloucestershire, GL5 1BJ
United Kingdom

Tel: (01453) 757040
Fax: (01453) 751138